The Manager as Motivator

Recent Titles in
The Manager as ... Series

The Manager as Change Leader
Ann Gilley

The Manager as Mentor
Michael J. Marquardt and Peter Loan

The Manager as Politician
Jerry W. Gilley

The Manager as Facilitator
Judy Whichard and Natalie L. Kees

The Manager as Leader
B. Keith Simerson and Michael L. Venn

The Manager as Motivator

Michael Kroth

The Manager as...
Jerry W. Gilley, Series Editor

PRAEGER

Westport, Connecticut
London

Library of Congress Cataloging-in-Publication Data

Kroth, Michael S.
The manager as motivator / Michael Kroth.
p. cm.—(The manager as . . . , ISSN 1555–7480)
Includes bibliographical references and index.
ISBN 0–275–99018–4 (alk. paper)
1. Employee motivation. I. Title.
HF5549.5.M63K764 2007
658.3'14—dc22 2006028063

British Library Cataloguing in Publication Data is available.

Library of Congress Catalog Card Number: 2006028063
ISBN: 0–275–99018–4
ISSN: 1555–7480

First published in 2007

Praeger Publishers, 88 Post Road West, Westport, CT 06881
An imprint of Greenwood Publishing Group, Inc.
www.praeger.com

Printed in the United States of America

The paper used in this book complies with the Permanent Paper Standard issued by the National Information Standards Organization (Z39.48–1984).

10 9 8 7 6 5 4 3 2 1

To Lana, Shane, and Piper Kroth

Contents

PART III
Skill Development

Publisher's Note

The backbone of every organization, large or small, is its managers. They guide and direct employees' actions, decisions, resources, and energies. They serve as friends and leaders, as motivators and disciplinarians, as problem solvers and counselors, and as partners and directors. Managers serve as liaisons between executives and employees, interpreting the organization's mission and realizing its goals. They are responsible for performance improvement, quality, productivity, strategy, *and* execution—through the people who work for and with them. All too often, though, managers are thrust into these roles and responsibilities without adequate guidance and support. MBA programs provide book learning but little practical experience in the art of managing projects and people; at the other end of the spectrum, exceptional talent in one's functional area does not necessarily prepare the individual for the daily rigors of supervision. This series is designed to address those gaps directly.

The Manager as ... series provides a unique library of insights and information designed to help managers develop a portfolio of outstanding skills. From mentor to marketer, politician to problem solver, and coach to change leader, each book provides an introduction to the principles, concepts, and issues that define the role; discusses the evolution of recent and current trends; and guides the reader through the dynamic process of assessing their strengths and weaknesses and creating a personal development plan. Featuring diagnostic tools, exercises, checklists, case examples, practical tips, and recommended resources, the books in this series will help readers at any stage in their careers master the art and science of management.

Preface

I wrote this book because I had to motivate *myself* for parts of my career. I worked for a few leaders whom I would follow almost anywhere. I wish there had been more who really tapped my desires, energy, and talent.

I wrote this book because I have seen managers struggling to cause the living dead just to twitch.

I wrote this book because I have studied what managers can do and have done to develop highly motivating work environments. I want to share their stories. I wrote this book because I believe that inside every person there is a match waiting to be lit. Sometimes the person who can light the fire and give it kindling is the boss. I want to see people blaze.

This book is written for the supervisor who has to show up every day and figure out how to "motivate" the folks who work for him or her. Corporate downsizings, rightsizings, uprisings, and capsizings might be happening all around, but the average day-to-day work has to get done. Bills have to go out, repairs have to be made, and customer calls have to be answered. Each day, people are on the line to make things happen through other people. Inside are practical ideas to help do that. I hope that you enjoy reading this book and that it makes a real difference in your ability to motivate others.

WHAT YOU WILL MISS IF YOU DON'T READ THIS BOOK

The Manager as Motivator will give you timeless motivational principles that are simple to understand and execute in your work environment. You don't need inborn magical qualities or the ability to make an inspiring pep talk to motivate people. This book will give straightforward approaches you can apply to all aspects of your life.

This book is meant to be used, not read and put on a shelf. It's a personal coach to pick up anytime you are wrestling with the best way to help employees reach their fullest potential. Unlike others, this book focuses not only on how to cause excitement in your employees, project team members, and other coworkers, but also on how to build a *sustainable* motivating work environment.

Acknowledgments

Patricia Boverie and I began studying passionate work in 1999. I had been focusing my efforts on understanding personal power and mission but was looking for something I could feel even more strongly about studying. Patsy suggested the study of passionate work, and I immediately jumped on board. I will always be grateful to her for uncovering that path.

My thinking about passionate work as described in this book originated in the work that Patsy and I pursued together over the last seven years, and I continue to be influenced by what we have learned. A number of the stories and examples you will read here were first described in our newsletter, *Leading with Passion,* or in our book, *Transforming Work: The Five Keys to Achieving Trust, Commitment, and Passion in the Workplace.*[1] Other examples came from our research with organizations and leaders. "Occupational intimacy" is a concept we developed together, and it is described in detail in *Transforming Work.*

Writing a book takes many hands. My 2005 leadership class helped my initial thinking—I owe thanks to Kolby Cordingley, Jeremy Crook, Jason Flora, David Fry, Shane Goodwin, Dustin Harris, Brian Howard, Garth Jensen, Janiel Nelson, Ellen Rogo, Donald Schweitzer, Cynthia Strong, Li Su, and Greg Venema. Pam Twilegar read parts of the book and gave me useful feedback. I owe a special debt to my coworkers, especially Jim Gregson and Marty Yopp, who supported and encouraged me throughout. Thank you to the many people who contributed their stories and perspectives—you provided the emotional foundation for the book. I call Valerie Aker my editor-in-chief. She voluntarily edited much of the book and gave me many valuable ideas for improvement. The book is significantly better because of her.

Finally, my gratitude and love goes to my family and friends, especially my parents—Roger and Jane Kroth—who always encouraged me, believed in me, and were the sources of much of my thinking regarding what is really important about motivating people. My wife, Lana, and my two children, Shane and Piper, are my life. This would not be possible without their love and support.

PART I

Introduction to Motivation

ONE

Tools for "Noncharismatic" Leaders

WHAT YOU WILL FIND IN THIS CHAPTER

1. Who the book is written for
2. What this book is not
3. Why workplace motivation is important today and to you

INTRODUCTION

Have you ever had a manager who saw something you didn't see in yourself? In 1998 I was working as an internal organizational consultant. I carried emotional scars from moving up and down the corporate ladder for over 20 years. Those scars were limiting my motivation and self-confidence. I wasn't making nearly the contribution to the company I was capable of making. I had been passionate about my work for years but had been burned—and had burned myself. By 1998 I was getting by but was not able to recapture the love of work with which I had started two decades prior.

My manager at the time was bright, knowledgeable, and sensitive. He wasn't a rah-rah, inspiring leader with a magnetic personality, but he cared about his employees and knew his stuff. One day, he called me

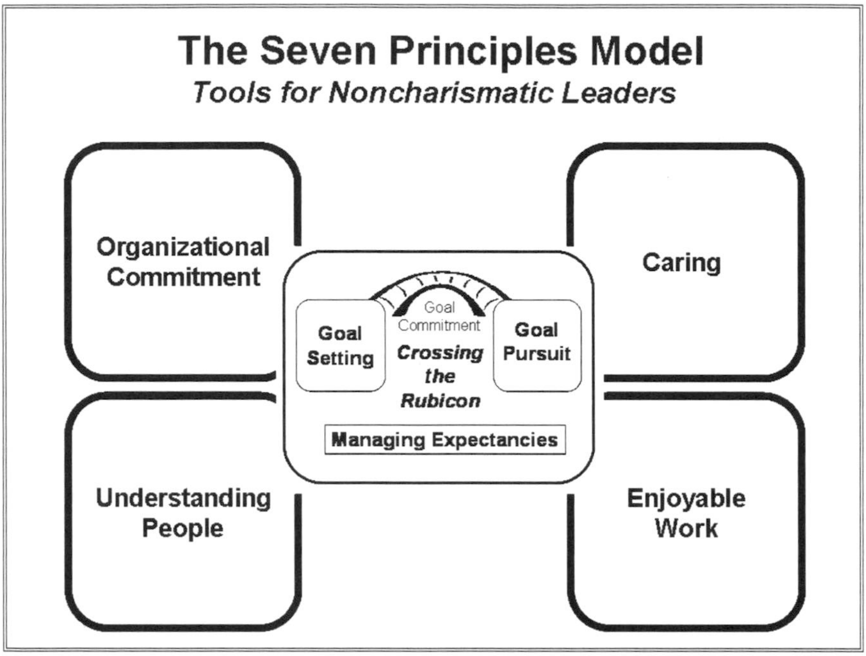

into his office and asked if I would be interested in developing a leadership program for the company. He knew I was interested in leadership development. He also knew I was leery of senior management. I didn't want to take the project, but he moved me forward in steps. He first asked me to research similar programs. Then he gave me support from an outside expert who not only helped me understand leadership development, but who also gave me confidence. My boss encouraged me and gave thoughtful guidance along the way. I became increasingly interested and excited about the program and was soon deeply involved with senior managers and their hopes and plans. The program I designed was soon adopted by our executive leaders, and I became the administrator. My respect for our senior leaders was renewed. I felt that my contribution was significant. I never enjoyed work more at this company.

The manager's name was Art Armano, and the consultant was Kate Mulqueen. I will always be grateful to them. Art embodied the qualities of motivational managers described in this book.

CHARISMA IS OVERRATED

Actors with charisma seem to have a "presence" on stage or screen that establishes a connection with the audience. They are magnetic.

Charismatic leaders are passionate and able to communicate their vision vividly. They develop strong emotional attachments with followers and have the ability to draw fervent effort from them. People wish they were born with charisma, and leaders hope to acquire it. Charismatic people attract people and power.

But charisma is not the leadership panacea it is often cracked up to be. An excellent motivator doesn't need it. Sometimes it causes more harm than benefit. Charisma thrives on crisis, and sometimes leaders create calamity just to play the hero. Such leaders may polarize rather than build consensus. What happens when the crisis goes away?

Jim Collins studied the performance of over 1,400 companies on the Fortune 500 list from 1965 to 1995 and found 11 that became truly great companies, with sustainable, long-term success. His 2001 book *Good to Great* reported that none of those companies were led by a charismatic leader. In fact, they were led by what he called Level 5 leaders.[1] Level 5 leaders have two qualities—humbleness and a powerful drive to succeed.

Long-term, sustainable motivation comes from those willing to put time and effort into creating a healthy, supportive, challenging, generative environment, not from charisma.

YOU HAVE THE ABILITY

You have the ability to be a great motivator. You have the potential to tap the exceptional creativity, productivity, and enthusiasm residing in each employee. Oliver Wendell Holmes said, "Many people die with their music still in them." You can bring it out.

Your hands may be tied by corporate policies and problems. You may be frustrated with the support you receive. You may have few resources and many challenges. You can still be a powerful motivator.

You may be shy. The thought of giving a pep talk may mortify you. You can still be a powerful motivator.

You may have employees who don't seem to care at all. You can still be a powerful motivator.

IS A MOTIVATING WORK ENVIRONMENT IMPORTANT?

Do you believe there is a relationship between passion and productivity? The answer is yes. It isn't a one-to-one relationship. Someone twice as motivated isn't necessarily twice as productive. There may be obstacles. Resources may not be available. All things being equal, however, the more motivated people are, the more productive, creative, energetic, and catalytic they will be.

How does that play out in the workplace? There is plenty of evidence that you have the tools at your disposal to motivate your workforce. Some examples from the research follow:

- Personal support from leaders is likely to result in "above the call of duty" effort from employees. Job satisfaction and fair treatment produce the same result.[2]
- Eight aspects of organizational climate seem to be related to subsequent productivity, including employee beliefs about how supportive their supervisor is and how concerned the company is about them, and whether or not said employees receive performance feedback.[3]
- Hundreds of studies with thousands of subjects in different countries have proven that goal setting works any time people can control their performance.[4] Specific, difficult goals in most cases lead to higher performance than asking employees to do the best they can.[5]
- Employees are more likely to seek feedback from sources they believe are supportive, and employees who seek feedback have higher performance.[6]
- Employees emotionally committed to the organization have higher performance than those who aren't and are absent less. Fewer quit their jobs. Employees develop emotional commitment when they believe the organization and their supervisor care about them.[7]

  You don't hold the reins of motivation entirely in your hands, but much is within your influence or direct control.

Employees are increasingly the true source of sustainable competitive advantage. They also have more choices about where and whether to work. Top employees can work anywhere. The challenge is to hire, keep, and support these already highly motivated people. Average employees may be working at half-pace or less. They will have a more difficult time job-hopping, but these employees could be a worse nightmare—they might retire on the job. The challenge with them is to infuse energy and increase their effort.

"The more you give away, the more you get back" is an old rule that works. Steve Wilkes, an elementary principal turned successful consultant, never had a problem attracting and keeping the best employees. He was a magnet. Principals apparently hold on to their best people as if they are hoarding food on a desert island. Steve's strategy, alternatively, was to do everything in his power to develop and promote the people working for him. As a result, the finest people in the school district lined up to apply for jobs in his school. Top employees want to work for the person who can help them grow the most, not the one who will keep them down.

Step back for a second and look at yourself honestly. Do the best employees want to work for you, or do they want to escape you?

MANAGERS ARE KEY TO WORKPLACE MOTIVATION

Employees inevitably point up when asked why the workplace is such a miserable environment. It's the boss, they say, or their boss's boss who makes it a depressing place to work. There is only so much you can do about the management chain, but my question to you is, "Are your employees pointing their fingers upward at *you*?"

A manager has more opportunity than any other organizational influence to directly motivate an employee. He or she has the most power to set the department's organizational climate. Managers set the tone, translate organizational strategy into employee performance and developmental plans, provide the clearest link between rewards and punishment, and in virtually every other way stimulate (or retard) employee action more directly than any other force can.

Formal or informal team leaders have direct contact with employees who make or break the project. These leaders influence behavior by listening, communicating, rewarding, punishing, setting goals, involving members, providing feedback, and reinforcing excellent performance more directly than anything else and sometimes more persuasively than the direct supervisor.

MOTIVATING WITHOUT RESOURCES OR CHARISMA

Many must look for ways to motivate workforces without the resources or the much-ballyhooed charisma of leaders described in the media or popular business books. Most managers aren't Jack Welch or Herb Kelleher, yet they have to get the job done day after day anyway. Managers can get similar results without the reputed "aura," "radiance," or "charm" of charismatic leaders. The tools are available to anyone.

The senior executives upstairs have expensive consultants to advise them when facing morale problems. Wouldn't it be nice to hire a $5,000-a-day consultant every time you need advice? Perhaps that is not an option for you. Pick up this book instead. Consider it your personal employee motivation consultant.

This book is meant to be dog-eared, underlined, passed around, filled in, smudged with worker dirt, and ... just ... used. The ideas, examples, and practices inside are meant to be cussed, discussed, kicked around, tried, and adapted to meet your own situation.

HOW TO GET THE MOST OUT OF THIS BOOK

Not much learning occurs unless people do something with what they are presented. Sure, it's nice to read useful information, and yes, sometimes such reading causes "aha" moments that change behavior. Real results come from taking what is read and applying it to real situations. To get the most out of this book, follow these steps:

1. Find a journal to capture your thoughts, ideas, and reflections about motivation. You will find examples, role models, and opportunities all around you when you focus on motivation. Don't miss or forget them.
2. Complete the "Initial Motivational Assessment" and "Motivating Others Starts with You" activities (found in chapter 6).
3. Set initial goals.
4. Read this book. Plan to mark it up. Underlining, highlighting, and writing notes in the margins are effective ways to remember things. So is reflecting upon what has been read. Highlight what is most important as you read. Write possibilities for applying those ideas in the margins of the book or in your journal.
5. Practice the concepts and complete the assignments.
6. As you work through this book, talk with employees, the boss (if appropriate), and other observers to help apply motivational skills.
7. Prioritize your most important learnings from all these activities.
8. Review and update your initial assessment.
9. Reassess yourself and update your goals.

ARE YOU THE FLAME?

Inside every person is a candle waiting to be lit. Every person is born purposeful. Every person needs other people. Every person has to live. Every person longs to do something special with his or her life. Every person has dreams. Life has snuffed the flame out of some people and dimmed it for others. You have the power to light candles. Just as importantly, like the wax surrounding the wick, you have the ability to protect the flame, to prolong it, to keep it burning bright. Managing people is a sacred trust. Individuals' lives are in your hands. The future of their families, their careers, their lifestyles, and their dreams can be crushed or lifted up in small or large ways through your actions.

The heat of your own candle will not light every other candle, but like a candlelight service, where the room begins to glow as each person passes the light to another, so will your workplace begin to shine. In the midst of the most terrible war this nation ever experienced, Abraham Lincoln lit the emotional embers of soldiers immersed in gruesome, hellish circumstances and kept the spirit of a nation buoyed during its darkest hours. He did not succeed by denying the horror of war, or by drawing upon the aura and reality of power, or even by decree. He stoked the flame by tapping into the humanity of people and their innate sense of humor and desire, by deeply understanding them, and by demonstrating a depth of care and humbleness in every way. The elegant words he spoke at Gettysburg on November 19, 1863, dedicating a battlefield and cemetery, are powerful today.

I was deeply moved when I recently read Doris Kearns Goodwin's book about Lincoln, *Team of Rivals.*[8] With his death, a great light was tragically snuffed out. We are unlikely to match Lincoln's eloquence or the leadership he displayed during such dark hours. But we can emulate his care for the people who gave so much to the job facing them.

Are you the flame lighting your employees' work? Are you dousing it? Candles that relight themselves are rare. Are you shielding their tentative hopes and desires and joys from those in your organization who would blow them out? Are you expecting each candle to light itself? You have the match. You must light them. You must protect the flame.

WHAT THIS BOOK IS NOT

This book is not about corporate incentive programs, mission statements, succession planning, strategic objectives, or hiring programs. It is not, in other words, about matters most managers are unlikely to influence, but it *is* about what they can influence.

It is not about how to manipulate people to get their best and then to discard them or about treating people as "resources" or "capital" to be leveraged or shifted around to meet your goals. It is not, in short, about motivational techniques—no matter how effective—that consider employees to be cattle waiting to be prodded into action. It *is* about releasing the full potential and humanity of each person. It is about creating and maintaining a *sustainable* motivating work environment.

It is not about charisma or power or celebrity. It is not about qualities or attributes that only a few of us have—but it *is* about what anyone can do.

It is not a book about theory, though it is based upon theory and research. It is not about simplistic how-to guides, though there are many exercises you can use in your day-to-day job. More accurately, it is about using theory and research as the foundation for practical tools that can make a difference in the workplace.

WHO SHOULD READ THIS BOOK—THE NONCHARISMATIC LEADER

The theme for this book came to me on an airplane, sitting next to a young man dressed very corporately—nice, neatly pressed white shirt and tie—and obviously quite serious about his work. I asked how he motivates his employees. He told me he wasn't a charismatic leader, wasn't the kind of person with a lot of "personality," and didn't naturally inspire people. He was, however, very successful. His employees achieved significant goals regularly, he had moved up the organizational ladder quickly, and he was now in charge of an entire region. That made me curious.

Many books about leadership are written from the perspective of what people at the top of the organization can do to create highly successful work environments. But what do you do if you are just an average Joe or Jane who has to get the packages out on the loading ramp every day or close the books before 5:00 on a Friday afternoon or get the inventory completed overnight? Sure, you might be lucky enough to be in a great corporate environment that pulls the best out of its employees. But it is more likely you are not. Your boss may be a jerk, or the company may have taken away retirement benefits, or the place might just be dull. Then what do you do? Pull out the guitar and sing songs together? Get a bunch of plaques to give out at monthly meetings? Tell your folks that their jobs are as important as Mother Teresa's work?

I think not.

When was the last time those ideas got *you* moving? Do you think your employees will think any differently? In the right setting, those tactics might help, but when taken by themselves they are superficial and often counterproductive. They are Band-Aids.

But you have a few tools at your disposal. You have your own skill and experience. You have whatever support you can get from your organization. You have the people you work with. Anything more is a gift. If that's your story, this book may be able to help.

The Purpose of This Book

The purpose of this book is to give simple, practical, motivational tools that are based on research and theory and that work.

WHAT MOTIVATION CAN AND CANNOT DO

The seemingly impossible can be accomplished with time, motivation, and will. Nearly anyone can get a college degree, run a marathon, learn to make cold calls, or move employees to greater achievements than thought possible, but there are some things motivation cannot do.

Motivation can't control outcomes. It is frustrating and even debilitating to put every ounce into something and still not reach the goal. That often happens by setting goals that are outside the ability to control. Winning a race is out of anyone's control. The world record could be broken and the runner still lose. Getting the next promotion is also out of an individual's control. The job may go to the boss's daughter even after you developed the skills and experience to be the best candidate. Getting an "A" grade may be beyond a person's control. Even scholarly work might result in a "B" if the professor only gives the top grade to 10 percent of the class. Getting the sales contract is not guaranteed. The best proposal might go for naught when the sales contract goes to the owner's golfing buddy. Those are examples of goals that depend on what other people do. Sometimes, goals are even more outside anyone's control. I once saw a departmental goal that was dependent upon the weather—how motivating was that?

Note what highly motivated people do when not reaching an out-of-their-control goal. They say, "I didn't get this job, but I am prepared for three other jobs in the marketplace." "I learned at a doctoral level." "We surpassed every requirement they wanted." Their fallback positions are what they really do control—the effort, focus, and persistence exerted to accomplish something important.

Motivation cannot magically provide abilities or characteristics that a person doesn't possess, and it can't assure the accomplishment of what is uncontrollable. It can, however, take a program to levels not thought possible through exertion not thought obtainable.

KEY POINTS

1. *You can be a powerfully motivating manager.* You can create a highly motivating environment, no matter your rank in the organization or your level of personal magnetism. Take charge of your situation.
2. *Learn by doing and reflecting, not just from reading.* To capture anything of value in this book, you must put it to use. The learning cycle progresses from reading to reflecting, to applying what you've learned to a real situation, to reflecting on what you learned from that, and then to starting the cycle again.

TWO

Overview

When the opportunity arose to write a book about motivational strategies for managers, I knew it was something I wanted to do. Motivation has been studied, discussed, theorized, and explained for centuries.

Research and theorizing in the field of workplace motivation is burgeoning. Topics being studied include self-determination theory, goal theory, equity theory, self-efficacy theory, expectancy theory, self-regulation, organizational citizenship behavior, organizational justice, perceived organizational support, organizational commitment, volition, attribution theory, and more.

These are the foundation for the seven principles introduced in this chapter and elaborated on in chapters 3 and 4.

WHAT YOU WILL FIND IN THIS CHAPTER

1. An introduction to motivation—All motivation is not the same
2. The four don'ts—What managers should *never* do
3. An overview of the seven principles, goals, and practices of workplace motivation

The word *motivation* comes from the Latin word *movere* for "to move." What is it that moves people to action? What causes them to persevere in difficult times? Can managers actually motivate employees? How about demotivate them?

Everyone has motives—those emotions, desires, plans, or needs that cause action to occur in certain ways. Motivation is compelling. It may be inspiring or desirable, or it may have to do with the need to escape hurtful, dangerous, or unpleasant situations.

Sometimes, pleasure motivates. A craftsman enjoys the act of making furniture. An accountant enjoys working with numbers. My wife loves to dance and choreograph—which she does for pure joy. My grandfather, a farmer, loved to rise very early in the morning, stroll to the barn, heft several bales of hay onto his truck, and go out to feed the cattle. It always gave my dad pleasure to go with my grandfather on horseback; "fixing fence," as my dad calls it; looking for jackrabbits along the way; and, as importantly, enjoying the simple satisfaction of father–son companionship. My grandfather would tell my dad, "Let's ride the range," and that was motivation enough.

Sometimes the promise of a future reward motivates present action even when the action seems counter to immediate interests. Russ may work as an accountant, a job he hates, for 30 years so that he can retire to his dream cottage on the Oregon coast. Sue may endure the shakes, nausea, and fear of Toastmasters in order to speak effectively in future business meetings. Bill may take his grandmother to church because he might end up in the will.

"HAVE TO" VERSUS "CAN'T WAIT TO" MOTIVATION

All motivation is not the same. There is *have to* motivation, and *can't wait to* motivation.[1] Which do you suppose extracts the most creativity and productivity? Which the most enjoyable?

Can't wait to motivation has a sense of eagerness and anticipation. There is an air of enthusiasm, jumping right in, and choice. Regret reigns when such a project is complete.

Have to motivation gets people off their seats, but there may be a feeling of resignation and obligation. When such a task or project is complete, people move to what they want to do. *Have to* work comes with every job. Paying people creates a have-to relationship. All jobs have joyless tasks that must be done well.

How much better it is when a can't-wait-to environment surrounds have-to tasks. Then boring or difficult work passes quickly and is completed with a spirit of contribution instead of resignation or bitterness.

It has become fashionable to say that no one can motivate another person. That's ridiculous. It's a cop-out. Parents motivate children. Friends motivate friends. Workers motivate coworkers. If I promised you a million dollars to do 25 sit-ups, you would do them. If you saw one of your children about to be injured in the street, you would rush to pull her aside. If you could take your pick of seats on an airplane flight, you would get to the airport two hours early just to stand at the front of the "B" line. We *can* powerfully influence others to act in specific ways.

Motivated people are easy to spot; they are often bustling around or intensely focused. The seemingly unmotivated are easy to spot as well. "He is sitting on his can" or "She'll never get done in time," one thinks. In truth, every person is motivated all of the time. The engineer lazing around during the day may be saving energy for the evening intramural basketball game. He is eager to be the star again. The blasé employment coordinator is graduating this semester and could care less about reducing the error rate on her project. She has sent job applications everywhere. Her mind is on homework. Because all people are motivated all the time, the trick for managers is to figure out what will move each employee to do what needs to be done.

THREE QUALITIES OF MOTIVATION

Motivation has three qualities: energy, direction, and sustainability.[2]

Energy

People expend energy for two reasons—they either enjoy doing something or are rewarded for doing it.

Some say they are the luckiest people in the world because they get paid for what they love to do. A manager's goals should be the following:

- Find what energizes each employee
- Find ways to furnish that kind of work
- Reward them for doing it

Direction

Working with employees to set and commit to goals is an indispensable part of work motivation. Goals give direction to work by indicating what needs to be done. Goals have been a major focus of motivational research for decades. Goal setting is practical, and it works. Goal setting is a uniquely human endeavor. It relies upon the ability to imagine, plan, anticipate, and evaluate. It requires making choices. Those choices and commitment to them are dependent on how skills are evaluated and on the situation.

Sustainability

Sticking with something is called volition or, more commonly, willpower. Most understand the significance of willpower in late January, when goals happily set on New Year's Eve are tested.

Setting goals is just the starting point. Maintaining commitment and the energy to accomplish a target is just as much a challenge as effective goal setting. Energy can wane as time passes. Other organizational goals and distractions pop up. Personal issues intrude. Obstacles get in the way. Sustaining motivation is essential to success.

I remember walking out of the auditorium feeling ecstatic after spending a day watching the best motivational speakers in the land. Zig Ziglar, Tom Hopkins, and others had pumped me up. My handout was covered with notes. I had written some specific, exciting goals that I was sure would change my life. I had resisted the urge to spend several hundred extra dollars on CDs, tapes, and books offered at the back of the room, but I couldn't wait to return to work and get started. Life was going to change. I had specific goals and the annoying "true believer" enthusiasm of smokers who quit or dieters who drop 20 temporary pounds.

Three days later, it was pretty much business as usual. After a week, it was for sure. After a couple of months, I didn't think about my new life-changing goals at all. In fact, I forgot them totally until I remembered this story while writing this section.

What happened? I actually did accomplish a limited number of the goals I had written down, but it was luck, or osmosis, that caused that to happen. Some goals turned up on other goal lists made from time to time until they were finally accomplished. Some slid off those lists never to return. Some I never thought of again after that heady day.

On the other hand, when I returned to graduate school I vowed not to quit. I told others, my journal, and of course myself time and again that the only way I wouldn't graduate would be if I died. Two years later, I crossed the stage to receive my diploma. Four years after that—having made a similar vow—I did the same for my PhD.

I had not only committed to graduate, but this time, I had also sustained motivation by using a variety of strategies that kept my motivation strong. That's what you will need to do when summer arrives and your employees want to be outside, when the reorganization changes reporting relationships, or when the compensation or retirement package is modified. A variety of strategies is often needed to keep motivation strong.

YOU MAY BE DEMOTIVATING EMPLOYEES AND NOT EVEN KNOW IT

A new job is exciting. Anticipation is high. Anxiety and hope share the stage. The desire to do great work soars. Dreams are vivid and the future is bright. Often, after a few months or weeks or even hours, expectations plummet. Getting out of bed each morning becomes akin to dragging yourself to a hanging. Hopes turn to work apnea—you gasp for life each day and choke on petty policies. Twice-(or thrice-)baked projects stick in your craw. You do just enough to get in, get paid, and get out. If you have some pride and confidence, you get on. If not, you get by. What happened? You probably have a poor manager.

Perhaps your experience was similar to this person's: "I had a new job. I was left alone, with no direction, and no mentor. I was told to 'just find your niche.' I needed assistance but didn't get it. I was physically isolated—'Out of sight, out of mind.' I had no support and struggled to find my way."

Marcus Buckingham and Curt Coffman conducted research studies of over a million employees. They emphasize the importance of the manager–employee relationship in their 1999 book *First Break All the Rules.*

> The talented employee may join a company because of its charismatic leaders, its generous benefits, and its world class training programs, but how long that employee stays and how productive he is while he is there is determined by his relationship with his immediate supervisor. (pp. 11–12)[3]
>
> Remember—*you* are the most important motivating and demotivating factor for your employees.

THINKING IS BEHAVIOR

Thinking is behavior. Employees act inside their heads all the time. Each gauges whether she cares enough to act and has the skills to do what the task requires. Then she considers the odds of being rewarded if she completes the task. Sometimes this is done instinctively and quickly, and sometimes it takes years.

In the excellent *Primal Leadership,* Daniel Goleman, Richard Boyatzis, and Annie McKee say that the most important job for leaders is to create "resonance—a reservoir of positivity that frees the best in people" (p. ix).[4]

They report that up to 20–30 percent of business performance is the result of the emotional climate—how people feel about working there.

More importantly for managers, *employees attribute 50–70 percent of the organization's emotional climate to their boss*. The manager, more than anything or anyone else, establishes the working environment. The authors of *Primal Leadership* found that at one international hotel chain, talking with someone in management put employees into bad moods more than did unruly or rude customers, oppressive policies, personal problems, or work pressure. Nine of 10 interactions with management caused frustration, anger, sadness, hurt, disappointment, or other bad feelings. As a manager, you have an excessive amount of power to stop employee motivation cold, and you may not even know you are doing it.

Yet it happens all the time. Supervisors do to their employees what they would be embarrassed to tell their minister. It is sometimes meanness, but often just obliviousness. It is easy for even the well-intentioned to act in ways that reduce motivation. Managers often don't have the slightest idea that what they are doing is counterproductive.

Some managers are less than demotivating. They are actually dehumanizing. If you are one of those people, please get out of management today, do some serious reflecting about who you are as a person, or see a therapist. *There is no room in our society for leaders—people who have power over other people—to treat people as less than human beings.*

Giving feedback to managers about how they are perceived by their employees, boss, peers, and customers—known as 360-degree feedback—taught me that leaders often have blind spots about their behavior. Discovering what managers do that demotivates is simple. Just ask employees. If not your own, ask others.

The following are typical quotations from employees I have interviewed:

> I had a private office for years. When I was on vacation, they decided to move a person in with me. Rather than work with me, they went behind my back.

> I got thrown into a project, and it was sink or swim. I wasn't ready, and the boss didn't provide support. It hurt my self-esteem. I was floundering. My boss didn't provide what I needed.

> It was out-and-out rudeness. The person I reported to resented me, so he was very mean to me. I received poor treatment from my coworkers and the supervisor—out-and-out rudeness. Condescending. I told them that I didn't like it, but it went on so I had to move to another job.

> One supervisor was a real nice guy but had no spine. You couldn't count on him to come through.

> My boss got into the mode of having me do a bunch of gofer work. I got tired of it. Younger guys came in and got promoted above me. I said, "Time to move on."
>
> I used to do volunteer work. [My boss] nagged me about that. I kept log books in case he came back so that I could prove I wasn't taking away from his work. He mentioned it all the time.

Gathering data yourself is as easy to do as reading the many studies about what demotivates or energizes employees. Informal places such as cafés, lines you may be standing in, or planes are excellent research locations. I often ask enthusiastic employees why they like their work and those who seem unhappy why they don't. One time, I was on a long flight and went to the back galley to stretch my legs. Three flight attendants were huddled in deep discussion. Although friendly while moving through the cabin, here they looked stressed. "Our company is in the middle of bankruptcy and we don't know if we'll have jobs next week," one volunteered without prompting. "Worse, they may take away our retirement benefits." This data was certainly easy to collect.

Actions taken may lie dormant now but come into play later when asking a worker to take on an additional duty. Employees are continuously weighing, consciously or unconsciously, the level of effort to put into a given task. They calculate how much they trust you, how much they like you, and the weight of past benefits in anticipation of future ones. Do you think insecure employees will be enthusiastic? How about when their pension is threatened? Most people will share their stories in casual conversation on a plane, in a restaurant, or in other informal settings.

Do some research. Gather data over the next few days. Ask people what their bosses do to motivate or demotivate them. Do it in a variety of away-from-work situations. Make it casual conversation when talking to a waiter, waiting in line to buy a ticket, or chatting between church services. Keep a record of what people tell you.

To these folks, you're not a manager looking for data, but just someone who happened to ask what they like or don't like about their work in the middle of another conversation. Say something like, "When you've had a great boss, what did he or she do to motivate you?" "What have managers done to demotivate you?"

When asked that way, the person doesn't have to openly expose his or her current supervisor, even if that is the example the person gives.

Activity

Complete the exercise "Field Research: What Managers Do to Motivate or Demotivate Employees," found in chapter 6.

FOUR "DON'TS"

Four ways of treating employees must be avoided at all costs. These may confer short-term results but over the longer term will eviscerate your effectiveness.

Don't Treat Employees Like Dirt

You have the reins of power, and power seems to corrupt character. Being rude, talking down, acting superior, expecting people to kiss your proverbial ring, treating them as pawns in a chess match, or failing to respond in a timely way are all forms of making people feel unimportant. I once observed a CEO make sure all his senior officers were in the room waiting before he would enter meetings, guaranteeing they all knew their place. Don't do it. No one will want to work for you.

It is not hard to find examples of managers treating employees poorly. Here are a few:

> Just because he was a doctor, he was "above" me.
>
> I remember one time I had to move something, and he refused to help me—and I was working for him!
>
> Being treated as a piece of political pork.
>
> Not valuing people as people, especially people with fewer degrees, salary, or grade level.
>
> Being manipulated.
>
> They don't look at you as a person. Your time is not as valuable as theirs.

When I first began my career, our manager regularly had employees pick up laundry and do personal chores for her. That certainly put people in their place.

Employees are *people,* not objects to be moved around on a whim, not to be looked down on, and not to be disrespected. It's the little things that signal worth. Although the intent may be admirable—to try to show the value of employees—I generally dislike using the terms "human capital," "assets," or "resources" (as in, "let's move some resources over to help old Jim out") to refer to employees. It is objectifying.

Treat the people you count on the most—your employees—like gold, or, more importantly, like human beings.

Don't Say One Thing and Do Another

Saying one thing and doing another is lying. It is a short-term strategy, doomed to defeat the ability to motivate in the future. It destroys trust and over time wipes out the ability to lead. Don't do it.

A technical specialist told me his motivation disappeared when his boss said he would be promoted by working at a higher level. He did perform, but he wasn't promoted. The boss said the rules had changed. The employee checked out.

Expectations are a motivational filter. I expect to lose weight if I diet and exercise. I expect to learn something interesting if I read the paper each morning. I expect my spirit to be more serene and my body more supple if I take a yoga class (and I expect to laugh each time I describe my body as supple). If any of those results don't occur, I am less likely to pursue what I have been doing.

How do expectations change when a coach, teacher, or parent promises a child something in return for effort and doesn't follow through? Go back on your word enough times after promising a movie to your children in return for bedroom cleaning, and see how many times rooms are cleaned in the future.

Don't say you will reward based on performance and then give raises and promotions based on tenure, gender, age, friendship, a bell curve, or anything else but performance. Don't send out questionnaires asking for ideas or opinions when the decision has already been made.

It is not just a matter of trust—though trust is crucial—it's that people will not be motivated by *any* expectations you try to set up. They won't believe you. Carry out what you promise consistently, or your power to motivate through rewards will vanish.

Sometimes organizations and managers say nothing yet create expectations. Unspoken expectations must still be honored. Claiming nothing was verbalized or written may technically be correct, but it is still—in the eyes of the employee—a broken promise.

Feeling underappreciated, in one sense, is the result of the unspoken, broken promise that the organization will honor us personally and publicly if we do well. One scientist was deflated by her organization and in particular her manager because she won an award and no one announced it in the company newsletter. Another clinical supervisor has employees who hold national leadership positions in their fields, but have never been thanked or rewarded by company management. They've done their company proud and expected to be showered with praise. They were more than disappointed.

One manager deliberately made his expectations unclear so that he could reward employees as he wished. He became known as a manipulator, and no one trusted him. Relying on unclear expectations to motivate is a short-term strategy. First, it doesn't motivate effectively because people are scurrying around trying to figure out what to do to make you happy. Second, people think you are devious and insincere.

This "don't" goes far beyond motivation, however. It strikes at the heart of all relationships. If you tell your child you love her, and make plans to spend time with her, and those plans always get sidetracked by work or other responsibilities, she will match your words with your actions—and believe the actions.

Go to the ends of the earth to keep your word.

Don't Micromanage or Abandon Employees

Too much support is called micromanaging, and employees hate it. Too little support is called sink-or-swim, and most employees hate that too. Consider the following example from my own experience:

> If memory serves after all these years, it was a fall day, and it seems an overcast Kansas sky and a street strewn with leaves set the stage. What I do remember clearly is sitting on my new, red, shining Schwinn bicycle. I was terrified, but learning to ride a bike was a boyhood skill that was way beyond motivating—it was life or death.
>
> I didn't need a mission statement or a performance review to risk scrapes and shame. Every pal I had was already riding his bike. I sat there shaking, tears close to the surface, with my jeans cuffed up at the bottom (a habit that one future day saw me spattered all over the cement, tangled in the chain, but for now was of little concern).
>
> My dad had his hand on the seat and told me I could do this. He said exactly what to do—keep the wheels straight and don't stop pedaling.
>
> "I can't!" I cried.
>
> "Yes you can," he said. "Let's just go a little way."
>
> As I slowly started pedaling, he moved with me, hand on seat, and told me again I could do it—"Yes, you're doing great!—keep pedaling!"
>
> I realized somewhere down that narrow lane that my dad had let go, and I was on my own. I got to the end of the road, put my brakes on, and stopped. I scooted my bike around.
>
> "Good job!" and a thumbs-up from up the street. I pushed off and rode back to meet him.

Examples of how parents, teachers, and coaches gave just the support we needed at the time are everywhere. The next time I rode my bike, I sure didn't want my Dad's hand on the seat of my bike—I wanted to ride on my own. Employees are no different. The complaint I hear more than any other from employees is that managers micromanage.

The most useful model I have found for providing the right support for an employee at the right time is the Situational Leadership model, developed by Ken Blanchard and Paul Hersey.[5] The model shows what a leader should provide as an employee moves from an enthusiastic beginner to a peak performer. An enthusiastic beginner has plenty of motivation but needs lots of direction from her boss because she doesn't have experience or knowledge. As the employee learns more, according to the model, and finds that the going will be more difficult than anticipated, she needs both direction and support, which is called coaching. She is a disillusioned learner. Support includes encouragement, praise, listening, and problem solving. As she develops further, she becomes an emerging contributor. She needs less direction but still encouragement. At that point, the leader mostly supports and encourages her. Finally, she develops into a peak performer, and the leader can delegate with little need to provide support or direction.

Giving too much direction to a peak performer who knows how to do the job is called micromanaging. This is not only demotivating, but also can be humiliating. Giving too little direction to an enthusiastic beginner is called sink-or-swim or abandonment and leaves potentially productive employees hanging. It's a good way to lose high-potential people.

Scaffolding is another metaphor for the same concept. A scaffold is a supporting framework. It's a platform for workers to stand on while working on a building. Think of yourself as the scaffold—providing what your employee can't yet do and then, as he learns and grows in confidence, moving to lesser levels of support until you can pull away almost completely.

How do *you* feel when you are micromanaged? It reduces creativity, makes a person feel undervalued, and undermines initiative. After a while, most people become dependent and give up. Now think about being abandoned. How did that feel? One scientist said,

> "I've had so many managers who did nothing to develop me. One just left us to flounder. For two or three years I had no idea what to do. I had to find another. My own manager was worthless."

Most people do not operate at their best when they don't have the skills, confidence, or experience needed for the task at hand. They are afraid and may hesitate. Fear can paralyze, causing missed opportunities.

The art and skill of management is to provide the right challenge and then to provide the right amount of support throughout the project. That will vary for each employee and each situation. The best managers stake out the area, get resources, and let employees do the work. They give direction and are available as needed, but they don't micromanage.

Give employees what they need when they need it.

Don't Be Unfair

What is "fair"? Each person has a different reference point than you, the organization, or even other fellow employees. It is a difficult question to answer sometimes because fairness resides in the eyes of the employee.

- Is fairness based on giving the same amount and type of work to each employee? Or should work be delegated according to skills, interests, developmental potential, enthusiasm, the situation, or some combination of these?
- Should promotions be based on experience, educational level, work produced, community or organizational service, or some combination?
- Should more opportunities be given to younger workers than older ones because they will make more of a contribution in the future, or should older employees get the opportunities because they've earned those opportunities through past contributions?
- More basically, a workers asks, did I get a fair shake for the contribution I made?

These are not easy questions for a supervisor to sift through. People who feel like they are in an inequitable situation lose motivation or go someplace they believe will be fair to them.

"I can do as much or more than people with a degree, and then they progress and I don't. There is no recognition of experience," one employee told me.

Another said, "After a person is here 10 to 15 years, managers feel they won't leave, and so the tendency is not to reward the stellar performance of older workers as much as the younger. They think they have you. You feel trapped."

"Work is distributed unfairly and unevenly, and projects are taken away for political reasons," explained still another.

It is not always easy to discern how an employee will frame fairness. Fairness may be judged not only by how the final reward was allocated, but also by the process that determined that reward. When the process for determining the reward is not overtly stated, even the perception of what the process *may* have been can be demotivating. Fairness may also be judged by the results. For example, some people might not be happy with what they receive when compared with what others have received.

They wonder what their salary increases and totals are relative to people in other departments or other companies or in their profession.

A supervisor often has limited ability to affect the equity of the company compensation program and can't directly control other organizational recognition and rewards. Be fair and open within your own abilities. Your employees then will be motivated to follow your leadership, even if they feel the larger organization is treating them poorly.

WHAT TO DO

... can to act and communi- ... e acting fairly.

... ns are made concerning ... ny other issue that affects ... ployees to help you decide ... tions and shifts is always a ... lem by letting her employ- ... e made. Not only were em- ... nd solutions the supervisor

Be Consistent

No one trusts the manager who blows in the wind with each decision, rewarding based on one criterion one time and another the next. If you are consistent, employees will be able to adjust their behaviors and attitudes accordingly. Otherwise, they will scurry around trying to figure out why you did what you did. No crystal ball can help them if you are inconsistent.

Be Aware and Make Aware

An individual's perception of her performance may be much different than how you see it. What a group of employees (accountants, journeymen, nurses, etc.) believe that others are paid in the labor market in your region may be very different from what you believe or what is true. Your employees may believe you are paying less than other managers in your organization pay.

- If you are truly compensating unfairly, change it.
- Work hard to be aware of the perceptions of those who work for you, and make them aware of what they are truly paid relative to others.

Leave favoritism at the front door.

IN SUMMARY

1. Don't treat people like dirt. Treat the people you count on the most—your employees—like gold, or, more importantly, like human beings.
2. Don't say one thing and do another. If you want to motivate people, go to the ends of the earth to keep your word.
3. Don't micromanage or abandon your employees. Give employees what they need when they need it.
4. Don't be unfair. Leave favoritism at the front door.

The rest of the chapter outlines what *to* do. Seven principles are introduced that, when applied, will give you a road map for building a highly motivating work environment.

OVERVIEW OF THE PRINCIPLES, GOALS, AND PRACTICES OF WORKPLACE MOTIVATION

There are principles that can be used by anyone to energize, direct, and sustain workplace motivation. Although this book is for noncharismatic managers, the irony is that following these may make them more charismatic.

There are two important areas managers can influence in their day-to-day work arena. One is the backdrop for work to be done, and the other is the process for setting and pursuing goals. The areas can be thought of as "setting the environment" for motivation and "crossing the Rubicon."

SETTING THE ENVIRONMENT

Healthy, great places to work are being recognized and valued more than ever before.

- Each year, *Fortune* magazine lists the 100 best places to work.
- *Working Mother* has done the same for the last 20 years.

- Since 1999, Psychologically Healthy Workplace Awards have been presented to state and other regional organizations with support from the American Psychological Association (APA). Applicants are evaluated on their efforts in five areas:
  1. Employee involvement
  2. Work–life balance
  3. Employee growth and development
  4. Health and safety
  5. Employee recognition
- The APA presented its first annual National Psychologically Healthy Workplace Awards to six organizations in March 2006.

Highly competitive organizations have been able to succeed in the past because they had access to resources, knowledge, market share, or technology that others didn't. Employees are becoming an even more important sustainable source of competitive advantage. Although research has produced differing results regarding the relationship of employee happiness to productivity, it consistently shows evidence that organizational climate affects corporate market value and productivity. Companies that are great to work for may be more productive than their counterparts.

The paradox is that many workers are still not working in healthy work environments. Work for these people may be 24/7. Because of technology, they may be under more constant surveillance than was possible a few years ago. The way they approach tasks may be more prescribed than before. Employee perspectives may be more bounded. The organizational ecosystem may be more survival-of-the-fittest than a place for long-term sustainability and growth. This is a time when many employees are still told what to do and not to think.

The challenge—to develop healthy work environments—may be just as important today as it was when Studs Terkel wrote *Working* 30 years ago.[6] His description of work as being "about violence—to the spirit as well as to the body" (p. xi), isn't much different than Barbara Ehrenreich's graphic description of the "working poor" in her 2001 memoir, *Nickel and Dimed.*[7]

"Guilt," she says when describing how we should feel about these employees, "doesn't go anywhere near far enough; the appropriate emotion is shame—shame at our own dependency, in this case, on the underpaid labor of others" (pp. 220–21).

In many cases the workplace hasn't improved. The tragedy is that the people Terkel interviewed who described themselves as "caged," "a machine," "a mule," "a monkey," or an "object" could have been many employees today. Employees are still treated like property in organizations across the spectrum. Are you? Are the employees who work for you?

OCCUPATIONAL INTIMACY

Patricia Boverie and I developed a model for creating and sustaining a passionate work environment. We call the model Occupational Intimacy (OI).[8] "Occupational intimacy" is the term we developed to represent work that people love to do in an environment that cares for them. A full description of OI and how we developed it appears in our book, *Transforming Work.*

OI has three qualities:

1. Meaningful work
2. Enjoyable work
3. Nurturing workplace

Meaningful Work

What is significant for one person is different than what is for another person. Meaningfulness differs for each of your employees, and may come from a variety of sources, including vocation, challenge, relevance, relationships, making a difference, or competition. An effective manager finds, for every person, what makes work mean something.

Enjoyable Work

What makes "I can't wait to get to work" work? What makes it fun? When work feels as comfortable as your old rocking chair, when you find yourself laughing and smiling all the time, and when you feel pure joy in going about your day-to-day business, work is enjoyable. That is when work generates its own motivation.

Nurturing Workplace

A nurturing workplace finds employees continuously learning, growing, and developing. There people are supported, cared for, and valued. Employees know they can count on getting the compensation they deserve, and the recognition. Relationships in those places are strong and people feel—yes—loved, or at least believe the organization is interested in them as persons and not just as cogs in the machine.

These three elements—meaningful work, enjoyable work, and nurturing workplace—can be thought of as overlapping, much like a Venn diagram. Sometimes work is enjoyable, for example, because it is meaningful;

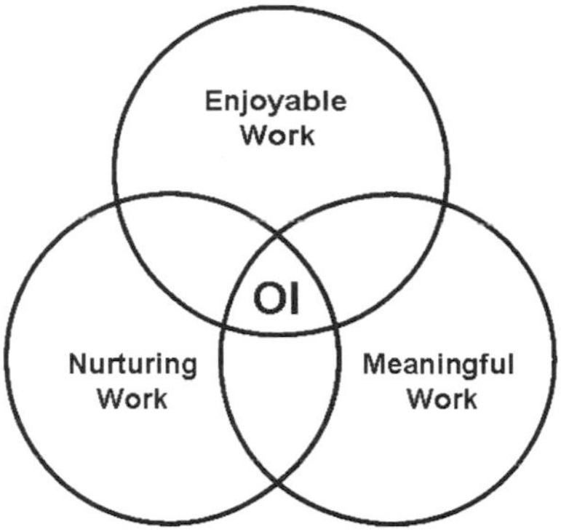

Figure 2.1 Occupational Intimacy
Source: Adapted from Patricia Eileen Boverie and Michael S. Kroth. *Transforming Work: The Five Keys to Achieving Trust, Commitment, and Passion in the Workplace. New Perspectives in Organizational Learning, Performance, and Change.* Cambridge, MA: Perseus, 2001.

and sometimes work is meaningful because of nurturing relationships. Sometimes work may be nurturing because of enjoyable relationships. Sometimes, work is all three.

OI has the potential to make a real difference in leadership development and organizational effectiveness. Margo Karsten, for example, a Colorado State University PhD candidate, recently applied OI theory to job satisfaction for medical doctors. Her complete findings will be available about the same time this book will be published, and I am excited about her results. She has developed an empirically tested job-satisfaction tool that measures meaningfulness, nurturing environment, and love of work. I think her findings could be very helpful for managers and Human Resource Department (HRD) consultants. This tool allows organizations the ability to identify where they may have gaps in these three OI dimensions. For more information on Karsten's research, you may contact her at mak@karstenconsulting.com.

Setting the environment provides the climate for employee motivation. Most managers don't have the power to change corporate policy, but there is much that can be done to create a great place for their own employees. The "Setting the Environment" chapter in this book describes how to do so.

Four principles are included in "Setting the Environment":

Principle 1: Organizational commitment motivates powerfully.
Principle 2: The more you care, the more they will care.
Principle 3: The more you know about people, the more you will know what to do.
Principle 4: Do what you love, and the motivation will follow.

Figure 2.2 Setting the Environment

CROSSING THE RUBICON

The story of Julius Caesar crossing the Rubicon, a small river in northern Italy, on his way to Rome, breaking a law forbidding it and making battle certain, has come to symbolize making an irreversible commitment. Caesar was undecided as he approached the river. When he did cross the river, he supposedly said the now famous phrase, "The die is cast." Today, "crossing the Rubicon" means passing the point of no return.[9]

I chose the metaphor "crossing the Rubicon" to describe the process of effectively creating and sustaining motivation to achieve goals. The model is adapted from an article written by Lyn Corno in 1993.[10] The model helps to explain how the powerful goal-setting and goal-pursuing process works.

In much the same way, setting and keeping goals is a process of approaching a problem or opportunity requiring a decision or course of action. Before making the decision, we are uncertain, hold different alternatives in mind, and weigh the risks and returns of choosing one option over the others. At some point, we make a commitment—yes, we'll lose 15 pounds by the reunion; no, we won't take the job; yes, we'll increase production 10 percent by the end of the month. Once we've made that commitment—crossed the Rubicon, in this metaphor—our thoughts then turn to how to make the promise we've made to ourselves or others come true.

Unlike Caesar, our commitments are usually less irrevocable. Vows have varying degrees of resoluteness. The determination to close the books by the first Friday of every month with zero rework and no overtime may dissolve during March Madness.

One choice is to set easy-to-accomplish goals. In that case, commitment is easy, but the results underwhelming. Another choice might be to set stretch goals. Commitment is then harder to gain in the first place but once obtained results in highly motivated behavior. Keeping employees motivated in the face of conflict, obstacles, and personal distractions is paramount in that situation. The leader's job is to provide the right support and direction for effective goal setting, goal commitment, and sustaining the effort to achieve them.

Chapter 4, "Crossing the Rubicon," describes how to do that. Most managers don't have the power to change the strategic objectives of the overall organization, but much can be done to set and support the goals in their own programs or departments. Three principles are included in this chapter:

Principle 5: Belief in personal capability enables goal setting and goal pursuit.
Principle 6: Great goals get people going.
Principle 7: Willpower is the engine for goal pursuit.

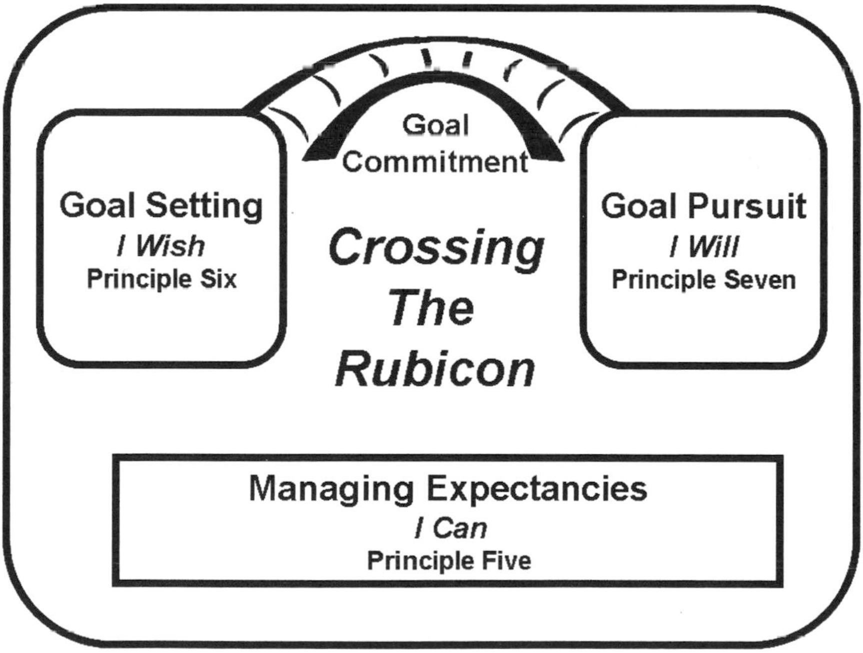

Figure 2.3 Crossing the Rubicon

Table 2.1
Seven Principles for Motivating Work

Setting the Environment: Create a Motivating Workplace		
Principle	*Goal*	*Practice*
1. Organizational commitment motivates powerfully.	Develop commitment to your organization.	Tap the heart, strengthen the connection, and make your organization hard to leave.
2. The more you care, the more they will care.	Develop "beyond-the-call-of-duty" motivation.	Give a darn!
3. The more you know about people, the more you will know what to do.	Understand what motivates employees.	Treat everyone the same and treat everyone differently.
4. Do what you love, and the motivation will follow.	Create work that generates its own motivation.	Design enjoyable work.

Crossing the Rubicon: Build and Sustain Motivation to Accomplish Workplace Goals		
Principle	*Goal*	*Practice*
5. Belief in personal capability enables goal setting and pursuit.	Build self-efficacy.	Be an expectancy manager.
6. Great goals get people going.	Set challenging goals.	Master the art and science of goal setting.
7. Willpower is the engine for goal pursuit.	Sustain motivation.	Use strategies to strengthen and support willpower.

PRINCIPLES, GOALS, AND PRACTICES

Chapter 3 discusses setting the environment, chapter 4 covers crossing the Rubicon, chapter 5 describes the roles and responsibilities of the noncharismatic leader, and chapter 6 contains assessments and development plans. Before moving into the seven principles, please evaluate your own practices in each of the areas. The "Motivational Self-Assessment" survey will begin to examine strengths and weaknesses. It will also be helpful to know what others think about your ability to motivate. The exercise "Learning about Yourself from Other People" is a tool to help you gather that information from employees, peers, your manager, and others who know your work.

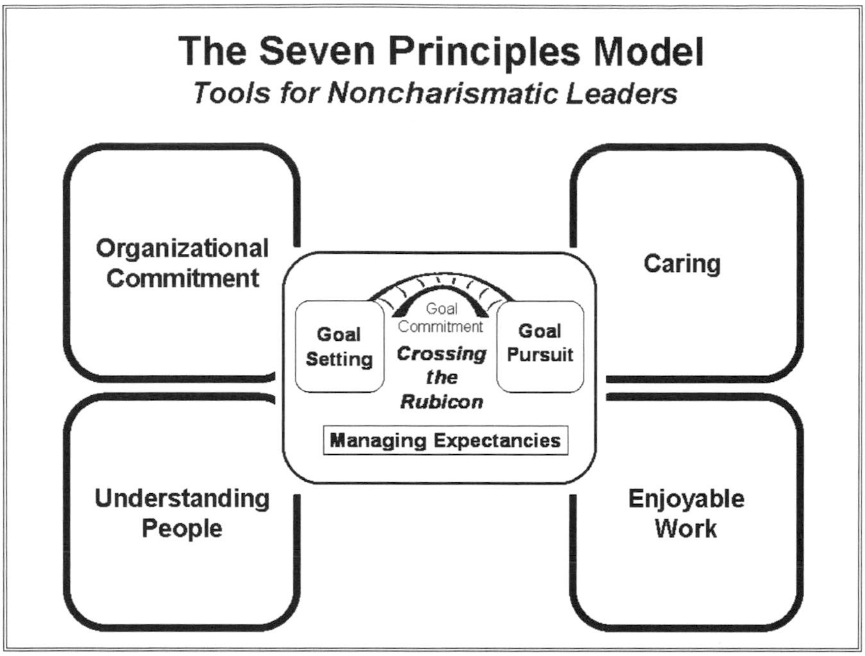

Figure 2.4. The Seven Principles Model

Activity

Complete the survey "Motivational Self-Assessment," found in chapter 6.

Activity

Review the interview guide "Learning about Yourself from Other People," found in chapter 6.

KEY POINTS

1. Incorporate "can't-wait-to" motivation into your workplace.
2. Avoid demotivating employees by treating them like dirt, saying one thing and doing another, micromanaging or abandoning, or being unfair.
3. Create and sustain workplace motivation by establishing the right environment, setting goals, and then pursuing them.

SUMMARY

There have been thousands of studies about motivation and hundreds of theories, but for our purposes, it all comes down to getting employees to do what you want them to do *over time.* In the short run, you can prod employees like cattle in a pen or fool them into working for some illusory reward or scare them into compliance. Fear is a powerful motivator. Punishment today is an unsustainable strategy, however. Labor flows more readily than ever to where rewards are available. Employees will go where they enjoy the work if the ability to compensate is equal. You will have to pay a premium to keep them if you are a jerk. No one will want to work for you. Even when employees were handcuffed by 30-year pension programs and a tight labor market, a manager could rarely use fear to sustain the highest creative, industrious, loyal effort possible.

Providing a positive, affirming, challenging environment, on the other hand, will draw the best employees. It shouldn't be a surprise that a place like that sets up longer-term success. Your reputation will go before you even if you are promoted or transferred, and the likelihood of success will continue to improve as the best talent flows to you.

A motivating work environment entails more than just keeping employees happy. Happy employees are not necessarily more productive. Employee productivity comes from a supportive work environment that is both enjoyable *and* challenging.

PART II

Principles and Practices

THREE

Setting the Environment

WHAT YOU WILL FIND IN THIS CHAPTER

1. Four principles that set the environment for workplace motivation
2. Three types of organizational commitment
3. The importance of caring—How to care when you don't care
4. The differences in employee motivation
5. Steps to design enjoyable work

Ecology is the branch of science concerned with interrelationships between organisms and their environments. Ecosystems can be as big as a desert or as small as a pond. They are dynamic, responding to changes either inside or outside themselves. A change to the outer environment, say a flood or a fire engulfing the system, will change the relationships inside. A change inside, such as when a mutation occurs or a species dies out, also changes the ecosystem.

A river is an ecosystem. Humans can change the river in negative ways (e.g., pollute it, kill its fish) or in positive ways (e.g., clean it up, protect fish spawning grounds). A farm is an ecosystem that a human (farmer) intentionally influences in order to produce something (grain, cattle, vegetables). A farmer creates many of the conditions to get wanted results but cannot control everything affecting the farm. For example, the weather and governmental policies are pretty much out of the farmer's control. A farm can be managed for sustainability or milked for shorter-term profits.

YOUR WORK ENVIRONMENT IS A NATURAL ECOSYSTEM

Your organization is also an ecosystem.[1] You can view it from an organization-wide perspective or as smaller units, such as your area of responsibility. Similar to an ecosystem, external forces affect your department, and its success will be at least partially determined by how well the organization adapts to those changes.

Like a farmer, you have great influence over what happens inside your organization, and at the same time, you have little influence. Your decisions can send tsunamis throughout the organization, but you will never be able to control all the complex internal interrelationships, dependencies, informal processes, and interactions that occur. Those emerge as people and things interact together. Nor can you control or probably even influence greatly the forces outside the department.

Consider your organization—at whatever level you manage an ecosystem. What do we know about your organization just from that? First, your organization is made up of interdependent parts that interact continuously. Second, your department is part of the larger organization and depends on it for food (compensation and resources) and protection (security and safety), just as the larger organization depends on you. Third, like ecosystems, your organization's ability to adapt to changes (lay-offs, restructurings, new technology, and new initiatives) will be the key to its survival. Those that can adapt may survive; those that don't, won't.

You have choices to make. One will be the role you wish to take within your own ecosystem. Will you be the polluter or the conservationist? Will you manage for sustainability or short-term gain? Will you wear out your employees with unachievable demands or create the conditions for sustainable and self-renewing employee motivation?

Organizational culture is the "way we do things around here" and a vital aspect of your ecosystem. Collins and Porras describe the importance of organizational culture in their thought provoking book *Built to Last,* which describes the qualities of visionary companies.[2] They found the culture of highly successful companies almost "cult-like." Visionary companies and cults have four common characteristics. Those are

1. a fervently held ideology,
2. indoctrination,
3. tightness of fit—employees either fit well or don't fit at all, and
4. elitism.

The way employees perceive their organization has been described as the organizational "climate." The number of dimensions that make up climate depends on the researcher describing them, but the qualities are similar. The so-called Organizational Climate Measure proposed by Malcolm Patterson and others has 17 dimensions.[3] They found that some characteristics of organizational climate predict productivity. Among them are

- supervisory support,
- concern for employee welfare,
- skill development,
- innovation and flexibility,
- quality, and
- performance feedback.

A HEALTHY WORK ENVIRONMENT IMPROVES PERFORMANCE

The reasons to give attention to organizational climate are compelling. The quality of work life positively impacts business performance. A great working environment results in financial performance that is as good as and often significantly better than competitors. The market values of companies listed as *Fortune*'s "100 Best Companies to Work For in America" exceeded those of similar firms not on the list.[4] Companies on the list have higher growth rates than companies on the S&P 500 list.[5] The 56 publicly traded companies on *Fortune*'s 2006 list beat the S&P 500 significantly over 1 year, 3 years, 5 years, and 10 years.[6] Employee attitudes at the "100 Best" are both highly positive and stable over time. Accounting ratios of companies on the list are generally better than a matched comparison group, and their stock returns outperform the board market in cumulative returns.[7] Other research supports the idea that a healthy work environment improves business performance. Michelle Arthur, for example, found that shareholder returns improved for companies announcing work-family initiatives.[8]

As Susan Bednar notes, a poor work climate has the opposite effect. In child welfare agencies, for example, employee attitudes about their work environment may affect the risk of child abuse by staff, service quality, and client outcomes. One review of research found that job stress and burnout, powerlessness, high anxiety, lack of training and professionalism, poor organizational directives, and poor supervision, among other factors, increase the risk of child mistreatment by child welfare staff.[9]

Improvements to organizational climate can result in improved employee and customer satisfaction. A poor work environment can harm productivity and quality and increase turnover. Like the farmer, a manager can till the earth, plant the seeds, and provide the nourishment leading to success. A manager can root out the weeds that will strangle the harvest.

There are many factors that affect employee motivation, including the relationship employees have with the organization, the relationship they have with their supervisor, the depth of understanding the manager has of them, and the enjoyment they find in their work.

Setting the climate consists of four principles that provide fertile ground for top employee performance. Following these principles will create a more positive environment for employee motivation. The principles are as follows:

Principle 1: Organizational commitment motivates powerfully.
Principle 2: The more you care, the more they will care.
Principle 3: The more you know about people, the more you will know what to do.
Principle 4: Do what you love, and the motivation will follow.

PRINCIPLE 1

Organizational Commitment Motivates Powerfully: Tap the Heart, Strengthen the Connection, and Make Your Organization Hard to Leave

COMMITMENT

Commitment influences nearly every source of motivation found in this book. Committing to something is a powerful motivational force. It ties a person to some thing or some action. An employee can be committed to people, goals, the organization, a task or job, or an ideal or value. A worker can be strongly, weakly, conditionally, or unconditionally committed. Making a commitment is like crossing a line. Before the decision, there are alternatives. What to do is up in the air. Afterward, choices are different. They concern how to fulfill the promise and remain motivated to accomplish it. Principle 1—organizational commitment motivates powerfully—focuses on building commitment to your department or program.

Table 3.1
Setting the Environment: Create a Motivating Workplace

Principle	*Goal*	*Practice*
1. Organizational commitment motivates powerfully.	Develop commitment to your organization.	Tap the heart, strengthen the connection, and make your organization hard to leave.
2. The more you care, the more they will care.	Develop "beyond-the-call-of-duty" motivation.	Give a darn!
3. The more you know about people, the more you will know what to do.	Understand what motivates employees.	Treat everyone the same and treat everyone differently.
4. Do what you love, and the motivation will follow.	Create work that generates its own motivation.	Design enjoyable work.

John Meyer and Natalie Allen developed a model to describe organizational commitment that has been widely studied for over 20 years.[10] It applies to occupations, supervisors, teams, programs, or customers as well as to the organization. They found three forms of commitment, which they labeled affective, normative, and continuance.

- *Affective commitment* represents emotional attachment. Employees with strong affective commitment believe their values are those of their employer, identify with the organization, and feel involved in it. Employees with a strong affective commitment stay with an organization because they *want* to.
- *Normative commitment* represents a feeling of obligation. It develops from cultural and organizational socialization. Employees with normative commitment feel they *ought* to stay with an organization.
- *Continuance commitment* represents the cost to leave an organization. It develops because employees build up an investment in the organization over time that would be lost upon leaving. Employees with continuance commitment feel they *need* to stay with the organization.

The most positive form of commitment is affective, which I call "adoring" commitment. Employees who are engaged in something because they *want* to be feel better about it and put more energy into it than they would if they only *had* to do it. Why might an employee emotionally commit? Shared values or mission is one reason, and relating to another person or the leader is another. Desire to commit also can come from involvement in an important project or program.

Table 3.2
Forms of Commitment

Meyer and Allen	*Qualities*	*Kroth*
Affective	Emotional Attachment "I want"	Adoring
Normative	Obligation "I ought"	Choring
Continuance	Cost "I need"	Storing

Source: Meyer, John P., and Natalie Jean Allen. *Commitment in the Workplace: Theory, Research, and Application. Advanced Topics in Organizational Behavior.* Thousand Oaks, CA: Sage, 1997.

Another source of commitment comes from the expectations of others—that is what I call "choring." Doing work because you're supposed to is kind of like milking the cow on a frosty morning. It may not be fun to get up at 5:00 A.M., but you feel a sense of responsibility. You know that people (and the cows) are counting on you. Some expectations are internalized your mother told you to always finish a job you started, and so that is what you still do. Some expectations come from external sources—you're part of a group, and the team asked if you would "volunteer" to work the late shift this week. You are then committed not because of eagerness to complete the task but because you feel you ought to do it.

The third reason for commitment is the prospect of losing something. I call that "storing" because a worker holds herself hostage in order not to waste something, say retirement benefits, that have been stockpiled over time. When someone is storing, commitment comes not because of desire or obligation, but because the cost of leaving is so high. An employee might remain in the organization an additional five years to earn a full retirement and do just enough not to get fired. The cost of breaking up a relationship may be too high both because of monetary factors or because valued friends would be lost. The objective, then, would be to do just enough not to get dumped and to find true enjoyment in riding the Harley with friends. Employees are more likely to stay with an organization they don't like if they have seniority, benefits, a social network, and accumulated vacation that would be lost upon leaving than they would be if they didn't have those investments stacked up. The price would be even higher if the costs of leaving meant relocation expenses and leaving parents behind.

Expect employees to feel imprisoned and resentful if storing is the only form of commitment provided. A mid-level professional said to me, "After a person is here 10 to 15 years, managers feel you won't leave, and so the tendency is not to reward stellar performance of older workers as much as younger. They think they have you. You feel trapped." How motivated is this employee? Does he put anything but the minimum level of effort into his work?

Organizations depended on the handcuffs of pension plans to keep employees in the past. Those kinds of strategies are less likely to succeed with portable benefits. More emphasis must be placed on developing adoring commitment. It's good business sense. Linda Rhoades and Robert Eisenberger say it strongly: "Employees who are emotionally committed to the organization show heightened performance, reduced absenteeism, and a lessened likelihood of quitting their job" (p. 698).[11] A highly motivating manager can't afford to miss that type of commitment.

Leaders should try to build all three forms of organizational commitment. An organization's mission and vision statements can contribute to emotional commitment (adoring). Organizational values ("This is the way we do it here") reinforce what employees feel they ought to be doing or what they "owe" to the corporation (choring). Competitive salaries, educational reimbursement plans, and defined retirement plans make it costly to leave (storing). A person who likes working there, who feels a sense of obligation, and who also knows he or she wouldn't be able to find another job that paid more has strong motivating commitment that results in high productivity over time.

*Commitment: Dominic Sedillo**

It's been a long, freezing day. Your flight was late, it took you forever to find the shuttle to your hotel, and you're nervous about the meeting tomorrow. Your girlfriend (or boyfriend, spouse, boss, employee, etc.) snapped at you just before you hit security at the airport, where you got the wand and remembered, too late, that you had worn your steel soled shoes. You are tired and irritable, and you feel as if life is out of control. Then you see the unsuspecting bellman holding the hotel door open. You glare at him, complain all the way to the top floor, and then somehow "forget" the tip. If the hotel room isn't just right for you, he becomes a little less than human. If your bellman was Dominic Sedillo, however, by the time you checked out of the hotel, you were all smiles, you left an inordinate tip, and you went out of your way to find the customer survey card so that you could tell management what a great employee they have.

Dominic absolutely loves his work. "Every aspect of this hotel is wonderful," he says. "I love coming to work every single day. I enjoy the people I work with. It pushes me to go forward, and to know that I am recognized makes me want to strive even further than anybody expects of me." Maybe it's his boss. It's not just promotions, he says, but his managers saying he is doing a good job. "Little, tiny things make me enjoy my job."

Within a year of joining the Old Town Sheraton as a bellman, Dominic had become a front desk supervisor and employee of the year. Now the

---

*This story was adapted from an article, "The Bellman," originally published in the February 2004 issue of *Leading with Passion*, by Michael Kroth and Patricia Boverie.

bellmen report to him. Dominic is only 21 years old but is on his way up the ladder because he loves what he does and is good at it. He takes risks—"I put myself out there," as he says it. He is self-motivated. "I take pride in what I do, and I take pride in myself, and I take pride in everyone around me." One of the most important reasons Dominic loves what he does is the work environment at the Old Town Sheraton. "I love everyone I work with," he says, and he lists them all—guests, banquet personnel, housekeeping, the kitchen staff, and management. "Management is always on a high note," he says, "and they are always willing to coach. And they don't put you down. Adrian [Sheraton's GM] is one of those people that make folks love what they do."

Activity

Review Dominic's situation and answer the following questions:

1. Dominic has an emotional attachment (adoring) to his work. What are some of the reasons?
2. Think of a time when you were emotionally committed to a team, organization, or project. What were the reasons you developed that commitment? How did it happen? What was the role of the leader?
3. What are sources of adoring, choring, and storing in your work area? Do you depend on one more than others? What could you do to create more balance?

When employees like Dominic have a strong emotional commitment to the workplace, they may be motivated to support the organization beyond what they are asked to do. These kinds of activities are called organizational citizenship behavior.

ORGANIZATIONAL CITIZENSHIP BEHAVIOR

Organizational citizenship behaviors (OCB) are "above the call of duty" actions performed by employees in your organization. They are completed for the good for the organization but are not required. They are a matter of personal choice—a gift, if you will, from your employees.

OCB can be focused on helping another coworker or on helping the organization as a whole. Jumping in to help someone who has a deadline approaching or praising the company to someone outside the organization would be examples of OCB. They are voluntary and intentional actions. They are also not directly rewarded by the organization.

Counterproductive work behavior (CWB) is just the opposite. CWB actions are intentional actions that hurt the organization or coworkers. Examples might include gossiping about another employee, taking long breaks, or calling in sick when feeling well enough to go play a round of golf.

Employees are more likely to go beyond the call of duty and do extra things for the organization when they: believe that the organization is fair, are satisfied with their jobs, believe their leader supports them, and are committed to the organization.

Employees are more likely to "work to the contract" and, in fact, consciously or unconsciously sabotage the organization and other employees when they believe the organization treats employees unfairly, they are not satisfied with their jobs, their leaders don't support them, or they aren't committed to the organization. OCBs are not just soft, extraneous activities. They have a real impact on performance.

The message is clear. The more you can motivate employees to go beyond the call of duty—their specific job and goal commitments—the more productive they and your program will be.

Sources: R. S. Dalal, "A Meta-Analysis of the Relationship between Organizational Citizenship Behavior and Counterproductive Work Behavior." *Journal of Applied Psychology* 90, no. 6 (2005): 1241. LePine, J. A., A. Erez, and D. E. Johnson. "The Nature and Dimensionality of Organizational Citizenship Behavior: A Critical Review and Meta-Analysis." *Journal of Applied Psychology* 87, no. 1 (2002): 52.

Activity

Complete the exercise "Organizational Citizenship Behaviors," found in chapter 6.

Adoring commitment is the most likely to improve job performance and OCB. It makes sense—the stronger the emotional attachment, the harder people will work and the more they will do voluntarily for the organization. Choring also improves performance, but storing not so much. In fact, when people feel trapped—think they have to stay—they may put in just enough effort not to get fired.

Creating the conditions for commitment to the larger organization is less under your control than opportunities within your own program. Employees entering the marketplace are less likely these days to give loyalty to organizations over their own interests. Still, organizational commitment is a significant source of employee motivation.

Create Your Own Oasis

Have you ever been in an organization that was dysfunctional? Did you notice there were pockets in the middle of that poisonous atmosphere where groups were clearly motivated, excited about their work, and having a great time? In those cases the supervisors, or maybe even members of the group, took matters into their own hands and sowed the seeds for growing their own living, generative, healthy work environments. Despite toxicity all around, they refused to be pulled into sick interpersonal, group, and departmental behaviors. Don't become a victim of the larger organization. Be the farmer. Create your own oasis. Protect your farm from the environmental forces, viruses, and contamination that would destroy it. Nurture life instead.

You Can Do It

Two employees within the same organization had very different experiences. One 24-year veteran had to escape her manager. "When I transferred out," she said, "it was like a ton of bricks off my back getting out from that environment where I was criticized for everything thing I did and his boss reinforced it."

Contrast that employee's experience with another one who had worked for over 20 years *in the same company.*

He said, "My boss has an energy level and enthusiasm that gets us passionate. He never asks us to do anything we shouldn't. He's above board, follows the rules, and has integrity. He's very supportive of my professional development. That's important to me professionally and personally." The work itself isn't all that great for this employee, but the supervisor makes all the difference.

"Not a day goes by," the second employee said, "that my boss doesn't say something nice or humorous. He recognizes you for a job well done, gives you a pat on the back, and salary reinforcement. He's passionate about his work."

Be the farmer. You will harvest much over time. The best talent will flock to you, and work will be more fun.

EXAMPLES OF ORGANIZATIONAL COMMITMENT

If you wanted to create unbreakable bonds of commitment to your team, if you wanted to lower your turnover and instead attract top, committed talent to your organization, what would you do? The Navy Seals and Poudre Valley Health System are two examples of how organizations do exactly that.

Case Study: Navy SEALs[12]

The Navy SEALs' origins go back to World War II. The first two official SEAL teams were commissioned in 1962, when President

Kennedy decided the country should develop unconventional warfare capability, and were made up entirely of underwater demolition personnel. SEAL stands for "Sea, Air, Land," and recruits go through what many consider the toughest training in the world. Candidates must pass rigorous entrance requirements and then a six-month basic course, three weeks of parachute training, and 15 weeks of advanced training period *before ever becoming a SEAL.*

Navy SEALs work in high-performance teams. Once a SEAL has been accepted, the desire for individual success is high. Importantly, the new SEAL has the same unshakable commitment to the team to which he is assigned. I wanted to know what creates that commitment from a SEAL's perspective, so I talked to AO1 (SEAL) Garrick Fernbaugh.

The Need to Know Who You Are—Developing Relationships

Counting on a coworker to complete the report when due seems imperative at the time, but counting on another person to save your life doesn't leave much room for regret if he doesn't come through. I was impressed when talking to Garrick about the importance of getting to know other SEALs at a deeper level than many of us experience with our colleagues. Interestingly, one of the places that understanding develops is after work. "It used to be that your reputation would suffer a lot if you were not out socializing with the guys, which meant drinking until the bars closed," Garrick says. "Guys wouldn't trust you because they didn't know who you were really." Going out together humanizes everyone, even the leader. "It bumps them off their pedestals and allows them to connect with us," he says. These days, socializing after work occurs less in bars and more with families, but it remains an important key to building organizational commitment.

SEAL leaders develop and support strong interpersonal relationships on the job too. There is a strong emotional commitment to each other and to the team. Much of it comes from carrying out extraordinarily demanding activities together. "You might not even like a particular guy," according to Garrick, "but if you've done a number of very difficult things, you've got a bond. You have a common denominator because you've accomplished these things together."

Being the Best

Standards of performance are extremely high from day one. SEALs are the elite. They are the best, and they know it. "People feeling special is a motivating factor," Garrick says. "Coming out of training and feeling like you're best is huge."

"I always felt that to be an effective leader, you needed to give those under your direction something to respect. That will give them another reason to follow your lead," he says. He would always give his best, no matter the situation. "Peer pressure is a powerful tool," he says. "Expectations for excellence are high, and when members don't perform, they are shut out from the group to a certain degree. That causes them to step up their performance."

According to Garrick, "It is a community of perfectionists. Everyone is striving to do everything the best they possibly can. It is the standard of excellence that SEALs are taught to value from day one. "You maintain a group of people always willing to give it all. If at any point, even after you have been in the teams for a number of years, you show that you are not willing or able to give it all, you will be pushed aside," he says.

Selection and Training

SEAL candidates are expected to be self-starters. You don't get very far if you don't have resilience and willpower. As a SEAL instructor, Garrick knows what it takes to survive the seemingly inhuman tasks candidates must perform. Most of us cannot imagine undertaking what they do in their very first few hours of training.

It is during training that organizational and interpersonal commitment begins to develop. Though succeeding is very much an individual accomplishment, no one can without the help of others. "During SEAL training, you have to have constant propping up, or nobody will make it," Garrick says. "Everyone's always leaning on each other for support." Exercises are designed to force mutual support. Still, even the standards for helping each other are high. "People are supportive of each other to a point," according to Garrick. "If they try to support you for a number of times, and you haven't come through, they just kind of give you up."

Mixing It Up

Finally, SEAL leaders don't just delegate. They jump in. "As a leader, you gotta be willing to mix it up," Garrick emphasizes. "You gotta get in there and show them you're willing to work just as hard to do the dirty nasty stuff you're asking them to do." One day, his squad was looking for a river crossing in freezing weather. They couldn't find one and wasted hours looking. Every route ended in the river. Not even night-vision glasses helped. "We didn't know how deep the water was. It was in the 30s (degrees), and everybody's freezing. That night, I took my clothes off and got into the water to find out if it was passable. I earned a few points with the guys that night. They learned firsthand that I wouldn't ask them to do something that I wouldn't do. I knew as I climbed out of the water that there could very well be a time I would ask them to do something that would put their lives in serious jeopardy."

This is a way of life that is reinforced when opportunities present themselves. "There was respect in the eyes of the guys that night just because I did something I wouldn't ask them to do," Garrick says. Commitment comes from "mixing it up."

Summary

The culture of being the best, not letting your buddies down, and persevering despite every obstacle is reinforced by a belief in the greater good. "Patriotism is definitely a [motivating] factor, especially after you've been to war and come back," Garrick says. "You feel like you have sacrificed for the country." Values are the bedrock of organizational commitment, and leaders build it by jumping in and "mixing it up." "Trust is an important aspect of being an effective leader," Garrick says. "People don't want to follow your direction if they can't trust you."

Case Study: Poudre Valley Healthcare*

Although many leaders have still to discover the benefits of making their organizations worker-friendly, more and more have done so. One is Rulon Stacey, President and CEO of the Poudre Valley Health System (PVHS). Over an eight-year period under his leadership, PVHS reduced overall employee turnover from over 20 percent to 7.7 percent, including high-demand, low-supply occupations such as nursing. Key indicators, including mortality rate, patient satisfaction, turnover rate, net revenue, net assets, and employee satisfaction, also improved dramatically. PVHS has received numerous prestigious awards, including being named one of the nation's 100 top hospitals for superior clinical, operational, and financial performance. PVHS was the 18th hospital in the nation and first in the Rocky Mountain region to receive the Magnet Hospital designation in 2000.

How did PVHS do it? By giving employees reasons to love coming to work, according to Stacey. Ironically, quality and financial results were the third and fourth priorities when PVHS began their

*This story was adapted from an article, "Across the Centuries—Putting Employees First," originally published in the May 2005 issue of *Leading with Passion*, by Michael Kroth and Patricia Boverie.

strategy eight years ago. Instead, they put employees first on their list, then physicians, then quality, and finally finances.

"We believe that if we meet the needs of our employees and work with physicians to provide the proper clinical tools, we'll lower our turnover and vacancy rates," he said.[13] Getting employees involved is key to employee loyalty, and even when times are hard, the company builds trust with employees. PVHS, for example, doesn't send nurses or staff home when their numbers are low.

"The board wants to keep our employees here because that shows our commitment to them," Rulon said. "When employees trust us, they won't leave. When they are satisfied, they provide better care."

Margo Karsten, the senior executive at PVHS's hospital, told me that the first several years of transformation were easy. "The culture was open and ready to embrace a change of focus, one which was more informal. Rulon's expectation was that all senior leaders should be out of their offices talking with staff and making changes to improve the work environment, and that is exactly what we all did."

PVHS leadership then began to make improvements systematically. Culture became the number one strategic objective and the first agenda item in PVHS board meetings, unlike many organizations, where employee concerns are discussed last if at all.

Among many examples of putting employees first were the following: increasing the number of employee forums, changing the reward and recognition program, and changing the employee culture survey to capture what would make employees "jump out of bed in the morning." How many times have employee surveys in your organization been conducted, but the results disappeared into a black hole? PVHS focuses on improving the lowest dimension of the survey results. One year, the lowest rating was "listening." So PVHS created listening classes and recognized people who listened well. At the quarterly leadership meeting, departments that listened well were featured so that the rest of the company could learn from them. Acting on employee responses made the survey credible to employees and enabled tangible workplace improvements.

Putting employees first doesn't mean simply being nice. PVHS has high standards of performance and is continually raising the bar. They are shooting for world-class status. It does mean being respectful, making the workplace a healthy place to work both emotionally and physically, and helping employees be successful. The hospital does not tolerate any hint of a hostile work environment. Senior leaders spend loads of time with employees.

It must be working. Poudre Valley is in its fourth year of sustained customer improvement and satisfaction. Only 2 percent of organizations in the country are able to sustain this for three years.

Patricia Boverie and I were curious about what made this environment so successful. We interviewed 12 PVHS employees who had been employed there for over 10 years—well before the culture change started—to learn more about changes since employees were placed first in the organization. We asked them what PVHS is doing differently now. It doesn't take a charismatic leader to initiate what these employees described.[14]

- *Communication is emphasized.* Management takes the time to explain, listen, and make people feel comfortable. There are many more social events and information meetings than there were before. Problems and conflicts don't fester. They get solved. Leaders are both approachable and visible. Supervisors are expected to listen to and support employees.
- *Employees are valued.* Management cares more and expresses appreciation. Not only that, but *others* in the company appreciate employees' work. Barriers inside the company are broken down, and people with negative attitudes are gone. Rewards and recognition are encouraged throughout the organization. Pay and benefits are good. Learning—including personal learning—is encouraged. Employees feel respected and valued.
- *Work is meaningful.* Work in a hospital is pretty important—hospital employees are saving lives and healing people after all—but much of the work can be tedious, hard, and, when you think about it, pretty icky. Poudre Valley has made the work even more meaningful by shooting for world-class status, emphasizing excellence in work, and having a strong sense of direction.

Employees interviewed attributed much of the change to President and CEO Rulon Stacey. Representative comments included the following:

> I think it started when Rulon Stacey became our CEO. He could see that employees were very unhappy, and he's done a lot of changes; he definitely makes you feel like you are important.
>
> Rulon actually came down on a graveyard shift, in our unit, and was walking around talking to everybody, and I'm thinking, "Oh my god, that's Rulon. He's here at night." Graveyard shift, we must mean something.

Activity

The Navy SEALs and Poudre Valley Health System are quite different, yet created organizational commitment through a variety of methods.

1. Which of these are adoring methods, which choring, and which storing?
2. What methods do these organizations use that you could apply to your own organization?
3. What are the pros and cons to creating adoring commitment in your organization? Choring? Storing?

THE 100 BEST PLACES TO WORK

It costs money to provide day care, to have an employee bring lunch or coffee to other employees, or to provide other "extras" that could be going to stockholders or to improve operations. Why do you suppose companies spend money on employees that is not directly related to the bottom line? The answer is that making the workplace enjoyable is a source of competitive advantage. Those "extras" attract the best talent and then retain them. Productivity increases. Commitment is built. The motivation to be the best spreads. Why would anyone leave such a company?

Fortune publishes its list of "100 Best Companies to Work For in America" each year.[15] Take a look on the next page at what these companies do to create adoring, choring, and storing commitment. Actual examples are listed in each category.

WHAT YOU CAN DO: FIVE WAYS TO INCREASE EMPLOYEE COMMITMENT

Here are five quick starter strategies to increase employee commitment to your program. There are countless ways to put each of these strategies into practice—use your imagination.

Involve Your Employees

Involvement leads to commitment. The more involvement, the more commitment. Involve employees in decisions, activities, and planning. Ask for their advice. Obviously, all employees can't be involved in all things, but the more the merrier.

Table 3.3
***Fortune*'s 100 Best Places to Work: Examples of What Some Companies Do to Build Adoring, Choring, and Storing Commitment**

"For starters, most of the things that make a workplace great turn out to cost employers absolutely nothing" (Roth, 2006, pp. 121-22).

Adoring	*Choring*	*Storing*
Scientists and engineers are encouraged to spend 20% of each workweek pursuing pet projects. (Genentech)	Employees interview job applicants to make sure future colleagues will fit the culture. (J. M. Smucker)	Even part-timers can receive bonuses, and drivers are rewarded for service and safe driving. In 2004 one driver was given $5,000 for ten years of safe driving. (Container Store)
Regularly hosts environmental service projects. One worker said, "REI is a way of life." (REI)	Culture "rules." Sayings such as Every client, Every time and No exceptions, No excuses are everywhere, on posters, T-shirts, mugs, notepads, and portfolios. (Quicken Loans)	The firm will send you to get an MBA, pay your tuition, and double your salary if you stay with them. (Boston Consulting Group)
Everyone is expected to attend rock shows as often as possible and are reimbursed as long as they file a fashion report. Employees are expected to call buyers with tips. This makes salespeople feel as though they're not just selling products, but picking them. (Hot Topic)	Company is "legendary" for its Friday afternoon socials, summer cookouts, and beach parties at the end of the tax season. (Intuit)	Company pays the entire health insurance premium for employees and dependents, gives bonuses up to 12% of pay, and funds 401K retirement plans liberally. (Kimley-Horn & Associates)
Encourages employees to invent new ways to display food and then exports winning ideas to other stores. (Whole Foods)	Everyone, from the CEO to plant workers, wears "Quad Blues." The dress code was adopted in 1993 to remind all employees that they are production workers. (Quad/Graphics)	The employee retirement plan allows employees to replace up to 75% or more of their pay upon retiring.(Mitre)

Sources: Boyle, Matthew. "Happy People, Happy Returns." *Fortune* 153, no. 1 (2006): 100; Levenson, Eugenia. "Welcome to Our World." *Fortune* 153, no. 1 (2006): 114.; Levering, Robert, Milton Moskowitz, Eugenia Levenson, Jenny Mero, Christopher Tkaczyk, and Matthew Boyle. "And the Winners Are … " *Fortune* 153, no. 1 (2006): 89–108.; Morris, Betsy, Doris Burke, and Patricia Neering. "The Best Place to Work Now." Fortune 153, no. 1 (2006): 78.; Roth, Daniel. "Trading Places." *Fortune* 153, no. 1 (2006): 120.

One health care supervisor was having a horrible problem scheduling work shifts for her employees. There were quite a few variables involved, including the number of shifts, back-ups, and holidays. She couldn't keep anyone happy. Absenteeism was high, and people would come to work grouchy or late. She decided to let the employees put the schedule together. It worked wonderfully. Not only were the employees committed to making it a success—after all they had created it—but they also came up with creative ways to solve problems that this supervisor never would have. It was a win-win solution.

Create Symbolic Identification

A powerful tool to create an emotional tie to your organization is to use symbols. Words are symbols, logos are symbols, flags are symbols, and sometimes actions are symbolic. They are simple expressions of complex ideas or concepts. Symbolic identification is everywhere—shirts with the department name on them or program nicknames (the Tiger Team). People develop commitment to the group as they identify with it.

One leader did a number of things to create symbolic identification, including: adapting a slogan from the movie *Butch Cassidy and the Sundance Kid*; making coffee cups with every employee's name and hire date; asking people to write their life plans (going beyond their professional aspirations); asking each employee to put their handprint on the wall; and having an organizational chart that included not only employees, but also their families.

Symbolic identification is a powerful tool for creating organizational commitment. It doesn't have to take much money to make people feel part of the organization.

Build Networks

Relationships are being built when best friends sit in cubicles next to each other, when the softball team includes employees from various departments, and when people go to lunch together every day. People get to a point when they would never let their friends down and are committed to them even when not committed to the larger company. Those networks of relationships are powerful sources of organizational commitment. Social networks are influential information pipelines, and sources of competitive advantage. They can support not only the people involved but also the purposes of the organization. Make the power of networks a source of commitment by using them in the work of your program. Put people on task forces or teams, create social or learning groups, and otherwise encourage people to build relationships.

SEEK ALL THREE FORMS OF COMMITMENT

I discourage employees from becoming too dependent on organizations or from letting themselves get into situations that create penalties for leaving. Defined benefit plans, for all their security, effectively created indentured servants—people who felt they had to stay. These people had a strong commitment to keep their jobs, but that was about it. Many did the minimum and resented it. That's not the kind of commitment you want, and it is fertile ground for abuse by those in power and for subservience from those who aren't.

Create Powerful Organizational Values

Follow the wisdom of companies like Nordstrom, Wal-Mart, and Disney. These organizations have "cult-like" cultures.[16] They have a core ideology they reinforce in tangible ways. They "indoctrinate" new employees, making sure that newcomers know this is "how we do it" and "what we believe in," and create a sense of belonging to a very special organization. This can be accomplished in any number of ways, including orientation and training programs, socialization activities, the building of social networks, and celebrations. The organization you supervise can have a strong culture or value system even if the larger organization doesn't.

Compensate Competitively

People become committed to organizations that value them. Pay and benefits are one way to demonstrate value. If your pay is at least competitive with other organizations (that includes other internal departments or business units), then the costs of leaving increase dramatically. Not only is there no financial benefit from leaving, but furthermore, it probably would cost to leave.

Immediate compensation is only part of the compensation equation because employees know that the potential for future compensation is equally important. That's why hiring primarily from within, giving learning and promotion opportunities, and demonstrating that your area has a vision and potential for growth in the future are all strategies for increasing long-term employee commitment to your group. You may have limited ability to compensate your employees effectively. Fight for everything you can get. Make your case upstairs and to your compensation professionals. Look for informal ways to compensate your employees. Make it hard for employees to find a place that gives a better return for the time and effort they've invested, and they'll work harder to keep their jobs.

Activity

Complete "Assessing Your Organizational Commitment Strategies," found in chapter 6.

KEY POINTS

1. The form of commitment that produces the most productivity is adoring—when employees *want* to work for your organization; the second is choring, when they feel they *ought* to; the last is storing, when they feel they *have* to work there.
2. Organizational citizenship behavior occurs when employees go above and beyond the call of duty.
3. Employees are more likely to go above the call of duty and do extra things for the organization when they believe that the organization is fair, they are satisfied with their jobs, they believe their leader supports them, and they are committed to the organization.

PRINCIPLE 2

The More You Care, the More They Will Care: Give a Darn!

"Caring" is not just a touchy-feely term. It means someone or something is important. Caring a good deal is passion, and caring little is apathy. Caring too much is obsession, and caring too little causes laziness and sloppiness.

The principle is this—the more you care, the more your employees will care. The less you care, the less will they. Managers must care about their work and their employees to produce high, sustainable motivation.

Ralph Dennis wasn't a great coach, at least as far as I could tell. All he did was change lives. In 1998 I was preparing to give a keynote presentation for a teachers' awards luncheon. I decided to ask the members of the audience which teacher had made the biggest difference in their own lives and to pledge to write and thank that teacher. That made me think of my own teachers. The one who came to mind was Mr. D.

In 1968–70, when I was going to high school in Olathe, Kansas, Ralph Dennis was teaching history and politics along with coaching basketball and other sports. It was a time of unrest in our country. The Vietnam War was at its height, and emotions were running high even in our little school of 900. The debate resolution for high school competitors around the country that year was "Resolved: That Congress should prohibit unilateral United States military intervention in foreign counties."

To this day, I don't know Mr. D.'s political persuasion. He may have been quite conservative. He taught his Sunday school class for over 30 years and was an usher for over 56 years. He married his high school sweetheart and stayed married, with sons, daughters, grandchildren, and great-grandchildren. On the other hand, he may have been liberal and just found it hard to express that view in conservative Kansas in the late 1960s. What I do know is that I could express any opinion in class and feel like he listened and honored it. I really don't know if he was a great coach technically, but I have never met a person who wanted me to succeed, in the larger sense, more than he did. Maybe that is what the truly great coaches do, after all.

Wanting to set a good example for my audience, I wrote Mr. Dennis to thank him and to tell him how important he had been in my life. The letter I received in return made me realize why he was the one teacher I remember most. The handwritten note told me he'd retired in 1991 after 43 years. He said he still couldn't "get basketball out of [his] blood" and still helped out at the away basketball games. He told me about some of the students I had gone to school with and with whom he had obviously kept up. Jim Cumley, who knocked me out with one punch my first day at Olathe High School and who then became one of my best friends, was an assistant principal. (It was ironic, I thought, that Jim was now stopping fights instead of instigating them.) He told me that some of his old athletes had sent him and his wife to Europe. He didn't mention it, but I discovered later that he had been honored with all sorts of awards, including election to the Kansas State High School Activities Association Hall of Fame.

As I read through his note, tears came to my eyes when he said, "Mike, I wasn't a very good teacher and a poor coach, but if I had one thing going, it was my love for all you kids." He talked some more about taking a part-time job in retirement as a courier for a title company, about the route he drove every day, and about the $8.50/hour that he made. Then he wrote the real tear-jerking line.

"Thanks for being a teacher," he wrote. "I tried in my final years to see a little bit of God in all of my kids, and in doing so, it made it nicer for them and for me."

"Thanks for being a teacher." I couldn't have been prouder if the president of the United States had said it. I would have done anything he asked me to do, and so would thousands of his other students. He was a motivator because he cared.

Watch any great coach prowl the sidelines. If it's a Pat Summit, Bobby Knight, or Mike Shanahan, you can see the passion for their work. You don't have to imagine—they pump the air with their fists, scream at the officials, and get in the faces of their players. Even gentlemanly John

Wooden, who never spoke about winning but snagged 10 NCAA championships, was an intense, focused, driven coach.

Watch an artistic director at work, the choreographer in the studio, the director of a play, the conductor of the opera, or a great CEO. Do you think Jack Welch cared? These leaders exude emotion—anxiety, hope, fear, anger, love—and they demand your best. What they do is important. For some, it seems life or death.

The prerequisite for motivating your employees is that you are motivated yourself. If you don't care, they won't either. The more you care, the more will they. Business, military, educational, and artistic leaders from all walks of life go beyond caring. They are passionate about the results.

In a *Fast Company* article, Tom Peters says,

> Leadership, in the end, is all about having energy, creating energy, showing energy, and spreading energy. Leaders emote, they erupt, they flame, and they have boundless (nutty) enthusiasm. And why shouldn't they? The cold logic of it is unassailable: If you do not love what you are doing, if you do not go totally bonkers for your project, your team, your customers, and your company, then why in the world are you doing what you are doing? And why in the world would you expect anybody to follow you? (p. 136)[17]

PERCEIVED ORGANIZATIONAL SUPPORT

Perceived organizational support (POS) is the belief employees have about how much the organization values and cares for them. What is particularly interesting about POS is that it results from what employees believe the organization is doing *voluntarily*, by choice, to support employees. Giving pay raises or promotions because the organization *has* to does not result in increased POS.

The best way to increase POS is to treat employees fairly. That is because employees believe management can choose to be fair or not. Along that line, the more organizational politics (or unjustified, exorbitant executive bonuses), the less POS.

The second most effective way to increase POS is through supervisor support, and the third through rewards and positive job conditions. Rewards and positive job conditions have less impact on POS than fair treatment or supervisor support because employees believe that the organization more or less has to provide such incentives because of competition for talent.

High POS translates into high affective (adoring) commitment. When employees believe the organization cares about them, they are more likely to want to work for it. Those feelings are converted into higher performance and job satisfaction and less burnout and fatigue. People enjoy their jobs more. When employees have high POS, they are less likely to feel trapped (storing commitment) by the organization.

Organizational care makes a difference!

PERCEIVED SUPERVISOR SUPPORT

Supervisor support is essential for developing employee emotional (adoring) organizational commitment. Supportive relationships with supervisors increase performance, job satisfaction, and commitment to the organization. The degree to which employees believe supervisors value their contributions and care about their well-being is known as perceived supervisor support (PSS). PSS, like POS, includes employee beliefs about how much supervisors

- consider their goals and values,
- show concern for them,
- care about their opinions,
- provide help when there is a problem,
- forgive honest mistakes, and
- will or will not take advantage of them, given the opportunity.

When you care, your employees care—and business results improve.

Sources: Eisenberger, R., F. Stinglhamer, C. Vandenberghe, I. L. Sucharski, and L. Rhoades. "Perceived Supervisor Support: Contributions to Perceived Organizational Support and Employee Retention." *Journal of Applied Psychology* 87, no. 3 (2002): 565. L. Rhoades, R. Eisenberger, and S. Armeli. "Affective Commitment of the Organization: The Contribution of Perceived Organizational Support." *Journal of Applied Psychology* 86, no. 5 (2001): 825.

BEING FAIR

Employees who believe they are treated fairly are more likely to have higher job performance and go above and beyond the call of duty (OCBs).[18] Interestingly, if you were to double an employee's salary, give him a trip to Maui as a bonus, and also toss in an extra week of vacation, he would likely be thrilled. But if he then heard that others working at the same level had received more—say two trips, two weeks extra vacation, and three times the salary—he would condemn his own reward as "unfair." As a result, you would likely "hear about it," morale and performance would suffer, and he might leave. Fair treatment contributes more to employees' beliefs about whether the organization cares for them than any other factor.[19] That's because employees believe that the organization, including you, has the ability to choose how fair it will be. So what does being fair mean?

Organizational Justice

There are three ways employees perceive fairness in your organization: procedural justice, distributive justice, and interactional justice.[20]

- *Procedural justice* concerns the process for giving out rewards—that is, how the decision was made. Employees want to know if the basis for the decision was equitable.
- *Distributive justice* is about the end results—what was the actual decision? Was the result fair? Employees will compare what they received with what others received.
- *Interactional justice* refers to how employees feel they were being treated. Did they feel listened to and respected? Was the organization thoughtful?

What to Do—Treating Employees Fairly

Be consistent. Don't play favorites. Don't have them walking on eggshells trying to guess how you will react.

Do some first aid on your processes and procedures. Review the way decisions are made—who gets input and who's left out, what weighs most heavily, and why choices are made the way they are—to see if they need a shot of fairness.

Treat them with respect. Be sensitive, honor them as human beings, and be courteous.

Double-check job descriptions and assignments. Review the underlying basis for who does what work. Is someone carrying the whole load? Does the best work go to your buddies? Are some jobs seeded with tasks that will give a favored employee a promotion?

Listen deeply. Be empathic, try to see the situation from their view, and be sensitive to their feelings. To do it well, you have to be authentically interested in the other person.

Be transparent and communicate intentionally. Be clear about how decisions are made and about the basis for them. Make sure everyone understands. You won't please everyone, but it will force you to have a rationale in the first place and then to demonstrate your consistency in the second.

Make business-like decisions. Be unbiased and impartial in making decisions; make the decision based on the facts and the business outcomes you are seeking, not to favor a pet or to play politics.
Clarify expectations. Make sure everyone knows what the roles and responsibilities are and on what basis they will be rewarded. Don't play games by being ambiguous or manipulative.
Drop the superiority complex. Treat your employees like equals rather than inferiors, like human beings rather than animals or pieces on a game board.
Don't exploit employees. Don't prey on their need for a job. Don't take advantage of their dependency on you or of your power over them.
Be genuinely open. Unlock not just the physical door to your office, but also the gate leading to your preconceptions. Be receptive to the advice and feedback of your staff. Maybe you will learn something, and they will feel heard.

Treating employees fairly increases their belief that you care for them. In return you will get happier, more productive, more emotionally committed employees.

CARE ABOUT THE WORK

Randy Mascorella gave up a promising collegiate coaching career because she was profoundly changed the day her athletic director asked her to welcome three thousand athletes to the opening Special Olympics ceremonies held at her university. Randy spent the day watching the competition. She gave up the fame and money that comes with university-level sports because she was so moved, and she is now the executive director of Special Olympics New Mexico.

"It was a direct experience in my life that led to a revelation for me," she told me, "and it was so powerful that I knew that I would enjoy the work once I started it. But I didn't realize how much I would enjoy it and how much I would embrace it."

Can you imagine how motivating it would be to work with someone who cares so much about her work? Would you have been motivated to work for Bruce Spaulding? As his son, Rod, tells it, "My father was a railroad conductor for the Union Pacific Railroad. He worked for the railroad for 41 years. He never looked for another job outside his profession." Rod's dad loved his work because of the scenery and because of being with friends on the road, troubleshooting, and problem solving. He enjoyed fixing trains.

"Parts would break from the slack in the train," Bruce said. "Knuckles and draw bars would blow, switches would be improperly aligned, issues would arise from emergency brake applications. Everyday and every train was different. It was very interesting and exciting. I loved dealing with the unexpected!"

My favorite part is how Bruce described one of his trips.

> One time, I requested to take a train up to Yellowstone Park ... the rail was covered in snow. We had to have a rotary snow plow in front of the train so that we could get through the pass. It was a "branch track," so it was not used very often. As we were plowing out the track, we had to stop because there was a big bull moose running on the track. Because of the deep snow, it was easier for him to run. So we had to stop the train, thus taking a "moose break," and look out the window of the cab as the snow was coming down. Finally, the moose ran down the hill and hid behind a stand of aspen trees. It was cute [to] see the moose hidden behind a small branch with the rest of his body showing—he thought he was invisible. We got to Yellowstone Park and celebrated in the cook's car with a large T-bone steak. It was being together with the train crew, the wildlife and being in the beautiful country ... that is what I love!

Wouldn't you be motivated to work with someone who enjoyed his work so much? When is the last time you took a "moose break?"

CARE ABOUT THE EMPLOYEES

Hiring the best employees and keeping them is indispensable for competitive success. Showing them how much you care is essential. Ann Rhoades* has been the vice president of the People Department for Southwest Airlines, was executive vice president of Team Services for Promus/DoubleTree, and created JetBlue Airways' People Team in New York. It doesn't matter the position, Ann says; you have to have what she calls "A" players.

> You can be at the front line at McDonald's and make a difference, because I will go back to that person who is great. I want someone who really cares about making a difference while he or she is there.

JetBlue lost thousands and thousands of dollars once because the company would not put new airplanes into the air until it could hire an "A" level player in a key maintenance position.

"We said that it is better to wait for the 'A' player. We didn't want to hear ourselves mentioned on Jay Leno as being anything but great," according to Ann.

*This story was adapted from an article, ***Ann Rhoades,*** originally published in the September 2004 issue of *Leading with Passion,* by Michael Kroth and Patricia Boverie.

Housekeepers may be the most important employees in the hotel business because the number one item a guest wants is a clean room. At Doubletree, Ann decided it was important not to simply get warm bodies off the street, but to put the time necessary into hiring "A" players. So housekeepers hired housekeepers. The employees the housekeepers hired were exceptionally successful.

"The ones they hired were passionate. They kept their own homes clean enough to eat off the floor, and they wanted it to be the same way in the place they worked," Ann told me.

Do you suppose those housekeepers felt their opinions mattered? Involving them not only cut Doubletree's turnover; employees wouldn't even go across the street to a competitor offering more pay because they loved being part of a great team. "We supported them," Ann said. "We let them pick their own brooms and their own mops. That was a big deal to them."

Do you suppose these housekeepers felt valued by Doubletree? "'A' leaders have to be willing to spend the time and effort to develop and retain 'A' players because they will move if they aren't happy, being developed, and aren't being challenged," Ann said. You have to take care of your "A" people because it is difficult to find and keep them.

"Oddly enough, it isn't about money. Never has been and never will be," she says. You have to pay enough to show your best employees that you value them, but you don't have to be the highest payer in the market.

"I have a very good friend who is a critical care nurse," she says. "People beg her to come work for them. She is fabulous."

Her friend is paid less now than she was paid at her previous position elsewhere, but she is staying with her current organization. They let her take a day off if she needs it to care for her children. The doctors understand the value she brings.

> She said that everyplace she had worked, all they did was look down at her and the doctors never even talked to her in the hallways. She says that this is a different team environment and that she will stay even though she is paid less.... I think it is so easy to hire "A" players and then assume they are okay. But you have to constantly have a discipline about telling them they are doing a good job and defining what they need to do to improve, because "A" players never quit learning.

Show your employees you care and they'll stick with you and give you their best.

Activity

1. List the ways that Mr. D., Ann Rhoades, Bruce Spaulding, and Randy Mascorella showed they cared.
2. In what ways do you demonstrate care for work and your employees?

3. If I asked your employees today if you cared about them, what would they say? What examples would they point out? What evidence would they draw upon?

DOES IT MATTER THAT WE MATTER?

Mattering is the degree to which we believe we make a difference in the world.[21] We feel cared about when we feel we matter to someone else. We matter, for example, when

- someone pays attention to us;
- we rely on others for support or they rely on us;
- someone makes us feel better about ourselves;
- we have built a relationship of some kind with someone or something; or
- someone cares what we think.

In the 1980s Nancy Schlossberg and her colleagues developed scales to measure mattering for adult students in postsecondary education.[22] More recently, Gregory Elliott, Suzanne Kao, and Ann-Marie Grant developed a 24-item "Mattering Index" categorized by awareness, importance, and reliance.[23] Sample items include:

Awareness

People tend not to remember my name.
In a social gathering, no one notices me.
For whatever reason, it is hard for me to get other people's attention.

Importance

When I have a problem, people usually don't want to hear about it.
My successes are a source of pride to people in my life.
There are people in my life who care enough about me to criticize me when I need it.

Reliance

Quite a few people look to me for advice on issues of importance.
Often, people trust me with things that are important to them.
When people need help, they come to me.

If you want people to know they matter, pay attention to them, let them know they are important, and make them feel that you rely on them.

Activity

Complete the exercise "Do Your Employees Matter to You?" found in chapter 6.

HOW TO DEMONSTRATE CARING

If caring is important, how do we do it? We can learn from those whose business is caring. In the helping professions, losing the ability to care is a sign of burnout and ineffectiveness. The ability to relate to others is crucial for a therapist. When the ability to care is lost, so is the ability to be helpful

Nursing is a profession in which caring is particularly important. Leslie Wilkes and Marianne Wallis looked at how nursing students perceive caring and found eight themes:

1. *Compassion*—Actions demonstrating compassion include loving, having and sharing feelings, being a friend, and being concerned for others.
2. *Communicating*—Actions demonstrating communicating include listening, talking, explaining, touching, educating, and expressing feelings.
3. *Being competent*—Actions demonstrating being competent include assessing, watching for cues, having knowledge and skills, being responsible, and being professional.
4. *Providing comfort*—Actions demonstrating providing comfort include helping and assisting.
5. *Being committed*—Actions demonstrating being committed include loving, showing no bias, and "being there."
6. *Having conscience*—Actions demonstrating having conscience include giving the person dignity and respect and treating him or her as oneself.
7. *Being confident*—Actions demonstrating being confident include knowing what to do without hesitation.
8. *Being courageous*—Actions demonstrating being courageous include advocating for a person's needs and rights to treatment and intervening for and with the person.[24]

Kristen Swanson found five processes indicative of care for another person:

1. *Maintaining belief*—Conveying to other people that there is personal meaning to be found in their current situation. It includes a commitment to "stick with them," conveying hope and optimism.
2. *Knowing*—Striving to understand a person's situation, seeking information and cues. It involves avoiding assumptions and establishing a partnership.
3. *Being with*—Being emotionally present. It involves sharing feelings and showing that you are available.
4. *Doing for*—Doing for others what they would do for themselves. It consists of comforting, preserving dignity, and protecting, among other tasks.
5. *Enabling*—Helping others to practice self-care. It includes informing, supporting, and giving feedback.[25]

Do you want to demonstrate the care that you feel for your employees more effectively?

Activity

Complete the exercise "How to Care When You *Do* Care," found in chapter 6.

DARING TO CARE

Some have been burned and don't want to take the risk of caring again. A person experiencing enough bad relationships might not be willing to go "out there" again. He or she might not want to suffer another broken heart or to be let down again. This is also true about work. Hopes may have been crushed when the promotion didn't come through, a favorite project was canceled, or there was an undesirable job transfer. Caring involves emotions, and emotions make us vulnerable. Many are afraid to be hurt again. Some employees become "the living dead"—those who are alive physically, but dead emotionally, mentally, and spiritually.

Sometimes the work environment programs employees not to care. Some workplaces prove time and again that no matter what a person does, it won't make a difference. Employees hit their heads against the wall so many times that they give up. Why bother? They learn helplessness. They stop caring.

Are you one of those employees who have stopping caring? Are you a supervisor who is just putting in time? If you want to motivate your employees to do their best, *you have to care.* How else do you expect to motivate the people who work for you to do their best?

WHAT YOU CAN DO: HOW TO CARE WHEN YOU DON'T CARE

If giving a darn is so important, how do you make yourself care when you don't? Here are techniques you can use. They all involve intentionally making your work and the people you work with more important.

Set Standards

No one cares about shoddy work. Shoot for doing things well or even great. If the error rate is 10 percent, shoot for 5 percent. Now mistakes that didn't make a difference before are more important. If already terrific, look for ways to make it amazing.

Find Problems to Solve

Brainstorm five problems to solve this year. Then start figuring out how to solve them. Finding a challenge and discovering its solution increases care for the situation.

Develop Relationships with Employees

If you don't care about the work, find ways to care about the people with whom you work. Look for employees to mentor or teach. Find opportunities to learn more about them. Break bread together. One person said that when he started bringing doughnuts regularly to the break room, it broke down barriers, not only between his employees, but also between them and him. Get to know your employees. Be a catalyst for their success.

Set Incremental Goals with Deadlines

Sometimes it is hard to care about earnings-per-share targets when you are in charge of delivering the office mail on time. Year-end goals seem far away in February. Set sub-goals along the way and reward successes as they come.

Ask Those Affected by Your Work

Ask others what can be done better. Ask internal customers what their needs are and how your organization can meet them more effectively. Go see how the end-user applies what your group produces.

Ask Those You Are Affected by at Work

Go talk to the folks who supply your needs. Build relationships. Learn what they do, what their problems are, and how you can help. What do vendors and the departments upstream need? You depend on them. They should be important to you.

Look for Different Ways to Do Your Work Better

No matter how boring the work or how efficient the process, there are ways to do it differently, more creatively, or less expensively. Make it a challenge to accomplish any of those goals.

Think of Everything You Can Learn from Your Work

Some things can be learned from employees. Some of those won't have anything to do with the job. They will be about life. If Victor Frankl[26] could learn while in a concentration camp or Thoreau could learn sitting around Walden Pond,[27] you can learn on your job. If nothing else learn patience.

Draw from Deeper Sources

"Caring can be drawn from a reservoir," Chris Meade, Pastor at Grace Chapel in Boise, Idaho, says. "You could draw upon spirit, Spirit of God, or whatever your belief system is around God. And you could say, 'You know what, I'm meant to do this or I'm supposed to be doing this.' If you're Buddhist or Hindu you say, 'I should be mindful about this because whatever kind of work it is, it should be work done well.'"

Spiritual roots are an everlasting source of caring, no matter the situation or who is involved. Think seriously about what is important and the part work plays in your life.

Care Because You Have Character

Draw from your own values and work ethic to care about the work. The principle might be that work should be done well, that people are important, or that an honest day's pay deserves an honest day's work. Character is an important source of caring. Why leave it at the door on Monday morning?

Act Like You Care

As a last resort, act as if you care. Often, after going through the motions for a while, you will find yourself genuinely caring about the work and the people doing it.

Quit

Please quit if you can't find any reasons to care about your work. You will be doing yourself, your employees, your company, and your customers a big favor.

Activity

Complete the exercise "How to Care When You *Don't* Care," found in chapter 6.

KEY POINTS

1. Caring can be developed by finding ways to make something or someone important to you.
2. People feel they matter when others pay attention to them, depend on them, and believe they are important.
3. Employees perform better and voluntarily go beyond the call of duty when they believe their organization and supervisor care about them.

Principle 3

The More You Know about People, the More You Will Know What to Do: Treat People the Same and Treat People Differently

I thought once about writing a book called *Everything I Know about Motivation I Learned on the Farm.* There are so many lessons to be learned. There was one problem with that plan—I never lived on a farm. I still think someone should write it.

I did, however, spend many summers on my grandparents' farm, and my grandfather was a monumental figure in all of our lives. He knew not only the nature of the earth, but also human nature and what it took to motivate people. Young men working for him on a hot, sweaty, harvest day would look down and find a ripe watermelon he had planted for them months before just waiting to be cracked open, the juicy meat scooped up, seeds spit out, and used as an excuse for a spontaneous break. My dad, remembering, says, "Usually, we got so much sticky juice on us that we had to strip off our clothes and jump in the creek to get clean. You can't do that in Disneyland." For my grandfather, that kind of insight into what keeps young men working materialized from imagining what their experience would be that 100-degree day and planning for it months before it occurred.

Realizing that everyone is the same and everyone is different—and then acting accordingly—is the essence of motivating others. People are complex, and people are simple. A manager doesn't have to be charismatic to be a great motivator but does have to study human nature. It is vital to understand deeply the desires, needs, cares, and problems of the people with whom you work.

Stanley Weinstein looks deeply into the needs, wants, and desires of potential donors. He received the Association of Fund Raising Professionals' highest award for professionals in the field and is one of my longtime friends. I always marvel at how he convinces people to make million-dollar gifts and up, especially in a poor state like New Mexico. He was instrumental in the largest gift ever given to a nonprofit organization in New Mexico—$50,000,000.00. The secret is to *not* try to convince people.

"I'm convinced there is no such thing as persuading someone else to give a big gift because nobody wants to give away money," he says. "But people do want to make a difference in other peoples' lives." Instead, he looks deeply into their needs and wants. "You get into the mind of the donor and understand what unique things would be important to that person."

He told about a time he moved a prospect from a $50,000.00 gift to a $1,000,000.00 gift. First, he found out the donor's concerns. One worry was that the donor had given to capital projects before that hadn't been built. Stanley suggested making it a challenge gift instead of a no-strings contribution. Second, Stanley convinced the donor to describe the case for supporting the project. Then he asked the donor for permission to use that quote on materials produced for the campaign. Now it was the donor convincing others (and himself) to contribute to the organization.

"We answered every one of the donor's concerns and gave him the greatest flexibility," Stanley told me. The result was a million-dollar gift. The donor was so excited about the project that he then convinced a friend to give another million dollars.

The motivation to give such a large amount was possible because Stanley did everything possible to understand the needs and wants of the donor. He then found ways to involve and engage the donor in providing answers to his own objections. This was a very different approach than trying to persuade the donor of the merits of the gift from the organization's perspective.

How well do you know the needs and wants of your own employees? How well do you engage them in solving workplace issues *from their perspective?*

Researchers and theorists have studied people for many years, and philosophers have done so for centuries. We have learned much and yet in many ways know little more than a thoughtful, receptive, observer of human nature already knows through experience.

STUDY HUMAN NATURE—EVERYONE IS THE SAME

In the book *My Personal Best,* John Wooden, a basketball coach, shared stories about how he worked with players. He explained, "All of the preceding examples and many more resulted from my attempt to get better at understanding human nature—mine as well as other people—so I could be a better teacher. Understanding human nature is absolutely crucial to a leader's success.[28]

What is the same about people? We all think, we all feel, and we all strive. Psychologists and philosophers have said that all human behavior involves some combination of those three things. Those are cognition (thinking), affection (feeling), and conation (striving).[29] We are born with similar biological needs. We avoid pain and are drawn to pleasure.

Humans have beliefs, intelligence, and the ability to *think.* What we believe about the world affects what we do. To test this, ask if your actions would change if you discovered today that your company could not meet its pension fund obligations. Nothing else would be different. Your belief about the security of your money would change radically—and likely, so would your actions.

Emotions and *feelings* such as joy, happiness, and pleasure and also fear, anger, and pain are the result and the cause of what we do. All people have the capability for love, hate, envy, and passion.

All human beings are purposeful. All *strive,* want to achieve, and have desires. If that weren't true, no one would pursue what they think and feel about! All have the will and the ability to make choices. All people are motivated by the same things. What we know about human motivations varies depending on which theorist or author we happen to be reading, but there are some common things that most believe. Before I list some of those, let me test my own theory that a good student of human nature knows what motivates most people. Complete the next exercise before reading further.

Activity

Complete "What Motivates Everyone," found in chapter 6.

What Motivates Everyone

What did you list in the "What Motivates Everyone" exercise? If you included most of the following, consider yourself an amateur psychologist and a high-potential motivator. Here are some motivators that theorists past and present have suggested motivate all people:

Hedonism—Seeking pleasure and avoiding pain.

Instinct—Following inborn patterns of responses to various stimuli. Although psychologists today use the term *motivational forces* instead of the word *instincts,* at one time the list of instincts was nearly 6,000 (see Porter et al., 2000).

Drive—Pursuing energizers such as hunger, thirst, and sex move people toward or away from goals.

Need—Needs influence behavior until they are satisfied. They can be inborn or learned. They may include (according to Maslow) the need for survival, safety and security, belongingness, esteem, or self-actualization. They may also include the need for growth, achievement (including fear of failure and hope of success), power, affiliation, autonomy, or competence. Needs have been described in various ways, but the point is that people have them, and they motivate people to action.

Fear—Fears motivate powerfully. They include physical fear, the fear of failure, fear of looking or being incompetent, fear of being wrong, and fear of emotional pain.

Outcome expectancies—Outcome expectancies are beliefs that future rewards or punishments one cares about will occur based on his or her actions. In other words, if I train hard and eat wisely, I expect to lose weight. I'm motivated to the extent that I want the reward (a skinnier body), that I believe I can achieve it (performance), and that those outcomes are actually tied to what I do (healthy actions).

There have been many theories explaining what motivates all of us. Table 3.4, "A Sample of Motivational Theories," is a summary of some of the major ones.

STUDY THE HUMAN SITUATION—EVERYONE IS DIFFERENT

If what moves people is the same for everyone, why can't everyone be motivated in the same exact way? The answer is that although every human is motivated by hope, fear, reward, pleasure, and pain, every person is different. You were born with a different disposition than other people, and you look different. You're taller or smaller, faster or slower. You're an only child, or you have six sisters. You grew up learning different things than others. You learned that you could be a success at anything you tried or that people like you don't become CEOs. You learned to love or to withhold love, and you learned to hide or to jump right in. You wake up in a different house than others. Yours might be full of young children or aging parents; it might have a foreclosure sign on it, or it might have been in the family for a hundred years; it might not even be a house—it could be an apartment or maybe a car.

Table 3.4
A Sample of Motivational Theories

Theorist	*Theory*	*Mini-explanation*
Weiner	Attribution theory	Attributions are the reasons people give themselves to explain a result. Several types of attributions can exist to explain the same event: the cause of the result was either internal (my ability or effort) or external (others helped); it was stable (the conditions will remain the same) or unstable (things may change next time); and it was controllable (how I dressed, prepared) or was uncontrollable (luck, aptitude, age). What we attribute the event to will affect how we feel about it and our future course of action.
Adams	Equity theory	People compare what they have contributed and received with what others have contributed and received and develop a perception of equity or inequity. If perceived inequity exists, the person may try to reduce it by changing the amount of his input (lowering or increasing), altering the outcomes (more, less, or different), thinking differently about what is important or whom to compare with, leaving, or other strategies to reduce the perceived inequity.
Vroom	Expectancy and value	Individuals pursue tasks that they believe will result in rewards they value and that they believe they can perform. They have some degree of expectancy that their effort will actually result in the performance required. They also have some degree of expectancy that their performance will actually result in the reward or desired outcome.
Csikszentmihalyi and Csikszentmihalyi	Flow	Flow is a state of concentration that is totally absorbing. It occurs when someone is using his or her skills to overcome a challenge. When the skills do not match what is needed for the challenge, the task will be either too boring or anxiety-producing. Flow emerges when moderate-to-high levels of challenge are balanced with the needed moderate-to-high levels of skill.
Locke and Latham	Goal setting	Developed a comprehensive theory of goal setting that includes the process of goal setting and goal commitment.
Seligman	Learned helplessness	People develop learned helplessness when what they do does not affect outcomes. It occurs when the person believes that nothing he or she does will make a difference about what happens.

(Continued)

Table 3.4
A Sample of Motivational Theories *(Continued)*

Theorist	*Theory*	*Mini-explanation*
Boverie and Kroth	Occupational intimacy	Occupational intimacy occurs when a person is doing work he or she loves in an organization that cares for him or her. Organizations build renewing, passionate work environments through meaningful, enjoyable, nurturing work.
Maslow	Hierarchy of needs	Needs guide behavior until they are satisfied, starting from the most fundamental, physiological needs, and continuing to needs for safety and security, belongingness, esteem and ego, and finally to self-actualization.
Deci and Ryan	Self-determination	Types of motivation include amotivation (none); extrinsic motivation, stemming from rewards and punishment and other sources outside the work itself; and intrinsic motivation, derived from the interest and enjoyment of actually doing the work itself. Deci and Ryan propose that humans have needs for autonomy, competence, and relatedness.
Bandura	Self-efficacy	Self-efficacy is the person's belief about his or her capability to complete a specific task. Motivation depends on the person desiring something she thinks will occur (a reward or other outcomes) if she does something (her behavior) that she believes she can actually do.
McClelland	Learned needs theory	People acquire needs, which include the need for achievement, need for power, need for affiliation, and need for autonomy.
Dweck	Mastery versus performance goals	Mastery goals are related to learning, and performance goals are related to performing well on a task.
Skinner	Reinforcement theory	Behavior is caused by events external to the person. It is determined by the consequences of the action, which include being reinforced or punished.

Sources: Boverie, Patricia Eileen, and Michael S. Kroth. *Transforming Work: The Five Keys to Achieving Trust, Commitment, and Passion in the Workplace. New Perspectives in Organizational Learning, Performance, and Change*. Cambridge, MA: Perseus, 2001; Porter, Lyman W., Gregory A. Bigley, and Richard M. Steers. *Motivation and Work Behavior*, 7th ed. Boston: McGraw-Hill/Irwin, 2003.; Reeve, John Marshall. *Understanding Motivation and Emotion*, 4th ed. Hoboken, NJ: Wiley, 2005.

You are different than other people, and *every one of your employees is motivated differently*. Some of the differences each person brings to work are described in the following sections.

Different Times

What is important to a person changes over time. A 30-year veteran receiving six weeks of vacation a year is probably less interested in an extra day of vacation than would be a brand new employee with two weeks of annual vacation, young children at home, and a teenager with lots of away games. A young, single mother might find a flexible work schedule important, whereas the fellow who likes to put in his eight hours and go home to watch *American Idol* couldn't care less. The priorities of either the single mother or the eight-hour guy could quickly change, however, if something happened in their lives.

Different Personalities

One friend of mine gets her feelings hurt if you don't lavish her with attention on her birthday. It's important to her, mighty important. If you remember her birthday and remember that traditions are very important to her, she will follow you to the grave. Another forgets his own birthday and couldn't care less if anyone else does. Each employee is more or less secure, more or less needy, and more or less self-centered. This is part of being human.

Different Interests

One employee likes sports, another ballet. One likes school. Another hates school but is taking carpentry classes and remodeling her house. One likes Pepsi, another Coke.

Each employee may have a different interest in his or her job. One might need it for long-term, secure steady income and another as a quick stepping-stone to a different company or position. One might be interested because it's a learning opportunity; another may see it as the only place to socialize in an otherwise lonely world. The reasons are many and sometimes complex.

How Do You Find Those Differences?

Discovering those differences can be tricky. One way is to get to know your employees better. It doesn't mean becoming buddies or going on fishing trips together, though some do. It does mean studying people like you would any challenge. Here are four ways to learn more about employees:

1. *Ask*—Periodically ask employees what is important to them. When is the last time you did that? Ask what they enjoy, what would be an important reward, what made a difference in the past, what is coming up in their lives or careers that is important. Ask how you can meet those needs. Some will tell you more, some less.

2. *Hang out*—Be available, be around, and get in there and do the work together now and then. Be on the same softball team, or at least be a loyal fan.
3. *Talk to others*—Make a point to listen to what others are saying about your employees. Tuck their challenges, fears, and hopes into the back of your mind.
4. *Try things*—Test rewards, recognitions, assignments, and opportunities with employees. See what they respond to and what they just blow off. Don't keep hitting the same nail with the same hammer if they don't respond well to something. Try something else. There are more tools at your disposal than you may think.

Great motivators, be they admirals, T-ball coaches, teachers, or accounts-payable supervisors, recognize that everyone is motivated by the same things, and yet every individual is unique. You can be great too if you study both human nature and the human situation.

Activity

Complete the exercise "Finding the Differences," found in chapter 6.

DK Kroth: Treating People the Same Way, and Differently, in the Theater

My brother David, "DK" to everyone outside the family, has been a professor of lighting at the California Institute for the Arts for over 20 years. He teaches classes and, as importantly, develops student skills and techniques through a demanding performance schedule. He focuses on the dance program, and most of the students in his classes are there because they want to be professional dancers. Performers, especially college-age dancers, are notoriously egocentric, over- or under-confident, emotional, and otherwise difficult to handle. DK manages by treating everyone the same way, and everyone differently.

His rules and the way each show is designed, built, worked backstage, and then broken down afterward are absolute. The culture and unwritten norms are the same—the tech crew shows up on time, and no one leaves until everyone is done. He is a tough taskmaster.

He also treats everyone the same in a different way—as human beings who deserve respect.

"My fundamental philosophy and practice has always been to completely respect the people that I'm working with," he says. "Dealing with the artistic community, people can be temperamental. I think in general people initially are a little insecure and a little unsure of themselves going into new situations, and to acknowledge and respect somebody no matter what has put me on the best footing I can possibly think of." Every student is treated with respect.

He also treats everyone differently. Much of that can happen because he is so accessible. After a late rehearsal, he makes sure there is a social time afterward. Often, it's just 30 minutes spent drinking a beer together (all those involved are of legal age, and it is a private school). They relax and discuss what needs to be done next.

"Quite frequently, we discuss our problems," he says, "or I listen to problems. People support each other that way and become friends. Friends for years and years and years."

Graduates from around the country send their friends to him because they know he will be someone who will look out for them. One thing he believes particularly effective, which few others do, is "hanging out" in front of the theater.

"It's not a case," he says, "of the office door is always open if you want to come by. No, I'm having a cup of coffee sitting on a bench outside nearby, and you can come to talk to me about anything. This isn't me being the boss. That's being accessible. The social part is very important, and it doesn't take more than 15 minutes before a call or 10 minutes after class."

One student was an excellent carpenter but was failing his classes. He partied too much, stayed up too late, and was insecure about being in an art school.

DK recalls, "I say, 'Hey, you want to have some fun?' And he's like, 'What do you mean?'"

So DK gave him a problem to solve—how to get the sun to travel slowly on an arch behind the scrim. "I've got an idea how to do it," DK tells him, "but I don't have the whole idea. Can you solve it for me?"

He leaves the problem with the student. Later, during the performance, the effect the student created generated applause from the audience.

"It was during *Bolero*," DK said. "And as he's traveling across the stage, the crowd is just blown away. And suddenly, he's contributed something he can brag about. And he comes back for more. So we form a friendship. And I also used him for the next three years [and found] some very outrageous things for him to create and build. It changed him. It changed his self-image. He learned to supervise. Now he works for the theater department at a major university."

That kind of motivation comes from treating people differently on the basis of their individual needs.

Although everyone is born with needs that motivate, each is unique. Every employee is one of a kind, with needs that will change, becoming more or less important and relevant through his or her career.

WHAT DO YOU KNOW ABOUT YOUR EMPLOYEES?

Every person is special and unique. The organization may view employees as "resources," but each person has a story. Each wants to matter (see Principle 2). Each is motivated in the same way as well as differently. Your job, if you want to be a great motivator, is to find the keys to unlock the energy in each.

How much do you really know about your employees? How do you hope to motivate them if you don't know them well? The more you know, the better, as long as you aren't intrusive and don't move into someone's personal space. It is true there is and generally should be differences between a manager–employee relationship and an employee–employee or a friend–friend relationship. Managers generally err on the side of detachment instead of connection, however.

Activity

Complete the survey "How Well Do You Know Your Employees?" found in chapter 6.

KEY POINTS

1. Employees share similar needs, drives, fears, and expectancies that make motivating each person comparable.
2. Employees have different interests, personalities, and changing situations that make motivating each person unique.

PRINCIPLE 4

Do What You Love, and the Motivation Will Follow: Design Work to Be Enjoyable

Do you want compliant employees, or do you want them to take the initiative? Do you want the best of their creativity, problem solving ability, and energy focused on accomplishing the work ahead? If you find ways to provide the work they love, the motivation to do it will come from within.

One of my favorite books is Marsha Sinetar's *Do What You Love, the Money Will Follow.*[30] As Sinetar says, "It is this radical transformation of duty into love, fascination or pleasure which allows the individual to feel that he is at play. This is because he is fully present, as a personality, fully there in the moment. And because he has committed his heart, attention and intention to doing the work … he heightens his energies and intelligence, and thus is able to give his all to the job at hand" (p. 162). Now isn't that exactly what you want from your employees?

Work should not be drudgery. Kahlil Gibran said that work is love made visible. "Right livelihood" is what Sinetar calls work consciously chosen, leading to enlightenment, with full awareness and care. Most people don't think of their work in those terms, but it's true. We were born to do work we love. Let's see how and then explore how to tie in to this powerful human need in the workplace.

"Joy," Kay Redfield Jamison says in her marvelous book *Exuberance: The Passion for Life*,[31] "is essential to our existence." Exuberance is irrepressible and in the blood, she says. It "may ebb and flow, but the underlying capacity for joy is as much a part of the person as having green eyes or a long waist."

The job of motivator becomes infinitely easier when work is enjoyable. The desire to do the work then comes from within the worker. Action doesn't have to be forced. Even without reward, the task itself is so compelling, fun, and satisfying that it would be completed with more creativity, energy, and persistence than could be demanded through rewards or punishments. When the reward comes from doing the work itself, it is energizing rather than exhausting, stimulating rather than stupefying, and engaging rather than enraging.

It is in your best interest to create work that is enjoyable for your employees. "I'd do this without being paid" are the words you want to hear from your coworkers. Even if that is not totally true, it is the feeling you want from employees.

Happy employees are not necessarily motivated workers, however. Many times, employees can be happy as punch when chatting it up and hanging out—but not getting anything done! It is pretty easy to be happy when being paid to sit around and do nothing. Happy is good, but it is not enough. What we are talking about here is what makes *the work itself* enjoyable.

What, then, makes work pleasing? The answer is rooted in both our genes and our individual personalities. So again, enjoyment is the same for everyone and, at the same time, different for each person. My sister, Mary, loves accounting. I can't stand it. I love public speaking. Others find presenting akin to facing a death squad. It is your job to know those differences.

Work is enjoyable when the act of doing it is pleasurable. It makes sense to provide such work, but many are far more familiar with just the opposite.

TOXIC WORK ENVIRONMENTS

What is it like to work in a poisonous workplace? How motivated are people then? How productive? Upton Sinclair's classic *The Jungle* depicts factory life in the early 1900s and gives a vivid picture of work at its worst.[32] The passages describing the horrors that those workers endured cause a visceral reaction every time I read them. I cannot imagine human beings (management) treating other human beings (employees) in such degrading ways. One passage, typical of those throughout the book, describes work in the slaughterhouse:

> The men would tie up their feet in newspapers and old sacks, and these would be soaked in blood and frozen, and then soaked again, and so on until by nighttime a man would be walking on great lumps the size of the feet of an elephant. Now and then, when the bosses were not looking, you would see them plunging their feet and ankles into the steaming carcass of the steer. (pp. 83–84)

That was just the physical environment. The social and emotional indignities were at least as severe. One would think that matters surely have changed over time. Or perhaps not. Fast-forward nearly 70 years. Studs Terkel introduced his 1974 book, *Working,* which described the work of over a hundred people in different occupations, by saying, "This book, being about work, is, by its very nature, about violence—to the spirit as well as to the body.... It is, above all (or beneath all), about daily humiliations. To survive the day is triumph enough for the walking wounded among the great many of us" (p. xi).[33]

Surely the work environment must be better in this century, a hundred years after Sinclair described working in unholy conditions. We have the "best companies to work for" now, don't we? Or perhaps not. Barbara Ehrenreich's 2001 book, *Nickel and Dimed,* put us in the shoes of people in the workplace today. She went undercover to discover what it's like for low-wage workers to hold down a job.[34] In her concluding chapter, she says, "What surprised and offended me most about the low-wage workplace (and yes, here all my middle-class privilege is on display) was the extent to which one is required to surrender one's basic civil rights and—what boils down to the same thing—self-respect" (p. 208).

You may be saying to yourself, "That doesn't apply to where I work. We have highly paid professional workers here." Maybe so. But maybe not. Jean Lipman-Blumen describes toxic leaders as "those individuals who, by virtue of their destructive behaviors and their dysfunctional personal qualities or characteristics, inflict serious and enduring harm on the individuals, groups, organizations, communities and even the nations that they lead" (p. 2).[35] I have friends who have developed health problems because of mean-spirited bosses. I bet you know such people too. As a consultant, I have had people cry in my office because the people in their department treated them like dirt. What kind of workplace are you leading? Are you a nurturing or a toxic manager?

Nothing makes work less enjoyable or motivating than a toxic environment. Destructive, dysfunctional workplaces wreak serious, lasting damage to employees, teams, departments, and even to customers and vendors. The infliction of emotional pain, insensitivity, betrayal, rudeness, conflict, manipulation, and selfishness by leaders, fellow workers, or others in the larger organization is debilitating. Work, then, is not only unenjoyable, but intolerable, and productivity takes a nosedive. If you are a toxic leader, stop it now.

Toxic leaders love their power and their ability to mete out punishment and love making their employees feel less important so that they can feel more important. But it kills the human spirit.

If you notice backbiting, power plays, political gamesmanship, hoarding, or any toxic work behaviors, you have to stop them. Build trust, reward, and collaboration; oust cheaters; and take power away from vicious employees. Don't allow a toxic environment to poison your ability to enjoy your own work, much less the work of those who are your responsibility.

Obstacles to Work Enjoyment

Nothing makes work more frustrating—no matter how much you like it—than having to overcome unnecessary obstacles. Have you ever thought, "I can't wait to try this job out," and after a while thrown your hands up in disgust because there were so many hurdles to jump? Don't be penny-wise and pound-foolish. Work won't be easy if policies tie employees up like a boa constrictor, if employees don't have the tools they need, or if they are struggling just to get supplies, clerical support, software that works easily, or the right equipment—and it certainly won't be fun. Make doing the work as easy as possible. Work is hard enough. A manager has the unique role of representing management to employees and employees to management. Make sure you're doing an equally good a job for both. Make it as easy as possible for employees to do the challenging work they have been assigned.

GENERATIVE WORK ENVIRONMENTS

Toxic environments destroy the spirit and over time break down peoples' bodies, creativity, initiative, and spirit. Positive work environments, in contrast, are generative. They build a "can-do" spirit; an atmosphere of learning, building, and growing; and most importantly for you, motivation that emanates from within your employees rather than being imposed. What are some qualities of a generative work environment?

Nature—The Physical Environment

Nature draws joy, happiness, ecstasy, and tranquility from within people. It is the rare person who does not relate to nature in some wonderful way. There is evidence that aesthetically pleasing objects help people work better. They make people feel good and enable them to think more creatively. A client was having trouble with employee morale. One reason was because the offices were so horrid. Some were working out of closets. Do you think employees were embarrassed or proud when they took their spouses and children to see where they worked? A call center found productivity measures turned for the better when they replaced old, duct-taped chairs with new ones and made the cubicle-environment colorful and festive. The physical work environment is important.

It's not just the environment itself—it's how much ability employees have to make it their own. The Gallup Organization found that employees able to personalize their workspaces are more likely to be engaged in work and connected to their organization.[36] Giving employees choices is a powerful motivational force. Gallup found that employees who work in environments with comfortable temperatures are twice as engaged as those who don't. Interestingly, when employees felt their opinions counted at work, the percentage of disengagement dropped dramatically.

A pleasing work environment is different for different people. One person loves cars, the smell of a body shop, the feel of a wrench in his hand, and rock and roll music blasting away. Another person likes to work outside. To her, the idea of checking power lines every day is appealing because she doesn't have to sit behind a desk but can travel from site to site each day. Another person likes solitude, and the notion of editing books at home, sitting in front of a computer with a cozy fireplace, makes work pleasurable. Still another likes the hustle and bustle of people and a variety of sights and sounds. She can't wait to get to her sales job in the mall each day.

Challenge and Novelty

Dr. Gregory Berns makes the fascinating case that the brain thrives on challenge and novelty.[37]Although predictability and security may be what people think they want, survival over the centuries depended on the ability to adapt to change. Brains now have that capacity built in. Satisfaction, romantic love, and pleasure are all part of processes that take place through chemical reactions in the brain. This is important because this need for novelty and challenge—what seems intuitively true—is part of what makes work enjoyable. Employees want variety and change—to be stretched at work. That makes work more pleasurable. If you notice your employees doing the same thing day after day, ask how much they are enjoying their work. If they aren't, give them something different that tests them and see what happens.

Relationships

Marcus Buckingham and Curt Coffman's 12 elements needed to attract, focus, and keep the most talented employees, as described in *First Break All the Rules,* famously include having a best friend at work.[38] Half of waking hours are spent at work. Why wouldn't people want their best friends to be coworkers? It is just more enjoyable to work with people you like. Work will be more enjoyable if you encourage relationship-building in your shop. Whether it's through work teams, bowling leagues, or even those informal but influential go-to-lunch gatherings, the social network exerts a powerful positive or negative motivational pull. Put it to use.

Play

We were born to play. Children play not just for pleasure, but also to learn. Skills learned and instincts honed through play have increased the chance of survival throughout history. Play not only increases skill, but also develops relationships. How can play be useful in the workplace? One company uses games to learn new policies and customer information. The "winner" is always a large percentage of employees, so there are many rewards, but all have fun learning something important to the organization. In training, employees might role-play difficult or challenging situations. Using the imagination can be playful. Play encourages exploration, curiosity, and new approaches. Taking on new tasks is less daunting when approached as a game or a challenge.

Choice

We are born purposive. All humans seek food, drink, and warmth as they grow, and over time, they find that by doing certain things, they can make other things happen. Sometimes people have more dominion over their environments than they do at other times. People discover that they can make choices that affect what happens. That choice-making ability follows to adulthood. The environment—which includes parents, teachers, laws, and managers—either allows exercise of that capability fully or squelches it. If people perceive that they have few choices, they feel powerless; if people think they have many alternatives, they feel powerful. Hitting heads against the wall too many times causes people to stop trying.

Upbringing, life experiences, and toxic work environments leave some people needy and dependent, insecure, or with victim mentalities. In those cases, people may wish to be told what to do. But these are not inborn qualities. In the workplace, most employees want to choose their tasks rather than have tasks imposed on them. Being forced to take on activities and carry them out in prescribed ways is not what people generally desire. Most don't like to feel controlled, threatened, tied down, or watched. Most would rather make choices, have control over their actions, and make decisions.

Capability

We have a fear of being incompetent, and also fear being thought of as incompetent. We want to feel capable. There is a joy in developing the skills to do a job well. Moving from the bunny hill to the high slopes is a challenging, enjoyable task. Make sure employees have the training, experiences, talent, mentoring, and coaching to be successful. Imagine how your employees will feel if you give them something important that they don't believe they can do. Imagine how they will feel when they develop that power.

Learning and Development—Growth

As Patricia Boverie, coauthor of our book *Transforming Work,* often says, we are "learning organisms."[39] Humans were born to learn. Learning is a means of survival and also makes work more enjoyable. It is as natural as breathing. Boring, repetitious work is not enjoyable. It can be tolerable, but not enjoyable. Focus on learning. Find creative ways to give employees learning opportunities.

Much of John Wooden's success as, in my opinion, the greatest college basketball coach of all time came because he never focused on winning (rewards), but focused instead on each player doing his best (learning and performing). "It is never simply a case of win or lose," he says, "because I do not demand victory. The significance of the score is secondary to the importance of finding out how good you can be" (p. 177).[40] He won 10 national championships.

Accomplishment

Have you ever been assigned, like the punishment of Sisyphus, a task that has no known end to it? You do it day after day after day, and you don't know whether you are getting anywhere? That makes work unenjoyable.

One thing I love about teaching is that in 16 weeks, I have started and finished a project. I can see progress. I can look at my work, see what worked and what didn't, get the sense of satisfaction that something important was accomplished, and move on. I like that about my consulting work too. A project goes from a definite start to a definite finish (although I'm sure some of your consultants never quite leave), and in most cases, you not only met the goals, but also made a longer-term difference.

Work is enjoyable when people know what they have to do, know what the expectations are, know that they can actually do it, and know how they are doing along the way. They know when they are done and what they have done.

Meaningfulness

All tasks are directed toward a purpose, but many times there is a disconnection between what employees do and how they view the importance of the result. It's your job to help them see the connection. Better yet, discover what is important to employees (it may be different for each one) and give them work that meets those needs. The meaningfulness of much work was removed when workers moved off the farm and into factories. People couldn't see the result of their labors, and tasks became repetitive and monotonous. Even today, organizations trying to systematize excellent work processes can fall prey to the dangers of taking employee choice, creativity, and meaning out of the work.

Putting it together, work is more enjoyable and self-motivating when employees competently accomplish a variety of novel, challenging, meaningful tasks that fit their interests; work in an environment that gives them pleasure; work with people they care for and relate to; and continuously learn, grow, and develop. Getting paid to work or receiving a slap on the back makes it just so much better.

MAKING WORK MORE ENJOYABLE FOR YOUR EMPLOYEES

Each employee is the same as and also different from every other employee.

Activity

Complete the "Employee Work Enjoyment" worksheet, found in chapter 6, for each of your employees.

Intrinsic Work

Work that satisfies interests, the need for growth, and the desire to master challenges is called "intrinsically" motivating. It is an outgrowth of psychological needs. People who are intrinsically motivated do what they do because it is fun or enjoyable—they *want* to do it. People who are intrinsically motivated continue to work even when not monitored and when no rewards are offered.

Edward Deci and Richard M. Ryan identified a continuum of motivation, beginning with nonmotivation, moving to extrinsic motivation based on rewards and punishment, and then to intrinsic motivation, which they call "self-determined." Deci, in his 1995 book, *Why We Do What We Do,* contrasts the "control" that a system of rewards and punishment imposes with autonomy, which he says is an innate human need.[41] He believes that extrinsic rewards can actually undermine intrinsic motivation. "When people say that money motivates," he says, "what they really mean is that money controls. And when it does, people become alienated—they give up some of their authenticity—and they push themselves to do what they think they must do" (p. 29).

In early studies, Deci found that college students who were *not* offered an extrinsic reward (money) to solve puzzles would continue working longer to solve the puzzles than would those who were compensated. The rewarded students were far less likely to play with the puzzles just for fun. "Stop the pay, and stop the play," he found. "It seems that once having been paid, these subjects were only in it for the money. And that was with an activity they had initially been quite willing to do without rewards" (p. 25).

> *That is not to say that money, recognition, and other rewards are not important. They are valuable and often necessary motivational tools. They are not, however, the* only *tools, and relying solely on them reduces your ability to motivate people to their highest potential.*

You can build upon intrinsic motivators when working with your employees.

Activity

Complete the exercise "Doing Work for the Fun and Reward of It," found in chapter 6, and then complete the exercise "Doing Work for the Fun of It—Our Department."

JOB SATISFACTION

Job satisfaction has been one of the most studied topics in organizational behavior. Over 10,000 articles had been published on the topic up until the year 2000, and more have appeared since. Job satisfaction is the feeling employees have about such issues as how interesting, enjoyable, meaningful, and challenging the job is and how much variety it has.

Job satisfaction has been measured by simply asking employees how satisfied they are with their jobs or, more comprehensively, by inquiring how they feel about pay, opportunities for promotions, supervision, their coworkers, and the work itself. Interestingly, one's personality seems also to have a good deal to do with how satisfied an employee will be with the job, regardless of other factors.

There is evidence that job satisfaction contributes to both individual performance and organizational results such as profitability, productivity, turnover, customer satisfaction, and loyalty, though not all research has produced similar results. Happy workers are not necessarily more productive than those who aren't, but there is more and more proof that satisfaction really does impact performance and workplace results.

Sources: Harter, James K., Frank L. Schmidt, and Theodore L. Hayes. "Business-Unit-Level Relationship between Employee Satisfaction, Employee Engagement, and Business Outcomes: A Meta-Analysis." *Journal of Applied Psychology* 87, no. 2 (2002): 268–79. Judge, Timothy A., Joyce E. Bono, Carl J. Thoresen, and Gregory K. Patton. "The Job Satisfaction–Job Performance Relationship: A Qualitative and Quantitative Review." *Psychological Bulletin* 127, no. 3 (2001): 376

Passionate Work

If having "satisfied" employees is important, how much more motivating would it be to have employees who are actually *passionate* about their work? When Patricia Boverie and I began to study this in 1999, there had been very little discussion about such a "touchy-feely" topic, and you can imagine the eyebrows that were raised when we began to talk about occupational intimacy. Yet people do have relationships with their jobs, don't they? They love or hate them and are disgusted, frustrated, or excited about them. Occupational intimacy represents passion renewal in organizations and consists of work that is meaningful, enjoyable, and nurturing. The following article, published originally in the March/April 2005 issue of *Advancing Philanthropy*, describes actions anyone can undertake to create a more passionate work environment.

Nine Ways to Create a More Passionate Work Environment—Starting Today!

By Michael Kroth, PhD, and Patricia Boverie, PhD

Do you have any "living dead" on your staff—people who just get through the day? If so, what effect does this halfhearted attitude have on your donors and the fundraising goals your organization is trying to achieve? A passionate work environment is not only more enjoyable, but also more productive. In fact, how people feel about working in an organization can account for 20 percent to 30 percent of business performance. All things being equal, employees who are more enthusiastic and motivated will produce more, be more creative, and be more committed to organizational success than those who are not.

Passion can be defined in various ways, but for our purposes we will define it as a strong desire to do something. We asked people what causes them to be passionate about working in an organization. Their responses fell into three categories:

- Meaningful work
- Enjoyable work
- Being in a nurturing workplace

Following is a list of nine activities anyone can start tomorrow to create what we term "Occupational Intimacy," a more passionate work environment comprising the three organizational categories. It is not an exhaustive list—you may have others that work just as well or better for yourself or others you work with—but it is a starting place.

Meaningful Work

1. *Become the best.* It is hard to be passionate about something that is mediocre. A master craftsman who has worked for 38 years at the Waterford Crystal Factory in Ireland told us he is still passionate about his work because he knows he is one of the best in the world at his craft and because he works for the best crystal factory in the world. The process of becoming better makes many people passionate about their work, so that they either strive to develop into the best they can possibly be or they work to be the best in their class, occupation, industry or field.
   - What would it take for you or your organization to become the best you can be?
2. *Connect to your mission.* Capital campaign consultant and author Stanley Weinstein, ACFRE, explains, "Commitment to mission is the sine qua non of nonprofit fundraising success. Donors may give modest amounts because a respected peer asked, but major commitments become possible only when the donor believes in the organization's mission and the value of the philanthropic investment. Additionally, volunteers—even those who are inherently uncomfortable with fundraising—become motivated to make that personal ask when they

remember that the request for funding flows from their commitment to the valuable work of the nonprofit organization."

- How can you connect volunteers, staff, and yourself to the contribution you are making to the world?

3. *Create a challenge.* Why do organizations try to win the Malcolm Baldrige National Quality Award? Why does a manufacturing company set zero defects as a goal? Why do organizations set high fundraising goals? Challenges can ignite passion for the work of the organization or for an individual.
   - What challenge will spark the imagination of your organization?

Enjoyable Work

4. *Put the right people in the right job.* This activity is more difficult because it involves peoples' livelihoods. Each person naturally has work that he or she likes to do. Some like working with people, while others would rather work with a computer. Some have an affinity for numbers, others for engines. It is remarkable how often people take jobs—volunteer or otherwise—simply because they were offered and find they are miserable years down the road.
   - Does your organization strive to get staff and volunteers involved in the kind of work they truly enjoy doing?
5. *Create the best physical environment possible.* There is actual evidence that aesthetically pleasing objects enable people to work better. Music can soothe, inspire, or energize workers. Decoration can reinforce the atmosphere most conducive to the particular work needing to get done. On the other hand, dreary environments can drain energy and even depress the people who inhabit them. One call center we studied went from an error-prone place where employees sobbed on the elevators on their way to work to the best in their industry class. They did a number of things to make it happen, but one was to improve the physical environment. When they bought new chairs (the previous ones were held together by duct tape), their productivity numbers immediately went up and continued to rise. Now each individual colorfully decorates his or her office with plants, pictures, balloons, and other personal touches.
   - What can you do to make your organization a place that your staff and volunteers find cheerful, motivating, and productive?
6. *Give people permission to have fun.* We work with a 300-employee organization comprising mostly accountants and information technology (IT) professionals. We wondered if they would be fun to work with. As it turns out, they create activities to make work humorous, entertaining, and enjoyable. They have had a "Gong Show" event with employee acts, including the CFO dressed in prison stripes lip-synching "Jail House Rock." He brought down the house and made it comfortable for others to let their hair down. Fun does not have to be wild and crazy. It can be simple. For a leader, it means letting people know that it is okay,

even encouraged, to do things that make people laugh and enjoy themselves at work.

- How can you make your volunteers' and staff's work more fun?

Nurturing Work

7. *Learn constantly.* When we interviewed passionate people, we always found that they take risks and learn. When work becomes monotonous or, as one of our good friends says, when you have "baked the same cake too many times," passion fades. Organizations that proactively promote learning are more passionate. One Inc. 500 organization we studied (from *Inc.* magazine's list of the nation's fastest growing privately held companies) requires each member of its senior management team to take an hour each week just to read a book or article or view a video. Later in the week, team members get together and share information learned with each other. Other organizations rotate people into new positions, assign stretch projects, or send people to training to improve their skills or get new perspectives.
   - What can you do to introduce new learning opportunities into your organization?
8. *Build relationships.* Most fundraising, we have observed, involves social activity and relationship building. One of the most powerful roles that professional organizations such as the Association of Fundraising Professionals (AFP) play is to create a web of relationships that is constantly renewing, challenging, and supporting. While an individual's organization may not be doing its best to motivate staff and volunteers, often the professional relationships people have keep them energized about their field. For others, the relationships at work make the job enjoyable and meaningful. One of our clients reorganized its entire manufacturing organization. One group slated for dispersal was a group of women who worked closely together. Their informal role in the organization, however, was to serve as the social glue. The organization realized in time the huge mistake it would be to destroy this important group and made them the only exception to the newly decentralized organization.
   - Are you applying the principles you practice with donors and volunteers to your own staff?
9. *Provide recognition and rewards.* We almost did not include this because it almost seems like a cliché. There are so many ways to do it, but it is easy to forget. One high-tech company we looked at puts the names of not only its employees, but also their extended families, on its organizational chart to recognize the valuable contribution fathers, mothers, daughters, sons, cousins, aunts, and uncles play in making the organization a success. Each new employee also puts his or her handprint on the entrance of the building. Those handprints, together, symbolize the importance each person has as a part of the team.

- Undoubtedly you do a great job of recognizing and rewarding your volunteers and donors, but do you put the same effort into your fellow employees?

We have presented nine ideas you can implement today to create a more passionate, more productive work environment in your organization. You also can apply each one of them to yourself. They are not the only ideas that might work for you, nor will all of them apply to you or your situation. Each one has, however, been effective for others. Cumulatively they can be a powerful force.

DESIGNING ENJOYABLE WORK

There is not a job on earth that doesn't have something about it that is unenjoyable. Even CEOs, who have tremendous power to control their environments, have to face angry shareholders. Ministers have to share bad news or lead fund-raising drives. Athletes have to endure injury and failure and the constant toil of being on the road. Almost every job, however, can be made more enjoyable.

Job Sculpting

Timothy Butler and James Waldroop use the term "job sculpting" in a Harvard Business Review article of the same name.[42] They say that talented professionals will stay at the same organization if their job matches their life interests. "Deeply embedded life interests," they say, "do not determine what people are good at—they drive what kinds of activities make them happy. At work, that happiness often translates into commitment. It keeps people engaged, and it keeps them from quitting" (p. 146). Job sculpting steps involve the following:

1. *Managers identify each employee's deeply embedded life interests.* The eight interests Butler and Waldroop found in their research are application of technology, quantitative analysis, theory development and conceptual thinking, creative production, counseling and mentoring, managing people and relationships, enterprise control, and influence through language and ideas.
2. *Use each change in assignment as an opportunity to do some job sculpting.* A salesperson with a life interest in quantitative analysis might be

given responsibilities to do market analysis. For an engineer with an interest in influence through language and ideas, a manager might add responsibilities for helping the communications department design sales support materials or user manuals.

3. *Use the performance-review process.* Make job sculpting a part of the discussion. Systematize it within the career-development process. During the performance review, ask employees to play an active role in job sculpting. Ask them to write their views about career satisfaction, the kind of work they love, and what their favorite activities are before the meeting.
4. *Listen.* Listen more carefully to employees when they talk about what they like and dislike about their jobs.
5. *Customize the next work assignment accordingly.* In some cases that will simply mean adding a new responsibility. Sometimes it will mean more significant changes.
6. *Giving new responsibilities means taking some away.* The uninteresting part of one person's job may be perfect for another person.
7. *Sometimes the job cannot be re-sculpted to meet the employee's needs.* A talented employee may need guidance to leave the company.

Job Crafting

Amy Wrzesniewski and Jane Dutton, in a 2001 *Academy of Management Review* article, describe another interesting approach to job design. In this case, the employee is the job redesigner.[43] *In Crafting a Job: Revisioning Employees as Active Crafters of Their Work,* the authors say that work tasks and interactions are the raw materials employees use to construct their jobs. Employees can change the activities they engage in while doing the job, can change how they view the job, and also can control whom they interact with on the job. Doing those things affects the meaning of the work and how the person defines him- or herself at work. A hospital cleaner cutting out tasks and avoiding interactions with others is one example they give. "Job crafting," then, involves the actions employees take to shape, mold, and redefine their jobs, and job crafters are those employees who do it. Two people with the exact same job description may complete the work in very different ways.

Employees craft their jobs in order to have some control over them. They do it to create a more positive self-image regarding their work. They do it to fulfill a need to connect with others. Often they do it because they don't feel their needs are being met through the existing job design. In this way, employees make the jobs their own.

Job crafting is the mirror of job sculpting. With job crafting, the employee is using what freedom he or she has to modify the job, and with job sculpting, the manager is taking the lead. Job crafting makes work more meaningful to employees, gives them a sense of being proactive designers of their work, changes how they view themselves in the job, and also affects the relationships they have with others.

Job crafting is not, the authors say, innately good or bad for organizations. If employees modify their jobs in ways that are aligned with organizational goals, it will be helpful. If they modify jobs in ways that are not aligned with organizational goals, their motivation will not be directed in productive ways.

Job crafting will occur whether or not you want it to happen. Take advantage of your employees' need to make their work more intrinsically motivating. They *want* work that is enjoyable and meaningful. To make the most of what employees will do anyway, get involved using the following approach:

1. *Employees craft their jobs, and you sculpt them.* Make it an interactive practice between you and them to meet both organizational and human needs.
2. *Set the context for your entire organization.* Depending on your attitude and actions, employees will craft their jobs undercover, or they will feel enabled. Honor their desire to make their own work as motivating as possible.
3. *Actively acknowledge and encourage job crafting* because employees probably don't think of themselves as "job crafters." The goals will remain the same, but how the work gets done to meet those goals can change. Legitimize job crafting through training, rewards and recognition, creative work organization, and job design. Help employees make their own work meaningful by including them in strategic conversations about what you are trying to accomplish and why.
4. *Take some risks.* Let employees try things in their jobs. Give them training that *they* believe would give them desired skills for their work. Sure, you may waste a few training dollars, but your overall return may increase significantly.

WHAT YOU CAN DO: FOUR STEPS TO DESIGNING ENJOYABLE WORK

1. *Identify what each employee finds to be enjoyable about the work itself.* That means talking to him or her and listening deeply to what isn't said or perhaps even consciously known.

2. *Ask employees to help restructure their work to make it more enjoyable.* Involvement increases commitment.
3. Make the changes you can now, and plan for those you can accomplish later. Some job modifications will be relatively easy, and some changes to the work environment will be simple, but some will take more time. Start now and stick with it. Job customization could be as simple as asking someone who enjoys public speaking to make a presentation after the project or asking another who likes data management to develop a file system for a project. One possibility might involve giving more decision-making power to the employee, or another responsibility might be buying plants for the office. Other customizations will take more persistence and resources. Maybe someone needs additional training or perhaps a job rotation to give a new challenge. Changes such as those can cost money in the short run but pay off handsomely in work enjoyment—with associated commitment and productivity—later.
4. *Review and readapt.* Systematically check in with employees to see how they are doing. Performance review and developmental planning are the perfect times to do it on a yearly or quarterly basis, but also hang out, listen, and find out on a more informal basis what is making work enjoyable—or isn't.

KEY POINTS

1. Toxic environments destroy motivation.
2. Generative environments provide the energy for motivation that sustains itself.
3. Both managers and employees can design jobs and tasks to be more motivating.
4. Occupational Intimacy—a passionate work environment—includes enjoyable, meaningful, and nurturing work.

CHAPTER SUMMARY

The workplace either supports or restrains employee motivation. By capitalizing on the four principles described, you will prepare the environment for sustainable motivation.

FOUR

Crossing the Rubicon

WHAT YOU WILL FIND IN THIS CHAPTER

1. Three principles for setting and pursuing highly motivating goals
2. How to become an expectancy manager for your employees
3. The differences between process, performance, and outcome goals
4. How self-regulation training can improve performance

When Julius Caesar crossed the Rubicon in 49 B.C., he committed an irrevocable act. He couldn't unbreak the law he had just broken. He was set on a course of action. He crossed the tiny stream, announced "The die is cast," marched his army across, and called on his soldiers to pledge their loyalty. He went on to defeat the Roman forces and install himself as dictator, only to be assassinated on the Ides of March five years later.

The previous chapter (Setting the Environment)—Principles 1, 2, 3, and 4—provides the support for this chapter (Crossing the Rubicon). There are specific jobs and tasks that need to be accomplished. Some of those tasks are more naturally rewarding than others, but even the least appealing must be completed. Goal setting can be effective even when one or more

Table 4.1
Crossing the Rubicon: Build and Sustain Motivation to Accomplish Workplace Goals

Principle	*Goal*	*Practice*
5. Belief in personal capability enables goal setting and pursuit.	Build self-efficacy.	Be an expectancy manager.
6. Great goals get people going.	Set challenging goals.	Master the art and science of goal setting.
7. Willpower is the engine for goal pursuit.	Sustain motivation.	Use strategies to strengthen and support willpower.

of the first four principles are weak or even lacking. That is because you have rewards your employees want and punishments they wish to avoid.

Crossing the Rubicon involves three principles. Principle 5—developing the belief that goals can actually be accomplished—is the foundation for both setting goals and sustaining the effort to achieve them. Principle 6 is the process of creating motivating goals. Principle 7 is sustaining motivation through willpower. Between principles 6 and 7 lies the Rubicon—committing to the goal. The stronger that commitment, the more likely it is that the goal will be achieved.

*Cannon's Sweet Hots: Stepping off the Cliff**

Diane Cannon and her husband John founded Cannon's Sweet Hots to produce a specialty chile sauce based on one of John's recipes. They had no experience in the food industry, no inventory, no market for their product, and had never produced one jar of Sweet Hots.

Diane had to quit her full-time job to go into business. "We had to ask ourselves, what [do] we have to lose, what do we have to gain? My discovery," says Diane, "is that once you take that first step, that leap of faith, if you've done your homework, if you believe in the product and can convey that belief—they will buy it. You feel exhilarated. I personally was terrified. We felt crazy but said, 'Isn't this great?'"

Diane could have closed Sweet Hots for any number of reasons. She had brain tumor surgery, and it took three years afterward before she could work normally. She had gall bladder surgery. John had quadruple bypass surgery. There was no processing facility in their home base at

*This story was adapted from an article, "Bored? Take a Risk" originally published in the July 2001, issue of the *New Mexico Business Journal,* by Michael Kroth and Patricia Boverie.

that time. They had no training or experience in the field. They assumed personal financial risk and sacrifice. "We sold our stock, got a loan, and stripped our lives down to the bare minimum," she said. Their love for Sweet Hots gave them the determination to stay the course. Their line now has 25 products that are carried in 30 states.

When Diane quit her job, sold her stock, and borrowed money to go into business, she committed an irrevocable act. She couldn't go back. She was set on a course of action.

Creating highly motivating work environments involves (1) developing the confidence to take on difficult jobs, (2) setting challenging goals, (3) stepping off the cliff—as Diane and her husband John did in 1992 and as Julius Caesar did in 49 B.C.—and then, (4) sustaining the motivation to achieve the goals despite obstacles.

PRINCIPLE 5

Belief in Personal Capability Enables Goal Setting and Goal Pursuit: Develop Employee Belief in Their Capabilities

THE LITTLE VOICE INSIDE OUR HEADS

Every person has a little voice inside his or her head that says "I can do that" or "I can't do that." If you don't think you have that little voice, it's what you hear inside your head right now saying, "I don't have a little voice inside my head." Every person has a running monologue (some of us have dialogue or even group discussions) going on inside our heads all the time. How your employees answer the question "Can I do this?" will determine how much effort they will put into it, how long they will stick with it, and how high they will set their sights. Henry Ford's statement—"Whether you think you can or whether you think you can't, you're right"—is absolutely true.

That little voice is important. If accountants don't believe they can get the books closed in time this month, they won't put much effort into trying. If Sue doesn't think she'll get the promotion no matter what she does, she will put her efforts into something else, like finding another job. Jim will resist learning quality-management tools if he doesn't think he can figure out statistics.

On the other hand, if Sue thinks she's a good candidate for the promotion, she will work day and night to get it. If Jim took a mathematics class and received a good grade, he might volunteer to be your quality-control expert. Accounting supervisors will work 24-7 to close the books on time if there is a nice bonus involved and if they think completing the job is within their reach.

POWERFUL OR POWERLESS—CAN I DO IT?

People feel they have some degree of power, ranging from none to total, in both work and life situations. They believe they have the ability to make things happen, or they don't. Those beliefs will affect their behaviors and level of motivation. Two people with the same abilities will have different perceptions of them. That will cause each person to behave differently. One, thinking herself extremely capable, will put her heart and soul into completing the task. The other, lacking confidence in himself, will aspire to less and give up earlier.

If Rusty is assigned to change the corporate risk-management policy, and he thinks the policy is something outside his ability to change, he won't work very hard to get it modified. If Michelle believes that the policy is just another piece of paper that can be amended, that she has the ability to influence the change, and that the time is ripe, she'll be highly motivated to complete the assignment. The "facts" of the task may be exactly the same, but each person's perception of his or her ability to accomplish it is different. Therefore the motivation and subsequent actions of each are much different.

Powerful or Powerless—Will What I Do Make a Difference?

Shocks given in closed cages produce no response from dogs and cats after a period of time, even when the animals know a shock is coming. They give up trying to escape even when a door to the cage is opened. They develop "learned helplessness." Employees in your organization may also develop learned helplessness when they believe that

- they have contributed great work over the years and have still been passed over for promotions, recognition, and other rewards;
- none of the great ideas they have offered for workplace improvement have been adopted by the organization; or
- the great work teams they have developed have been disbanded every time there was a reorganization.

These employees have given up after days, weeks, months, or years of trying and now just put in their time. Just like the dogs and the rats, they sit and do nothing when you offer them an opportunity now. You wonder why they won't take the bait. They have been trained that it won't make a difference, no matter what they do.

Do you think you can get a date with a supermodel, have a traffic ticket dropped, or make the days cooler? If you think you can do those things, you are more likely to try than if you don't. Your perception of how much you control such matters is different from others' perceptions. Some people believe they can get that date, avoid the ticket, or change environmental policy. Their actions will be very different from those of people who don't believe they can accomplish these tasks. People develop beliefs through their experiences (turned down 10 times, had to pay every ticket, no pro-green candidates elected to Congress.).

Employees with learned helplessness have poor productivity or quit trying altogether. People with belief in their ability, however, learn from mistakes, think their efforts produce something, and don't blame themselves unnecessarily. That means it is important to give employees successes early in their careers, their jobs, or the assignments they are given. Those successes will inoculate them from the failures that are sure to come. It also entails coaching. When employees feel defeated or frustrated from knocking their heads against the wall, you should be there to help develop healthy beliefs about the situation and their abilities.

SUPERVISING FOR OPTIMISM

There are three ways people habitually explain good or bad events to themselves: [1]

1. As either stable or unstable (permanent or temporary). How long lasting is the cause of the event?
2. As either universal or specific. Will the event affect everything I do or just this one case?
3. As either internal or external. Did I cause the event or did something outside myself?

Pessimists think that bad events will last a long time (permanent) and will undermine all they do (universal) and that they are to blame (internal). Optimists think that failure is not their fault (external), that it was just a short-term setback (temporary), and that the causes of it were limited to just the one event (specific). The situation, other people, or bad luck caused it. Good events are explained in the opposite way. A good event for a pessimist is temporary, specific, and external. For an optimist, it's permanent, universal, and internal. Optimists view failure as a challenge and try harder. Pessimists are more likely to give up and get depressed.

A salesperson making 20 unsuccessful cold calls can interpret the event as a pessimist or as an optimist. If a pessimist, she might say, (1) "What's wrong with me? I'm just not cut out for this" (internal); (2) "Not only that, but I'm not good with people" (permanent); and (3) "And in fact, I'm just not good at anything a salesperson does" (universal). If an optimist, she might say, (1) "Heck, this kind of thing happens to everyone" (external); (2) "I think the big reason was because I'm still in training" (temporary); and (3) "Not only that, but my sales manager says it takes 100 calls to get 10 people to take a meeting" (specific).

Activity

How do you coach your employees? Try out the exercise "Supervisor Support to Increase Employee Optimism," found in chapter 6.

Optimism Isn't Just Nice to Have—It Pays Off in Increased Productivity

New salespeople at MetLife scoring high on a "learned optimism" test sold 37 percent more life insurance in their first two years than pessimists. Agents who scored in the top 10 percent sold 88 percent more than those in the bottom 10 percent. Optimists are better in sales, school, and work. They are healthier and live longer.

Not only is optimism an important motivational tool, but it is also within your ability to influence. Individualized leader support was found to increase optimism in sales people. Support activities include mentoring and coaching. Your employees have to be accountable for failures, but working from an optimistic approach will improve their chances of success next time.[2]

LEARNED HELPLESSNESS

Learned helplessness is a well-established concept within psychology. The theory was developed by Martin Seligman, who went on to write the 1998 best seller *Learned Optimism* and to become the leader of the Positive Psychology movement, which emphasizes what is right with people rather than what is wrong with them. How people interpret good or bad events will determine whether they are more likely to develop learned helplessness or learned optimism.[3] The good news is that pessimists can learn to be optimists. Seligman says that self-talk is the key, and he offers the ABCDE model as the process:

A = *Adversity.* Something bad happens.
B = *Beliefs.* How you explain the adversity to yourself.
C = *Consequences.* The feelings and actions arising from those beliefs. Feelings range from anger and joy and the actions from giving up to redoubling effort.

D = *Disputation.* Challenging what you initially believed caused the event. Changing your beliefs about the causes may also change the results. This involves stopping to reflect, think of alternative explanations, and contest negative explanations.

E = *Energization.* Doing this (ABCDE process) regularly should result in new energy and readiness to take on the next task.

Activity

Complete the exercise "Practicing the ABCDE Method," found in chapter 6.

SELF-EFFICACY—THE BELIEF THAT "I CAN"

"Self-efficacy" is an individual's belief about his or her ability to successfully perform a given task or behavior. Albert Bandura developed the theory and is the acknowledged authority.[4] People with low self-efficacy are less likely to attempt difficult goals than those with higher self-efficacy, even if their skills are the same. People with high self-efficacy are more likely to set higher goals and to persist in achieving them. People with high self-efficacy are more likely to perform better than those with lower self-efficacy. Self-efficacy also builds upon itself. High self-efficacy results in performance success, which results in higher self-efficacy, more challenging goals, and higher performance—a generative spiral. Low self-efficacy causes poor results and therefore lower goals and poorer performance—a death spiral. That is why self-efficacy and managing expectancies—Principle 5—provide the foundation for both goal setting and goal pursuit. Watch any team that expects to lose the game before it begins. They do lose. When a new coach comes in and changes the team efficacy, the team may begin to have small successes that build on themselves. Soon they have a winning team.

Activity

Think about times you helped an employee develop the confidence to complete difficult tasks. How did that happen? How has your own self-confidence been developed? Complete the exercise "Developing Self-Confidence," found in chapter 6.

Hundreds of studies have shown the relationship of self-efficacy to performance. Bandura identified four sources of self-efficacy beliefs:

Mastery experience. Succeeding on a challenging task is the strongest source of high self-efficacy beliefs.

Vicarious learning. This is learning by observing others. If I see a coworker with similar skills tackle and succeed on a project, then I have some confidence that I can do well too. The more similar the model is to the employee, the stronger the self-efficacy link.

Verbal persuasion. When someone I trust and think is competent tells me I can complete a task, I am likely to believe him or her.

Physiological and psychological arousal. When well-rested, your employees are more likely to feel "I can conquer the world." When tired, the opposite is true. Too much stress undermines performance. When stress is present, we are likely to doubt our ability to perform.

Mastery experiences have the strongest link to self-efficacy beliefs, vicarious learning the second strongest, verbal persuasion the third strongest, and physiological and psychological arousal is the weakest.

Developing "I Can" Beliefs: Stanley Weinstein

Imagine walking into a business or community leader's office and asking for a million-dollar contribution to your favorite nonprofit organi-

Table 4.2

Sources of Self-Efficacy Beliefs Proposed by Albert Bandura

Mastery experiences	Mastery experience is what we learn from our own personal experience with success or failure. Successful past performance provides the strongest information, leading to higher or lower efficacy beliefs.
Vicarious experiences	Self-efficacy can be affected by observing the experiences of others. If someone I relate to can do something, I'm more likely to believe I can do it too.
Verbal persuasion	Individuals form beliefs about whether they can or can't do something when people they believe give them verbal encouragement or discouragement.
Physiological and affective states	Anxiety, nervousness, a rapid heart rate, and sweating occur when people have challenges to overcome. Physical or mental states such as these affect whether or not people think they can do something, which in turn affects performance.

Source: Bandura, Albert. *Self-Efficacy: The Exercise of Control.* New York: Freeman, 1997.

zation. If you think motivating your employees is hard, try motivating a volunteer to ask a friend or community leader for a donation.

"I think it's easier to get people *to give* big gifts than it is to get people *to ask* for the money," Association of Fund Raising Professionals award winner Stanley Weinstein says. "That's the hardest thing in our field."

Stanley's challenge is to motivate volunteers to sit across the table from donors and ask for money. That is difficult because none of us like to be turned down, and we are taught it's not polite to ask for money.

Motivating volunteer fund-raisers is a process of making them feel capable of success. Stanley starts by assuring volunteers that they will never have to do anything they feel uncomfortable doing. He stresses that he will help them find that level of comfort. He meets one-on-one with volunteers to hear concerns, make them feel comfortable, and encourage them to raise that level of comfort.

Getting appointments and meeting with potential donors is difficult for volunteers. So Stanley gets his staff involved in making the appointments. Sometimes an experienced staff person will sit next to the volunteer and help him or her with the call.

Volunteers are asked to do the easy part of donor solicitation first. Perhaps they meet with a donor just to say thank you for a past gift. As they feel more comfortable, they are asked to try more difficult tasks.

Everything Stanley does is oriented to making volunteers feel they can do what they are asked to do. He provides training, emotional and task support, and loads of celebration and praise.

"If I sit before a group of volunteers," he says, "I could list all the reasons why people don't make solicitation calls. I could even tell them the solutions to each one. Instead, what we really do is say 'What are all the concerns?' I list them on a big chart even though I know what they're going to say." By asking the volunteers to come up with the answers, he gets them engaged and committed to the process.

"We help people find their own comfort level," he says. "We team them with people who have experience and give on-the-job training. We take easy baby steps first and, of course, thank them promptly and generously."

Let's think for a minute about what is happening here. Stanley takes a group of people who are afraid to make appointments with potential donors and develops them to the point that they can sit down with a potential donor and ask for a million dollars or more. More interestingly, as the volunteers grow more proficient and have more and more success, they enjoy it more.

To accomplish that, Stanley did the following:

1. Provided the support they needed at whatever level they were
2. Helped them develop the skills they needed to be successful

3. Modeled successful strategies and techniques
4. Gave them praise and recognition when they did well

He used proven strategies for making people feel they could be successful asking for money—a task people fear doing. Those are the same strategies that successful sales managers use to develop their salespeople, that organizations put into development plans for high-potential leaders, and that master craftsmen use with their apprentices.

Activities

Complete the exercises "Developing 'I Can' Employees—Fund-Raising Volunteer" and "Developing 'I Can' Employees," found in chapter 6.

YOU ARE AN EXPECTANCY MANAGER

It seems you should be able to just explain and delegate tasks, but you are also an "expectancy manager." You are a lens through which your employees see their ability to complete the task. They interpret past experiences through you too.

You can tell when someone has done a good job of being an expectancy manager. That person—a parent, coach, teacher, friend, or boss—has moved someone from low expectations and little self-confidence to a belief she or he can conquer the world.

Part of the trick is to create reasonable expectations. Your employee will fail and fail when he believes he has more competence than he really has. Then his self-confidence will erode. Alternatively, your employee will take on easy tasks and never grow or make the contribution she is capable of making when she believes she has less competence than she actually possesses.

EXPECTANCY THEORY

Expectancy theory says that people can be motivated if they believe that their effort will result in desired performance and that successful performance will result in a desirable reward or outcome.

People are motivated, in other words, to the extent they are working toward rewards that they want and that they think they can get by doing something they believe they can do.

Sources: Lawler, Edward E. *Motivation in Work Organizations,* 1st ed. The Jossey-Bass Management Series. San Francisco: Jossey-Bass, 1994.
Vroom, Victor Harold. *Work and Motivation.* Malabar, FL: Krieger, 1982.

Have you heard employees say the following?

"I was born with an introverted personality. I could never ... "
"The odds of getting done what corporate rolled down are about the same as winning the lottery."
"I've tried this several times and it didn't work. I must not be very good at ... "

A person believing the result is out of his or her control is unlikely to take responsibility for making the right things happen to accomplish the goal. Many times, these same people develop a victim mentality.

Contrast that with members of a high performing team. They—a Marine squad, an ambulance crew, a merger and acquisitions team, or a debate team—think there is very little they can't accomplish. They can learn it, acquire it, find it, or outlast it. They believe the responsibility for success or failure lies almost entirely on their shoulders. They attribute success or failure to their own efforts.

Which kind of employees do you want? You, as the expectancy manager, have to give tasks that build confidence and then coach your employees to believe they can accomplish them. Self-efficacy affects self-beliefs and therefore what will be attempted, how much effort will be devoted to it, and how long that effort will last. That is why the "I can" principle is foundational to both setting goals and sustaining the motivation to achieve them.

A FORMULA FOR SUCCESS

Putting aside for now the factors described in chapter 3, "Setting the Environment," employees are motivated to the extent that they think their efforts will result in successful performance, and that the performance will then result in a desired outcome. The amount of effort they will put forth depends on how much they want the reward, how high their expectations are about getting the reward if they complete the task, and how well they believe they can perform.

The previous discussions can be summarized with a simple equation. When BC = belief in my capability to achieve a task, OE = expectancy that achieving the task will result in an outcome, and DO = desirability of the outcome, then:

$$BC \times OE \times DO = \text{Motivation to perform the task}$$

That is, belief that I can do something (BC) times the belief that if I do that something, an outcome will occur (OE) times my desire for that outcome (DO) equals my motivational level to complete that task. Note that if *any one* of these qualities is missing, motivation is *zero.*

Belief I Can Do It		Belief That If I Do It An Outcome Will Occur		It's An Outcome I Want to Occur		My Motivation To Do It
10	X	10	X	10	=	1000
8	X	2	X	5	=	80
10	X	10	X	0	=	0
0	X	10	X	10	=	0

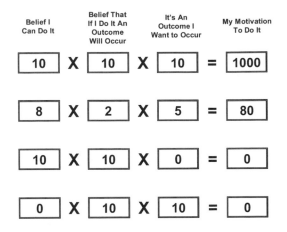

Figure 4.1 A Formula for Success

Let's say that I know I will get a promotion if I increase sales by 10 percent. I want the promotion desperately but don't believe there is any way I can accomplish the goal. My motivation to accomplish this task is zero. If I think I can do it and want the promotion, but have been passed over time and again when I've felt I'd earned it, my motivation is also zero.

The implications are compelling for managers. You have the ability to influence all three beliefs.

1. You can help build your employee's belief in his or her capability to complete the task.
2. You can assure that realistic expectations are created about the outcomes of successful performance (you'll make sure they receive their rewards if they perform).
3. By studying your employees, you will know what outcomes they desire and therefore what to offer.

You also have the ability to influence how your employee interprets successful or less-than-successful performance.

WHAT YOU CAN DO: "I CAN" BUILDING STRATEGIES

There are several ways you can build "I can" beliefs in your employees, which build upon Bandura's sources of self-efficacy beliefs.

Teach Them How to Do It

You can give your employees "baby step" experiences. If you give them too much too fast, before they have or can learn the actual skills to accomplish the task, they'll fail, and their belief in themselves will fall. Some of those learning experiences will mean sending them to a class; other experiences may be piloting a project, and still others will involve actually giving them "live" projects to accomplish. As they learn more, their belief in their own abilities will grow.

Over time, as the employee develops the experiences and competence and the associated confidence that she can do the job, a spiral of success will be created. Success will build upon success as she is willing to take on larger tasks with less need for oversight (or micromanaging) on your part. Note that this confidence is based on competence. Give her a different task in an area where she doesn't have competence, and you might be starting at ground zero again. A general pattern of success will produce an "I can" attitude that may transfer to other, new tasks. Competencies learned along the way may be applied to new tasks and may quicken the learning curve, thereby speeding an employee's journey to an "I can" attitude quickly.

"Learning to learn" skills are especially useful for employees. Problem-solving skills can be used in many new tasks, as can communication skills or negotiating skills. So can reasoning skills, creative thinking, and listening skills. If you give your employees the opportunity to build expertise in these areas, you are building *transferable confidence.*

Show Them They Can Do It

People learn by observing others. Learning can be accelerated by watching how others do it. I cut my learning time when I watch Emeril making a dish on TV. What would normally take me hours can be telescoped dramatically.

Mentoring programs, apprenticeships, internships, and rotation programs place employees with experts. All are ways employees learn by watching and increase the belief they can do similar things. The more "alike" the role model or mentor is, the more likely the employee will believe she or he can accomplish similar tasks. Watching someone fairly similar in look, age, experience, or background increases the likelihood that the employee will believe "I can do that too." Asking other employees to come and share how they successfully learned a similar task in similar situations can achieve the same purpose.

Tell Them They Can Do It

Confidence can also be increased by telling employees they can do it, but this approach is not as powerful as teaching or showing them how to do the job.

Highly successful and famed college basketball coach John Wooden believed in the hard work, perseverance, and skill building that prepared his team to play. In his book *My Personal Best,* he says, "There should never be a need for me to give a pep talk to instill motivation. The motivation must come from the players' belief—deeply entrenched—that ultimate success lies in giving their personal best. More than anything, I wanted players to love the process of doing that" (178).[5]

Telling someone they can complete a task is not nearly as powerful or long-lasting as developing the actual ability to do it but can be effective. Do you remember a time your favorite teacher or coach said you had the skills and talent to be successful? How did you feel then? Someone you respected claimed you could do it. Your confidence soared. You trained a little harder instead of giving up. You burned the midnight oil to finish your paper for the essay contest.

Your employee is likely to believe someone in his profession or craft saying he or she has the talent, skills, and personality to succeed.

Get Them into Physical and Emotional Shape to Do It

People who feel good physically often draw on their sense of personal power. When you wake up in the morning feeling refreshed, you are ready to take on anything. If you wake up feeling poorly, it's hard just getting to the office. People who are in good emotional spirits and surrounded by enthusiastic, supportive people have a positive outlook about the jobs ahead. Those who are overly stressed, conflicted, or depressed are less likely to feel like they can do just about anything.

Employees working exhausting hours week after week and month after month are being drained of their spirit. Be their strongest advocate upstairs. Get more workers or less work. If you have a toxic work environment, get rid of the poisonous people or clean it up. Make your organizational ecology generative and healthy.

Different people respond differently, but the more obstacles to a healthy work and emotional environment that are removed, the more positive and "can-do" the workplace.

OUTCOMES

Providing desirable outcomes is an important part of the expectancy manager role. What is desirable for one person may not be for another. Leaders have the ability to provide more than they may imagine.

LEADER–MEMBER EXCHANGE

Your ability to provide rewards may be much more comprehensive than you believe. Leader–member exchange (LMX) theory focuses on the relationship between leader and follower and is based on "exchanges" between them. When the relationship begins, exchanges are transactional—leaders provide followers what they need to perform, and followers perform. From there, the relationship may move to a higher level. Then social exchanges begin to occur. Those might include sharing information and resources on a personal and professional level. At the highest level, the leader and follower share mutual loyalty and support. The exchanges are emotional—trust, mutual respect, obligation—as well as behavioral.

At that stage, leaders depend on followers for help and constructive feedback. Followers can depend on the support of the leader. They are more satisfied overall and with the supervisor. Organizational commitment and performance improve, and turnover is reduced. Relationships are built on respect, trust, and mutual obligation.

Six types of resources can be exchanged in any human interaction: love, status, information, money, goods, and services.

When supervisors form exchange relationships with employees, good things happen. An employee who sees the supervisor as supportive, as discussed in Principle 2—"The more you care, the more they will care"—is more likely to have higher job performance, have reduced absenteeism, go beyond the call of duty, and be more committed to the organization.

Sources: Cropanzano, R., and S. M. Mitchell. "Social Exchange Theory: An Interdisciplinary Review." *Journal of Management* 31, no. 6 (2005): 874.

Teichman, M., and U. G. Foa. "Effect of Resources Similarity on Satisfaction with Exchange." *Social Behavior & Personality: An International Journal* 3, no. 2 (1975): 213.

Gerstner, C. R., and D. V. Day, D. V. "Meta-analytic Review of Leader–Member Exchange Theory: Correlates and Construct Issues." *Journal of Applied Psychology* 82, no. 6 (1997): 827–44.

Graen, G. B., and M. Uhl-Bien. "Relationship-Based Approach to Leadership: Development of Leader–Member Exchange (LMX) Theory of Leadership over 25 Years: Applying a Multi-Level Multi-Domain Perspective." *The Leadership Quarterly* 6, no. 2 (1995): 219.

PAY

Pay is important even when a manager may be quite limited in what he or she can give employees. There is a relationship between pay and the quality of the workforce a company attracts. Level of pay lets the workforce know whether it is valued.

One large grocery chain had 90 days to become profitable. The new leader discovered that 120 store managers in the chain were significantly derpaid. The leader decided the managers were important to the mpany's ability to turn around and gave them raises of 40–50 percent. ne success that followed was due in large measure to the store mangers. Instead of worrying about pay, they could focus on improving erformance.[6]

Edwin Locke, an authority on goal research, laid out four compensaon approaches:

1. *Stretch goals with bonuses for success.* Assign employees tough goals and give them a bonus for success. This motivates employees to high levels of effort but also can lead to shortcuts or cheating. Excellent performance that doesn't quite reach the goal is not rewarded, which can damage the ability to motivate in the future.
2. *Multiple goal and bonus levels.* This reduces the temptation to cheat because it is not an all-or-nothing bonus. It rewards just fair performance and doesn't necessarily push employees to their highest level.
3. *A linear system.* A variation on approach number 2, this strategy rewards compensation within tiers—say a 4 percent bonus for every 1 percent increase in sales. An employee is rewarded for exactly what he or she achieves, which also encourages stretching. Still, employees can settle at a certain level and not work at their capacity.
4. *Motivate by goals; pay for performance.* Employees are given specific goals, but the decision about how much to award is made afterward. Consideration is given to changes in the environment and to whether goals turn out to be more or less challenging than anticipated. This is a flexible approach but requires a knowledgeable and objective manager making the decisions.[7]

Many organizations combine approaches, depending upon their situation. Sales organizations may pay a salary, straight commission, or both. Compensation is one of the largest costs of doing business, and employee satisfaction with pay can affect morale, commitment, and motivation. Not surprisingly, pay satisfaction depends on employees' perceptions of fairness. If they believe there is a difference between the amount of pay that *should* be received and the amount that is *actually* received, they will be unhappy.

WHAT YOU CAN DO: OUTCOMES

Respect Expected Rewards

It doesn't take long for rewards to lose their motivational power when employees don't receive them when promised. That is why managers *must* clarify expectations about what will happen when employees accomplish a task. Then the expected reward must be awarded. Otherwise, promises mean nothing.

Never make a promise you can't keep (see the second "Don't" in chapter 2). Don't promise a bonus unless you have the power to give one. Don't hint at a promotion unless you can come through with it. If you're not sure what you can provide, be upfront with the employee about what you can and can't do, and also about what you're not sure of. Then do your best to honor what you said. If the company's rules change and you can no longer can keep your promise, let your employees know as soon as possible and renegotiate your agreement with them. The more you demonstrate integrity in this way, the more motivating will be the rewards you offer.

Offer Desired Outcomes

This is where all the good work you did with Principle 3—"The more you know about people, the more you will know what to do"—comes in. If you have studied human nature and also each employee's situation, you will have a good idea of what rewards each person desires. For some it is praise; they want to be told they did a good job. For others it is an opportunity to work on something different or more challenging. For still others it will be a chance to work on a team or with interesting people.

Money is always desired to some degree by people in jobs. That is one reason they are there in the first place. Its importance changes with time and situation. What was important to Jim a couple of years ago may not be so important today. His situation has probably changed. Desirable outcomes also include promotions, growth opportunities, recognition and thanks, any combination of these, and others.

Be Creative

The organization has constraints on what managers can offer, but there is more latitude when thinking in different ways. Children in a classroom receive stars or get to be the teacher's special helper or spend some extra time at recess. Surely a manager can offer flexible work schedules, or a write-up in the employee newsletter, or the chance to enter the company's leadership training program. Think in terms of all the possible forms of exchange—love, information, status, money, goods, and services. Use imagination.

Be Fair

Perceived fairness is an incredibly important part of the motivational task. Rewards should not be less than those of others doing similar work.

Employees want fair, equitable rewards in comparison with others doing similar-level work. Motivation becomes focused on being mad at the manager or the company and not the work when employees perceive unfair treatment. That could mean reducing effort to a level they think proportionate to other's rewards. They also might start looking for another job or simply stand in the way of others' successes.

Developing "I can" employees is the foundation for both effective goal setting and sustaining the motivation to accomplish them. Being an expectancy manager creates the conditions for high performance.

KEY POINTS

1. The way employees perceive their abilities may be as important as the skills they actually possess. Be an expectancy manager
2. A formula for motivational success is BC × OE × DO.
3. Honor promised rewards, make sure they are desirable, and be fair in how you give them.

PRINCIPLE 6

Great Goals Get People Going: Master the Art and Science of Effective Goal Setting

GOAL SETTING IS A POWERFUL MOTIVATIONAL TOOL

Setting goals is one of the most potent motivational tools managers have. Damon Burton, a sports psychologist at the University of Idaho, says that athletes who set goals systematically can count on improving their performance at least 5 percent, and that studies have shown 7–16 percent productivity gains in business and industry.

"Goal setting works," he says. "The consensus of more than 500 goal setting studies is that specific, difficult goals prompt higher levels of performance than vague, do-your-best, or no goals." That held true regardless of the complexity of the task, the setting, performance criteria, time span, or the gender, age, socioeconomic status, or type of employment of participants. "Goal setting," Burton says, "is arguably the most effective performance enhancement technique in the behavioral sciences."

Edwin Locke, considered the leading goal theorist over the last 40 years, found goal setting working in over 100 tasks, in time spans from one minute to 25 years, and with over 40,000 people in eight countries. Goal setting theory was rated the most important of 73 management theories by organizational behavior scholars. "We have learned," Locke says, "that goal setting is effective for any task where people have control over their performance."[8]

People everywhere are talking about setting goals, following goals, or describing how they either met or didn't meet goals. Goals are useful in almost any setting where things have to be done. Athletes want to break a world record or make the varsity squad. Actors want to get a sitcom or earn their SAG card. Business leaders want to get 50 percent market share (and a new employment contract) or increase speed-to-market by 10 percent. You want your department to make its sales goals or reduce turnover or get product out the door by 5:00 P.M. Goals should be set for whatever is important.

GOALS DEFINED

A goal is something a person wants to achieve. Goals affect what people do (direct their activity), the amount of effort they put into doing it (energy), and their stick-to-itiveness (persistence). Managers mobilize each of those qualities at differing levels when deciding the department will be the best in class, have zero defects, or reduce turnover by 50 percent. Sometimes people persistently follow a specific goal, such as getting a college degree, but don't put any effort into it. Thirty years later, the goal is still there, but they have taken very few classes. Other times, tremendous energy is dedicated to goal accomplishment for a short time and then abandoned. Persistence is low.

Goals are what a person, team, organization, or country wants to accomplish. They are intentions to act. A goal is the difference between what exists now and what is desired to exist. Sometimes we set them, and sometimes they are effectively set for us.

Goals draw upon abilities that animals and computers do not have. Goal setting involves the uniquely human capabilities of imagination, forethought, and choice. Goal pursuit involves the capability to plan and to exert willpower.

Goals can be difficult or easy, general or specific, short- or long-term. How we feel about ourselves influences how difficult a goal we'll accept, how long we'll persist in pursuing it, and how much energy we will contribute to it.

Goals can be simple or complex. One goal might require the accomplishment of many other subgoals to achieve it. Goals are always competing with other goals for attention, effort, and priority. Choosing one goal means not choosing another one.

Goal accomplishment involves assessing what goals are available, choosing a goal, planning to achieve the goal, and then staying the course until the goal is achieved.

WHAT ELSE DO WE KNOW ABOUT GOALS?

If you want high performance, set goals that are both difficult and specific. Challenges stretch skills, creativity, and effort. This is not infinitely true, of course. At some point, a goal can be so difficult that the employee just won't have the skills or the belief it can be reached. Then the person will give up. Breaking the goal down into manageable pieces or treating it as a learning goal may result in higher performance.

> *The more difficult the goal, the more important it is to develop the employee's self-efficacy—confidence that he or she can complete it successfully. (see Principle 5)*

Describing exactly what is wanted will target both activities and how success will be measured. Do you want it Friday at 5:00 P.M. or sometime this week? Do you want to improve the retention rate of customers, or do you want to increase it by 15 percent? Do you want something that looks nice, or a design that appeals to the 18–21 age group?[9]

If you want to increase organizational capacity and the growth of your employees, set "stretch" goals. Stretch goals go beyond difficult and specific. You don't know how to reach them when you set them. They are both performance and learning goals. General Electric set them in the early 1990s to hit targets but also to develop their employees. The company found that stretch goals can result in failures. Failure was not acceptable at GE, but they found that punishing people for failure guaranteed that people would lower their goal expectations. That was a dilemma. How to stretch and hit performance targets without failing? They decided stretch goals would be used only when the results weren't critical.

How do you evaluate success if performance isn't the measure? GE was creative. Stretch goals were evaluated based on *impact* (how did performance after compare to performance before?); on a *comparison* of GE performance with competitors' performance; and on *progress* (if the goal wasn't met, how significant was the movement toward achieving it?).[10]

Activity

Complete the exercise "Setting Specific Goals." found in chapter 6.

TYPES OF GOALS

All goals are not the same in their qualities or in their motivational power.

Promotion and Prevention Goals

People are motivated to seek desirable goals and are also motivated to avoid pain. What we *want* to do has been called a "promotion focus," and what we feel we *ought* to do a "prevention focus."[11] A prevention focus is related to security, safety, and responsibility. It is centered on fulfilling minimum requirements. A promotion focus is related to growth, accomplishment, and progress. It is centered on achieving the maximum possible. These are our hopes and aspirations. We are eager to pursue them. It is the difference between "working to the contract" and enthusiastically going above the call of duty.

Some goals we are eager to accomplish and put our heart and soul into carrying out. Some we have to do. Both are important, but which do you suppose will draw the most energy and the best work out of your employees?

Extrinsic and Intrinsic Goals

Intrinsic work is enjoyable. Extrinsic work is done for some external reward. Principle 4, "Do what you love, and the motivation will follow," emphasizes enjoyable work. Goals, however, do not depend on work being enjoyable. In some instances goals may even make work less enjoyable.

There are both intrinsic goals and extrinsic goals. Intrinsic goals are related to inner needs for health, personal growth, relationships, and contribution. Extrinsic goals are related to external rewards such as wealth, fame, image, and physical appearance or to the avoidance of punishment. An extrinsic goal (make money) can be undertaken for an intrinsic reason (provide a healthy, nurturing family environment).

You can frame what your employees are doing in terms of intrinsic goals, extrinsic goals, or both. Emptying the trash can be framed as making a contribution to the overall mission of customer service (intrinsic) or as the first step on the road to promotion (extrinsic). Intrinsic goal framing leads to better, more persistent performance.[12]

How do you do it? One way is to share the importance of the job. Help your employee see how the work is relevant to relationships, personal or career-growth, or to issues that mean something. He or she is apt to develop an interest in the work, learn more about it, and perform better.

Some goals will be *both* intrinsic and extrinsic—the employee gets wealthier and receives more approval (extrinsic) *and* grows, builds relationships, and learns (intrinsic). Different people need different things at different times, but framing goals both intrinsically and extrinsically would be motivating for most anyone.

Exercise

Intrinsic goal framing

1. Select a job or task, and frame it in intrinsic terms. What would make the job important, meaningful, or enjoyable to the employee?
2. Practice doing this with your employees—you will learn both what's important to them and what you can do to help make work more meaningful.

Learning and Performance Goals

You may give an experienced employee a tough target and let her go, but have you ever been assigned a difficult task you just didn't know how to do? Common knowledge for decades has been that setting high performance goals leads to the highest performance. That is not always true. Sometimes a high performance goal will cause such anxiety that performance is actually lower than it would be after just asking someone to go out and do their best.[13]

Employees can be so focused on the goal that they don't take the time to learn what is needed for success. When you have a high performance goal, and the employee doesn't have the knowledge or experience to achieve it, your best strategy may be to set a high learning goal rather than a performance goal. A performance goal might be "Speed up call center pickups by 30 seconds this month." A learning goal might be "Learn three new approaches to speeding up our pickup times." Performance goals *demonstrate ability*—but when the skill doesn't exist, learning goals that *develop ability* are called for. As ability develops, the focus can return to performance.

Don't set easy learning goals though—set stretch learning goals. Those bring out the creativity, inquiry, exploration, and imagination needed to expand organizational and employee employees. Learning goal failures spawn "How can we learn to do this better?" attitudes. Performance goal failures can cause people to feel inadequate, set lower goals in the future, or tell less than the truth about them.

Learning goals can have long-term organizational benefits because they force employees to strategize, plan, and learn new ways to accomplish tasks. To set up such goals, the organization has to have some "slack" in it. There is no time to learn, make mistakes, attempt stretch goals, or build organizational capacity if all employee time is spent in production. Motivation is more sustainable over time when employees are learning.

Process, Performance, and Outcome Goals

Sports psychologist Damon Burton identified three types of goals.[14] They vary in the amount of control needed to complete them. Athletes are often judged by criteria over which they have little control. A hurdler may run a personal best only to be defeated by an athlete running faster. The goal—to win the gold medal—is out of either athletes' control, yet they are judged "winners" or "losers" by society and often more tragically by themselves.

Set goals that employees can do something about. One company I know had a bonus that was dependent on the weather. How motivating was that? The result was entirely out of the employees' hands. In that case, the goal had no motivational power because employees knew they couldn't do anything to affect the result.

The three types of goals are as follows:

1. *Process goals* for athletes are related to improving form, technique, and strategy. These goals are most under the athlete's control.
2. *Performance goals* concentrate on increasing overall personal performance (running a faster time, hitting a higher percentage of free throws). These goals are less under the athlete's control.
3. *Outcome goals* emphasize outperforming other athletes and accomplishing an objective outcome (winning, being ranked in the top 10). These are least under the athlete's control. Outcome goals depend on performance goals, which depend on the achievement of process goals.

Outcome goals are the most rewarded by society (cheers, year-end bonuses) but are also the most penalized. "When athletes make the mistake of basing their self-confidence on winning rather than attaining process and performance goals," Damon says, "self-confidence is likely to be highly unstable." We brand silver medalists "losers," and if the marketing VP can't make a 50 percent share, we fire her, even if she doesn't control the cost or quality of the products she is given to sell.

Goals, Burton says, are best when they are most *controllable* and most *flexible.* Flexible goals can be raised or lowered so that athletes can regularly succeed when attempting challenging activities. Success develops the confidence (note Principle 5) needed to build and sustain the motivation to succeed in more difficult activities.

The same is true in organizations. If you wanted to be promoted to vice president of engineering and operations (an outcome goal), you would do everything in your power to make your numbers (performance goals). To accomplish that, you would work on your skills both as a manager and as an engineer (process goals). But even if you go to school, take on new assignments in order to learn everything you can, and make all your targets, [illegible] may not be chosen as the next vice president. Why? Any number of rea- [illegible] Someone else might be more talented or might have performed better. The new vice president might be the boss's daughter. Who knows?

One thing will be true. If you focused on building your skills and performing well, you will feel much better about yourself even if you didn't get the job. You will have accomplished much, and you'll be more hirable. Concentrating on building the skills and confidence needed to achieve process and performance goals will increase employees' motivation and make them more likely to achieve the outcome goals they want.

> *Concentrating on process and performance goals will give your employee more focus on what he or she can really control, a higher sense of confidence and accomplishment as those goals are achieved, and a higher likelihood that desired outcomes will result.*

It's not that outcomes aren't important. They are. It's critical to Southwest Airlines' success that it be the lowest-cost provider. What the company *can't control* is whether it actually is the lowest. What a company *can control* is how efficiently it books tickets, loads planes, buys and uses fuel, and manages all the other processes that add up to its total cost. It can control how it studies its competitors, technology, and potential legislation and then how it adapts and includes that information in its operations.

Try to set process and performance goals. Process goals alone aren't enough. Your employees could spend their whole lives in school or practicing. It's performance you want, and the outcomes will follow.

Activity

Complete the exercise "Process, Performance, and Outcome Goals," found in chapter 6.

Short-Term Goals Help Achieve Long-Term Goals

Running a marathon seemed impossible at first, but I did it by setting shorter-term goals along the way. It took two years. My first goal was just to run around the block. My subsequent goals were to run a mile and then seven miles, and then after six months, 13.1 miles—my first half marathon. Completing 26.2 miles—my first marathon—a year and a half after that was really a victory of short-term goals. I would have given up long before I reached such a difficult goal if I had concentrated only on the final objective.

Long-term goals are daunting and, unless tackled in smaller parts, can reduce performance. Near-term goals, say monthly versus annually or daily versus weekly, show that progress is being made. A short-term goal indicates progress better than comparing work-to-date with a longer-term goal. Receiving feedback on shorter-term goals shows the need to change tactics along the way. Each near-term goal may require different strategies than others. Breaking each goal down into such subgoals helps people focus on doing what is right for each task.

Coach employees to break difficult goals into parts. Accomplishing smaller goals will increase employee confidence, effort, persistence, and the likelihood of success.

Activity

Complete the exercise "Breaking Long-Term Goals into Short-Term Goals," found in chapter 6.

Using shorter-term goals increases confidence, focuses attention, provides better strategies, and boosts effort.

WHAT YOU CAN DO: GOAL SETTING GUIDELINES

Set Challenging, Specific Performance and Learning Goals

Challenging goals produce more motivation than those that are too easy. That seems intuitively true, doesn't it? Boredom is a great demotivator. Each of us wants to feel like we are doing something that tests our abilities. In interviews, people repeatedly say they want to be challenged. One technician said it was "the ability to accomplish the impossible" that motivated him, and a young professional said she is motivated when she "finds the challenge and conquers the challenge." In general, the more challenging the goal, the more effort employees will put in. When the goal is complex or difficult, use learning goals to start. Then use performance goals as employees develop their abilities and knowledge.

Goal commitment is key to achieving the difficult, specific goals necessary for high motivation. Why? Because such goals are hard work. It would be easy to give up without commitment.

Align Goals and Rewards

Organizational and individual performance suffer when goals conflict. If an employee has one goal to support her team and another goal to excel professionally, she may have to pick one over the other. It is a myth that one person can do everything, and sometimes the problem becomes more than just a juggling act. When one or more departments have conflicting goals, employees will be confused, diffuse their efforts, and may take sides. Employees are more likely to work together when assigned goals that require cooperation. Performance improves when team and individual goals are aligned.

Steven Kerr wrote a classic article titled "On the Folly of Rewarding A, While Hoping for B."[15] He tells how political, war, medical, educational, sports, governmental, and business goals are often sabotaged by rewarding different behaviors than those intended. He gave the example of elderly people facing a competency hearing in one county. Of 598 incapacity proceedings initiated and completed in the county that year, 570 ended with a verdict of incapacitation. That's not surprising when you consider what was rewarded. Experts who completed the evaluations were paid more—for the same examination—if the person was ruled incompetent. Align goals and rewards.

Give Feedback

Feedback gives employees clues about where they are and what they can and can't do. Feedback lets employees know if they are on course. It lets them know if they are on track to finish in time, are reaching quality or other standards, and if they are taking on the right things. Motivation plummets without feedback. Employees try to catch up or try something new when they think they are behind. Runners want to know their split times. Dieters check their weight regularly. Project managers track cost, time, and quality in order to complete the job.

Set Goals Employees Can Influence

Process goals are more controllable than performance goals, which are more controllable than outcome goals. Don't set weather-related goals if your employees can't change the wind or make it stop raining.

Setting SMART goals will accomplish much of what is needed for powerfully motivating goals: SMART is an acronym for specific, measurable, achievable, relevant (some use "results-based"), and time-specific.

Activity

Complete the exercise "SMARTer Goals," found in chapter 6.

Break Goals into Manageable Pieces

Take difficult, long-term, complex goals and break them into subgoal chunks that employees can learn from and accomplish. The chunks can be divided by time, by activity, or by some combination.

Limit the Number of Goals

No one can successfully juggle 10, 20, or more goals. Identify no more than five to seven of the most important for each employee. More than that will add to the difficulty for each one.

CROSSING THE RUBICON

Crossing the Rubicon is moving from goal setting to goal pursuit. The process of motivation can be divided into the time before goal commitment and the time afterward.[16]

Pre-Rubicon—Evaluating Wishes

Activities before a goal is chosen are related to looking at alternatives and considering the most important ones to pursue. Decision-making processes are called for at this stage, and there may be many questions to answer. What is the most desirable outcome to chase? How likely is success? What are the opportunities, threats, strengths, and weaknesses? How much effort will it take? Do we have the capability to accomplish it? What are the downsides? How will it affect the budget? What if we fail? What are the costs versus the benefits? What is the impact? How urgent is it? What will have to be given up to do this? This evaluation may be lightning quick or may take years. *It is the process of making choices.* The attitude at this point is one of open-mindedness, exploration, and evaluation.

The Rubicon—Moving from Wishes to Intentions

At some point a decision is made to pursue a goal. It may not be a life-or-death decision like Caesar made or a stepping-off-the-cliff-to-start-a-company decision like Diane Cannon made. It is the act of concluding to follow a particular course of action. It is characterized by resolve and intent. This commitment is what separates wishes and wants from will-do's. *It is the act of making a choice.* The attitude at this point is one of commitment.

Post-Rubicon—From Intentions to Actions

Once the decision is made, it is time to accomplish it. Now the challenge is to maintain motivation. The previous options are dropped. Attention is concentrated on how to accomplish the goal. The motivational problems now revolve around getting started, reducing doubts, staying the course, remaining energized, and keeping focused. *These are actions to implement the goal decision.* The attitude at this point is one of single-minded intent to accomplish the goal.

Theorists typically call pre-Rubicon activities "motivational" processes and post-Rubicon activities "volitional" processes. Volitional processes help sustain motivation for achieving the goal. They involve willpower.

GOAL COMMITMENT

Employees will more persistently and determinedly pursue goals as commitment increases. When commitment drops, performance drops. Understanding goal commitment is an important part of motivational leadership. The next principle to be discussed, Principle 7, "Willpower Is the Engine for Goal Pursuit," discusses sustaining commitment. Here I discuss how employees make the initial commitment to a goal.

Level of commitment varies and can vary over time. You might agree to a goal of answering 100 percent of customer calls within 30 seconds but six months later question your sanity. Or, like a sports team gaining confidence as it wins throughout a season, you may become even more determined over time to reach your goal as you experience successes. Commitment is most important when goals are difficult.

Leaders at Microsoft found that company goals had turned from commitments to hopes. They decided to turn that around. They started with company language. "Goals" became "commitments," which suggested a greater level of accountability. Managers began to record all commitments with employees and began to update them, to measure them, and to align them from top to bottom and across teams, the organization, and individuals.[17]

Goal commitment is crucial to goal achievement. Where, then, does initial goal commitment come from?

It comes from Principles 1–5: the stage for goal commitment is set by adoring, storing, and choring; caring; providing what the employee needs when he or she needs it; designing enjoyable work; and offering desirable outcomes for high self-efficacy performance.

GOAL COMMITMENT TIPS

Initial goal commitment is more likely in the following circumstances:[18]

- *Someone asks you to do it.* The employee is likely to do what is asked when the person asking is someone your employee trusts, likes, has an obligation to, cares about or believes to be an expert or person of authority.
- *The group influences you.* Coworkers, teammates, and other group members have significant influence over the goals employees will accept. It's a two-edged sword. The group can set the bar lower than you'd like it to be or higher than you expected. The group often will be more effective enforcing that commitment than you. High-performance group commitment comes from supervisor support, the members' own wants and needs, and how important the goals are to the team's success.
- *A role model influences you.* Veteran employees set high standards and reinforce commitment to achieving them.
- *You are given rewards you want.* Pay someone enough in money or recognition, and he or she will commit to incredible tasks. Have you ever watched any of the reality shows? Why would anyone in their right mind eat worms? Why do employees kowtow to their bosses? In general, the more dough, the more go. The more recognition, the same.
- *It fits your values.* An employee staying late to take care of a patient for no other reason than it's the right thing to do is committed to a value-based goal.
- *You are asked to help set the goal.* Employee participation doesn't necessarily lead to higher goals (people can underestimate their own capability or may want to assure success), but it can lead to goal commitment. Participation also helps employees start thinking about how to reach the goals they set.
- *You state it publicly.* I'm more likely to stick with my weight loss program if I've told my mom, dad, coworkers, friends, and the janitor that I'm losing 10 pounds by Christmas. Likewise, when an employee declares in a department meeting that she will take on the project and get it done on time and under budget, she's committed.
- *You believe your supervisor or organization supports you and the goal.* If you support them, they'll come through for you. Letting them know that the goal is something you care about increases employee commitment. If employees trust you and you insist upon success, commitment will increase too.

- *The task is within your control.* Employees won't be committed to something they can't influence.
- *You make it competitive.* Human beings are interesting creatures. Not only can cooperatively set goals increase commitment, but so can competition. Playing against another team, another company, or another country can increase goal commitment. For some reason, we want to win.
- *You believe you can do it.* The higher the self-efficacy, the higher the goal commitment.
- *It's challenging, interesting, or just plain fun.* Enough said.

KEY POINTS

1. The most motivating goals are specific, difficult, and have high employee commitment.
2. Commitment comes when the goals are important and people believe they can achieve them.
3. Set goals for outcomes you can control—there are process, performance, and outcome goals. Outcome goals are the most out of your control.

PRINCIPLE 7

Willpower Is the Engine for Goal Pursuit

Your employee just agreed to take on the goal you discussed together. This morning, he walked into the office with the best of intentions. He then confronted the other six priority goals you'd given him and dozens of other demands for his attention, not to mention the three career goals and five personal goals he carries inside his head that no one at work knows about. How will you help him remain motivated to pursue this particular goal when he is pulled in all directions? Principle 7, "Willpower is the engine for goal pursuit," will provide ideas to help you sustain the motivation created when the goal was set.

MAKING CHOICES AND WILL

How many New Year's resolutions lay dead in the water before January turns to February? How many three-ring binders full of training material gather dust on bookshelves long after the conference is over? How many times have you said, "I'm going back to school to get my degree," and instead watch March Madness, the NFL playoffs, and the World Series (or *Law & Order, American Idol,* and *The Apprentice*)?

We have an inborn instinct to strive toward meeting our needs and wants. If we didn't, humanity would not survive. We are born purposeful. Employees are purposeful each day they arrive for work. The question is whether they are motivated to achieve the goals of your organization or goals for other purposes.

WILLPOWER

In philosophy, willpower is known as "volition." It means strength of will. People with willpower do what it takes to get the job done. They are resourceful, self-directed, and determined. Despite difficulties, they persevere. People with the will to achieve the goals you set are the kind you want.

Think of people with willpower. The words *determined, committed, persevering, resolute, tenacious, dogged, steadfast,* and *obstinate* come to mind. At its most basic, willpower is brute determination to succeed no matter what the situation serves up. It is the act of keeping a commitment. It is an active choice that includes but goes beyond habit. Few have the kind of character Ernest Shackleton displayed when leading his men to safety from the ill-fated *Endurance,* though all have some degree of willpower. Many give up before they lose the 20 pounds they'd promised themselves. Many do not succeed in their dream business, turn around their organization, write their first book, or achieve excellence in their job.

Willpower: Ernest Shackleton and the Endurance

The ship was being slowly crushed, and there was nothing they could do about it. Captured by the ice, the ship was cracking like a walnut between frozen, massive pincers. Though the destruction seemed inevitable, the men pumped water out of the hold for hours. "About midnight," Alfred Lansing says in his true story, *Endurance,* about Ernest Shackleton's extraordinary Antarctic journey to safety, "after twenty-eight hours of ceaseless work, McNeish [the ship's carpenter] finished his job, at least as well as it could be finished. But it only slowed the water, and the pumps had to be kept going. Each spell was an agony of effort and when it was finished the men staggered to their bunks or slumped into a corner" (p. 58–9). The effort was futile.

Although the ship had already been imprisoned in ice for 10 months before it sank, the test of willpower had just begun for Shackleton and his crew of 27. The *Endurance* was destroyed. Their miraculous journey to safety took another 850 miles. It is one of the great true adventure stories ever told. Alfred Lansing's 1959 book is one of the most powerful I have read. What is it that causes some people and organizations to succeed when others give up? As a noncharismatic leader, what can you do to instill the motivation to succeed when times get rough in your organization?

FREE WILL

We are born with free will. Every day we make choices. We choose to get up at 6 A.M. and work out or choose to sleep in. We choose to take a new job or keep the same one. We choose to put our best effort into accomplishing departmental tasks or into sabotaging them.

We are free to choose our actions in any circumstance, but obstacles get in the way of our goals. Fear of failure or punishment inhibits what people choose to do. So do fears of rejection, embarrassment, or physical circumstances. Being out of shape, not having tools or equipment, or facing constrictive legal or corporate regulations may confront the best of intentions. Past successes or failures constrain future choices. Knowledge of alternatives limits perceived choices. If I don't know a calculator is available, the choices I believe available may be limited to counting fingers or using an abacus.

More insidious are diversions. More pleasurable opportunities—such as sleeping, watching TV, or shopping—may divert me from exercising. Other goals might arise that take attention from getting the project completed on time. The project assigned today may siphon energy from the 10 projects given over the last two weeks. Corporate problems—such as bankruptcy, reorganization, or mergers—may distract intention from the immediate goal.

The more difficult and complex the goal, the more employees must exercise their own powers of imagination, planning, problem solving, self-direction, and persistence. You can beat galley slaves into rowing your boat, but you can't force people, over time, to inventively and resiliently reach goals. If they do become inventive and resilient, they will use those qualities to sabotage, defeat, or leave you at the earliest possible opportunity. If they do not leave, your galley slaves will become the living dead, just putting in time until the final anchor is tossed.

Employees will use their inborn gifts to achieve goals when motivation is sustained in ways that honor and support them as human beings.

Forcing compliance results in dependency, submission, and just enough effort to avoid punishment or keep jobs.

WHAT YOU CAN DO: REDUCING THE NEED FOR WILLPOWER

Sports psychologist Damon Burton says the reasons people begin to exercise are very different from the reasons they continue exercising. People might start a program to lose weight, gain strength, or look better. The reasons they continue may evolve to include the social benefits, stress reduction, or good feelings that occur when exercising. "There are a variety of different things that pop up once you get into it that make it a lot more fun and enjoyable," Damon says, "and the interesting part is that some of these goals are real easy to accomplish." Finding an exercise partner or joining an exercise group is usually easy and creates a social affiliation that supports goal commitment.

The need for willpower is reduced when there are several reasons to complete a goal. Losing weight is easier when dieting with another person or group, when the choices of what can and can't be eaten are clear and specified, when there is an unambiguous target measured regularly, when the person is tied to an exercise program, and when friends and family know what is being attempted and the target date.

The same is true at work. Sustaining motivation to complete a goal will be easier with a variety of reasons to accomplish it. Think of the motives to lead a project to completion. They could include

- receiving a promised bonus when successful,
- working with interesting people,
- learning something new or stretching skills,
- making a real difference to the company or customers,
- being immersed in enjoyable work,
- feeling pride in doing something well,
- pleasing a role model or other leaders, or
- becoming better positioned for the next promotion.

Having multiple reasons to accomplish a goal can powerfully sustain motivation and reduce the need for raw willpower when things get tough. Help employees discover them all.

Willpower can be learned, and it can be strengthened. The need for it can be reduced.

WHAT YOU CAN DO—DEVELOP HABITS OF WILL

The need for brute determination is also lessened by developing habits. Those habits take two forms—habits of success and habits of action. Habits of success are developed when being less than successful is not allowed to be an option. The opposite—a habit of failure—is established when sloppy or incomplete work becomes the norm. Another habit of failure is to consistently make promises and not come through.

Contrast that with the person who says she will compete in the May Iron Man competition and does. It's a performance goal she can control. Further, she has a record of doing anything she puts her mind to doing. She has a habit of success. Take the department that consistently meets service deadlines and quality objectives. Those are performance goals it has considerable control over. Missing those goals would be unthinkable. It has a habit of success.

Habits of success decrease the need for willpower while strengthening it. Establishing expectations and patterns of success develop character. Doing what one commits to do becomes a matter of course and a matter of pride. It is almost impossible to be passionate about something that is mediocre. When someone has been the best, it is almost impossible to accept anything less. That is why it is so important for you to set goals for employees that are achievable and to insist they be achieved. Success breeds the confidence to set higher goals and develops a habit of accomplishment within your department. Anything less becomes unthinkable.

I have a student who is also the president of a large international company. He always does what he says he will do. Always. He always comes through, though he has many significant challenges pressing him. I have other students with far fewer responsibilities who can't finish a five- to seven-page paper on time. Who has the habit of success? Who is most successful?

Habits of action also lessen the need for willpower because they take the pressure off. They actually take advantage of the "unthinkable." The master craftsperson often doesn't have to think about cutting crystal beautifully. Her hands move automatically. The master teacher doesn't have to struggle to prepare an impactful lesson every day. After years of lesson preparation, he builds easily upon his stock of knowledge and experience to create a meaningful experience. Neither has to think inordinately about completing on-time work of the highest quality.

When goal pursuit is triggered by the situation, willpower hardly comes into play at all. You just do it. When the goal of friendly service becomes ingrained within your employees, they don't have to think much about it when a customer walks in the door. It happens automatically. Planning how you will put the goal into effect has the same power.

Establishing habits of success and habits of action makes goal pursuit much easier. It becomes a way of operating and requires less thinking and willpower. These habits may take a while and some effort to create. They require consistent reinforcement or will deteriorate. Akin to Newton's first law of motion, however, once routinized, habits will continue rolling along on their own with relatively little effort on your part.

THE POWER OF IMPLEMENTATION INTENTIONS

Starting work on a new goal is often a challenge. Other priorities, distractions, or anxieties may cause delay. Implementation intentions help get them off the blocks, especially when it is hard to get going for some reason. Employees are more likely to begin a project when goal intentions ("I will develop this software program") are combined with implementation intentions ("I will work on the new program every Tuesday and Thursday morning from 8:00 to 10:00 A.M. starting next Tuesday"). Determining when and where the goal will be pursued makes a difference.

Peter Gollwitzer is a leading thinker in volition research. He has found that people are more likely to pursue goal intentions—statements that a goal will be achieved—when also planning when, where, and how it will be done. These pre-decisions are called implementation decisions. Implementation decisions take the form of "If-then" statements.

"If I get the urge to smoke, I will chew a piece of gum" is an implementation decision. "If it is six o'clock, I will go to the gym" is another. "When I order food at a restaurant, I will order a salad with low-fat dressing" is still another. Advance planning leads to greater success. Implementation intentions increase performance when goal intentions are strong.

Source: Gollwitzer, Peter M. "Implementation Intentions." *American Psychologist* 54, no. 7 (1999): 493.

Difficult or disagreeable goals need extra motivational power. Who wants to eat greens or to sweat? Who wants to reprimand someone or complete administrative reports? Implementation intentions work. One hundred percent of the women in a study with both a strong goal intention ("I will do it") to perform a breast self-examination *and* an implementation intention ("I will do it Friday morning before I leave for work") actually did it. Only 53 percent of those who only formed goal intentions completed the exam. The same success has proven true with exercise programs and other health and disease-prevention programs. Programs such as these (trying to stop smoking, for example) are hard to follow in the short term because the benefits show up much later.

Implementation intentions are also effective when trying to avoid distractions. Saying "I won't be sidetracked by people chatting in the next cubicle" is not as effective as saying "When Joe and Sue start talking next door about their children, I will ignore it." Implementation intentions also help block other poor behavioral (automatically ordering fries) or emotional (getting angry when your ne'er-do-well brother calls) habits. They also help stop unwanted habits of thinking (automatic prejudging, stereotypical thinking)

Implementation intentions reduce the need for willpower because they turn the process of goal implementation over to the environment. Deciding ahead of time what will be done when goal distractions occur allows the situation to keep you on track. You don't need pure willpower.

Exercise

Practicing Implementation Intentions

1. Choose two of your goals. Write your goal intention (I will do this …) for each and then write an implementation intention (If this happens, then I will …) for each.
2. With two employees, choose a goal and do the same. Coach them how to write an implementation intention for their goal.
3. Check in with them at an appropriate interval to see if the implementation intention is working.

CONGRUOUS AUTONOMY

What gives people the willpower to pursue and persist in achieving life goals that seem so risky or unattainable that we can't imagine attempting them ourselves? It may be a combination of self-efficacy and doing what seems "right."

Karen Wilson Scott studied adults over the age of 50 who had maintained commitment to extraordinary involvement in new, compelling, and challenging life pursuits.[19] One woman sold her house and investments, purchased a boat, and sailed around the world. Another moved from a deficit income to a self-built business that she then sold to an international firm. One began bicycle racing at the age of 60 and won two world championships. Another left his career as a federal drug-enforcement agent at the age of 56 to write. He now has stories published in prominent mystery magazines and is pitching his first novel. Others followed equally challenging endeavors. All were selected for the study because they had chosen a new, difficult life direction in their later years.

"Congruous autonomy" is the term Karen coined to describe the qualities of compelling personal rightness and identity tied to an enduring belief in personal capability. She described it as "inspiring commitment to extraordinary involvement in a pursuit (rich in lifetime patterns and trends), despite sacrifice and risk, to develop one's highest potential" (p. 7).

What does congruous autonomy mean in your work environment? Can you create inspired commitment to accomplish exceptional results?

SELF-MANAGEMENT TRAINING

"Self-regulation" describes the processes for establishing, planning, moving toward, and revising goals. Self-management training consists of methods to (1) set clear, specific, challenging goals; (2) visualize obstacles to success and plan to overcome them; (3) self-monitor progress; and (4) self-reinforce in order to maintain motivation over time.

Self-management training improves performance. Employees in one study chose the behaviors they wanted to target. They chose job-related social skills, scheduling and organizational skills, and health and self-improvement skills. Self-management training sessions were conducted that included (1) defining behavior, (2) self-monitoring training, (3) self-assessment and behavioral principles, (4) intervention strategies and data graphing, (5) advanced behavioral principles, (6) behavioral contracts, and (7) relapse prevention. The self-management training resulted in improvements in 31 of 35 work-related problems.

Self-management training significantly improved performance of insurance salespeople. Self-regulation training in general has shown improvements in job, task, and team performance.

Sources: Kanfer, R. "Self-Regulation Research in Work and I/O Psychology." *Applied Psychology: An International Review* 54, no. 2 (2005): 186.
Vancouver, J. B., and D. V. Day. "Industrial and Organisation Research on Self-Regulation: From Constructs to Applications." *Applied Psychology: An International Review* 54, no. 2 (2005): 155.

Activity

Complete the exercise "Self-Regulation Training Checklist," found in chapter 6.

STRATEGIES FOR SUSTAINING GOAL PURSUIT

Goals have to be protected and maintained once they are set and the Rubicon of commitment has been forded. The process of deciding which goals to pursue may or may not have involved your employees, but the process of meeting them certainly will. What can be done to help them sustain the motivation for goal pursuit?

Emotional and motivational strategies sustain willpower.[20] Emotional control strategies help manage feelings that may sidetrack goal accomplishment. Anxiety, fear, feelings of inadequacy, and other emotions can slow or stop progress. Motivational strategies bolster the desire for goal accomplishment. They keep attention on the task when boredom sets in.

Ruth Kanfer and Phillip Ackerman found when studying air traffic controllers that emotional control strategies are more important when an individual is beginning to chase goals. At early stages, the goal may seem overwhelming. The fear of looking bad or failing gets in the way of learning what needs to be done to accomplish the goal. Motivational control strategies are more important when the skills to perform a goal have been acquired and your employee starts coasting.[21]

EMOTIONAL SUPPORT

There have been two times in my life when I've felt so overwhelmed I couldn't move. I was panicky. Both times I felt I had committed to something I had no business doing. I was in over my head. It didn't make a lot of difference that my boss in one case and my group of volunteers in the other thought I was quite capable of doing a fine job. All I knew was that I had goal committer's regret. I wished I had never said yes.

Employees may feel the same way. After agreeing to take on a task, they may ask themselves, their spouse, or their best friend, "What in the world was I thinking?" Anxiety can be paralyzing. Doubts and fears can cause hesitancy when the goal requires assertion. Your job is to provide emotional support until employees get their legs under them and have some training or projects under their belt. Here's what you can do:

- *Be a good listener and check in regularly* during the early stages to evaluate the emotional state of your employees. If you've done a good job of establishing a trusting relationship already, this will be much easier.
- *Encourage your employees.* Tell them that mistakes are normal and expected when learning how to do a task and that they shouldn't be concerned about them.

- *Remind your employees that they have strengths* and successful experiences to build on.
- *Make sure they know that you are there to help* and that they will have the resources needed to do the job.
- *Persuade them to find relaxation or other exercises to calm them.* Physical exercise is a great stress reducer.
- *Provide support when needed to boost confidence.* Would training help if they are unsure of themselves? Do they need an easier project to build confidence? Do they need a coach or a mentor to show the way?
- *Provide a healthy emotional environment.* Do they need less stressful surroundings? Relaxing music, plants, and pictures come to mind. Maybe they need stimulation—rock and roll and some good air guitar might hit the spot in that case. Humor can be helpful to diffuse stress and put things in perspective.
- *Visualize success with them.* Teach them to imagine performing assignments successfully in the same way that downhill skiers mentally go through the course ahead of time.

MOTIVATIONAL SUPPORT

When an employee doesn't need to learn many new skills to complete the assignment, the manager's job turns to motivation. It is easy in this situation for the employee to be diverted or become complacent. This is when having a challenging goal with desired rewards keeps performance high. If that is not enough, here's what you can do:

- Practice Principles 1–4. Build commitment, care, and enjoyment into pursuit of the goal. Know what lights the fire inside your employees better than they themselves do.
- Provide rewards along the way and remind such employees of the expected outcome for accomplishing the goal. Teach them how to reward or punish themselves for performance.
- Make it a competition (being sure not to set up conflict with other goals, employees, or departments).
- Create implementation intentions.
- Develop plans with challenging subgoal deadlines.
- Think through different, imaginative, or creative ways to accomplish the goal.

GIVE FEEDBACK

Feedback keeps attention on the goal, provides information about progress, and gives direction. It improves work performance.[22] It is information you, others, or the environment give employees about past performance. It is motivational when causing the employee to sustain or increase efforts to reach the goal. It is demotivational when causing the employee to stop or reduce his or her efforts. Here are four ideas to keep in mind about feedback:

1. *Motivation plunges without feedback.* Both positive (you're doing well) and negative (you are not doing well) feedback can sustain or increase motivation. Praise reinforces what is going well. Criticism lays out the gap between expectation and reality. Effective criticism is given with an attitude of respect and desire for improvement rather than blame. It gives employees the opportunity to get back on track. Be careful though. Remember Principle 5. Employees who doubt their capability may lower goals or give up when criticized. They may need emotional support and training. Every person is different and has his or her own insecurities, personal goals, ability beliefs, and history. How feedback is interpreted may differ. That is why you have to know your employees better than they know themselves.
2. *Employees are more open to and seek feedback when they think you are sincere, trustworthy, and competent.* Employees are more likely to want and use your feedback because it will help them succeed if they believe you to be honest, fair, interested in them, and knowledgable.[23]
3. *Tracking progress helps the employee keep an eye on the ball when there are many other distractions.* Don't wait until the week before the project is due to check in with employees. By that time, they may be mired inextricably. Simple advice and adjustments along the way might have kept them on track.
4. *Different employees need different levels and types of feedback and accountability.* Most experienced employees usually need much less feedback than those who are less experienced. Micromanagement is one of the most demotivating things you can do. Letting people sink or swim is equally perverse. It may seem like the best people will rise to the top when abandoned, but what really happens is that valuable time and talent are lost. The employees who survive a sink-or-swim strategy might not be the ones with the most ability. They may just know how to work the system or be emotionally hardened.

The feedback and tracking process can be as systematic as using project management software and daily updates or as informal as dropping by once in a while to see how people are doing. The more employees can track their own progress and evaluate their own efforts, the more they are taking charge of their own goal accomplishment. Train them to do that and watch their ability to direct their own efforts increase.

Activity

Complete the exercise "Listening for Success" and the "Giving Effective Feedback" checklist, found in chapter 6.

MORE STRATEGIES TO SUSTAIN MOTIVATION

Be a Source of Positive Energy

A manager can be an energizer or a downer. One manager delegates work with a sour look and a "here we go again" attitude. Another delegates work with enthusiasm and a positive "can-do" attitude. Who will be more motivating?

Even in the direst circumstances, people look to the leader for hope and validation. In a scene from the movie *Saving Private Ryan,* Tom Hanks's character goes off by himself, and only then does he allow himself to cry uncontrollably. He believed that the job assigned to his squad was dangerous at best, and that his ability to motivate them rested on the slender thread of their confidence in him.

Great leaders exude positive energy. Noncharismatic leaders have to draw upon their own enthusiasm for the task. That vigor is a catalyst enabling employees to sustain their own eagerness.

Visualize Success

Skiers go through successful descents in their imagination before they start their run. Spend time with your group imagining what a successful project will be, what the results will mean, and how work will be different and improved. Encourage them to visualize regularly.

Make the Goal Prominent

John Kennedy's famous goal—"Put a man on the moon and bring him back safely by the end of the decade"—was simple to remember, was clear as a bell, and rang in every citizen's memory. If it's important, make the goal so prominent that it is seen, known, and discussed.

Celebrate along the Way

Have fun when a milestone is achieved. Bring out the band and the bunting. Remind folks why they are spending all that time working toward a higher goal.

Pat people on the back any time you honestly can (inauthentic praise is easily spotted as insincere and has the opposite effect from what is intended). Even more powerfully, encourage employees to take charge of celebrating successes or progress. Congratulate them when they do and show support by supplying the resources necessary.

Prepare People for Obstacles

Engage employees in anticipating obstacles and thinking about ways to circumvent them prior to setting goals and then during goal pursuit. That will lessen fear and stress and improve the effectiveness of the response when barriers crop up.

PREPARING FOR OBSTACLES

In their 2003 article "Going beyond Motivation to the Power of Volition," Sumantra Ghoshal and Heike Bruch tell the story of an IBM subsidiary leader who noticed that most projects started enthusiastically, but only about 15 percent were completed acceptably. The leader observed that projects were presented over-optimistically at the proposal stage and didn't address the personal costs involved.

What strategies do leaders use to get volunteers or employees initially on board? Ghoshal and Bruch say that leaders trying to convince people to take on a job often paint rosy pictures, underline the benefits, and make light of the obstacles. In those cases, people signing up are only superficially committed. Leaders who cultivate a deeper commitment do the opposite. They underscore the difficulties that will be faced.

The subsidiary leader introduced a new process for selecting projects that included the business risks as well as the gains. The personal advantages and disadvantages for managers presenting the projects were also included. The project sponsors were asked once more after the project was approved if they were certain about continuing with the project in light of the risks and personal costs. As a result, far fewer projects were started, but 95 percent of them were successfully finished.

Remove Distractions in the Physical Environment

For some, physical distractions might be open offices where people can "drop by" or a noisy break room around the corner. Others, however, might be energized by having people around with whom to bounce ideas. Equipment that doesn't work, inadequate supplies, and out-of-date computer software or hardware are sources of frustration or even anger for everyone. They take attention away from the goal. Working in an ugly, overly hot or cold office seldom reinforces willpower and usually does just the opposite.

Each person is different. Find out what is distracting your employees.

Remove Other Distractions

Nothing quite distracts a person more than ongoing conflict or poisonous relationships. It doesn't help when employees are pulled one way and then another by manipulative or even well-intentioned leaders. Fighting or trying to circumvent onerous policies can be overwhelming. Employees fearful for their jobs, angry about their pay, or feeling disrespected will not give 100 percent of their attention to pursuing your important goals.

Find out what is distracting your employees right now. Ask them. Better yet, ask them to investigate how to remove those diversions. Then eliminate any distractions possible.

Make the Work Enjoyable

The importance of finding enjoyable work is discussed in Principle 4, "Do what you love, and the motivation will follow." It's not enough to passively sit by, however, and let the work generate its own enjoyment. Intentionally make the work more fun and enjoyable when possible. It is during the time between the excitement of goal commitment and the prospect of goal achievement that work can get tedious, hard, and exhausting. Be the manager who finds humor in difficult situations, who knows how to take strategic breaks to blow off some steam or grab something to eat together, who tosses a party in the middle of a long month, who rounds up a work crew to jump in to help jump a tough hurdle, or who creates a game or fun competition to make the work interesting.

Teach "Keeping on Task" Skills

Employees need skills to feel confident about completing the goal. To maintain motivation, they also need what I call "keeping on task" skills. Teaching time-management skills and work-organization skills help employees stay efficiently on tasks instead of wasting time and redoing work.

Goal-prioritizing skills help when employees must juggle competing priorities. Planning the most important activities and the best sequence of those activities reduces stress and the distracting worry of not knowing what's next.

KEY POINTS

1. Goal pursuit depends on building and sustaining willpower.
2. The more reasons there are to pursue a goal, the better.
3. Willpower comes from habits of success and habits of action.
4. Giving feedback is essential to maintaining motivation.

CHAPTER SUMMARY

Noncharismatic leaders can produce highly motivated employees by developing employee belief in their own capabilities, mastering the art and science of effective goal setting, and strengthening and supporting willpower.

PART III

Skill Development

FIVE

Roles and Responsibilities

THE SEVEN ROLES AND RESPONSIBILITIES OF HIGHLY MOTIVATING MANAGERS

The roles and responsibilities of the motivating manager follow the seven principles. Few master them all, but highly motivating managers constantly improve their abilities in as many areas as possible. The seven roles described in this chapter have been discussed generally in chapters 3 and 4. Chapter 6 will give you the opportunity to assess yourself and to develop a plan to develop the skills and knowledge you need to be successful. Throughout this book, I have suggested that you have the talent to motivate your employees. The roles you take on to do that are those of a Cultivator, Carator, Student, Designer, Expectancy Manager, Challenger, and Supporter.

PRINCIPLE 1: ORGANIZATIONAL COMMITMENT MOTIVATES POWERFULLY—CULTIVATOR

A farmer embodies the cultivator. I watched my grandfather create the environment where living things could grow. Every season he would prepare

Table 5.1
Roles: Seven Principles for Motivating Work

Setting the Environment: Create a Motivating Workplace		
Principle	*Goal*	*Roles*
1. Organizational commitment motivates powerfully.	Develop commitment to your organization.	Cultivator
2. The more you care, the more they will care.	Develop "beyond-the-call-of-duty" motivation.	Carator
3. The more you know about people, the more you will know what to do.	Understand what motivates employees.	Student
4. Do what you love, and the motivation will follow.	Create work that generates its own motivation.	Designer
Crossing the Rubicon: Build and Sustain Motivation to Accomplish Goals		
Principle	*Goal*	*Roles*
5. Belief in personal capability enables goal setting and pursuit.	Build self-efficacy.	Expectancy Manager
6. Great goals get people going.	Set challenging goals.	Challenger
7. Willpower is the engine for goal pursuit.	Sustain motivation.	Supporter

the field by plowing the earth and adding fertilizer before he ever planted the seeds. As the young sprouts grew he would remove or kill weeds that cropped up. Come the end of summer, he would harvest his crop. Some things were in his control, and some were not. My mom and dad remember Grandpa Milton getting on his knees and thanking God for rain. In earlier years, farmers grew crops and raised animals so that they could feed themselves. Now the yields are so high that farmers feed many others in addition to their families. Like a farmer, your role is to cultivate your environment, and your responsibilities are to prepare, fertilize, plant, weed, and harvest.

Prepare

Preparing the work environment means creating a culture that has strong, generative values. It entails building trust, which is the emotional glue for your organization. Preparing also involves asking employees to undertake work they are ready for and enjoy.

The leader also has to prepare him- or herself. My grandfather actually turned to farming in his mid-forties and had to learn from the county extension how to farm. He learned how and when to plant, what seeds to choose, and what kind of weather for which to prepare and considerably more. You need to do the same thing. Go to school, take classes, and learn from other leaders; do what you need to do to be the best leader you can become. Like the farmer who understands the life cycle well enough to know how to get the maximum out of every season, know your own organization well enough to look for hidden potential residing there.

Fertilize

Fertilizing is about nourishing your organization in every way possible. Hire the most talented, energetic employees available. Offer employees opportunities to learn and grow. Build relationships to pollinate the organization. Feed the organization by obtaining resources—pay, equipment, and knowledge. Effective leaders struggle to acquire the most wherewithal achievable so that the organization can grow.

A farmer tilling the land will plow the stubble from the last crop or use cow manure to fertilize the land. The motivational leader will look at all resources—even past problems—as organizational fuel.

Plant

Leaders plant the seeds of greatness in the work environment. Planting sets the bar high. Leaders plant ideas, hopes, and dreams, and they set goals that challenge employees.

Weed

One of the leader's most important responsibilities is to remove obstacles. Leaders eliminate threats to the organization and policies that choke productivity and remove employees or other people who poison the organization. In many ways you are the link to other leaders and resources outside the organization. You have to stick up for your employees.

Harvest

Too much fruit dies on the vine or is picked before ripe. Organizations have to harvest profits when products are hot and not sell too early or late. You are in the best position to know when it is time to ask a veteran employee to take on another challenging task or wait for a rookie to mature.

Pray for Rain

The leader buoys hope when everything seems bleak. Sometimes you and your organization have prepared, fertilized, planted, weeded, and harvested, and yet progress just isn't happening. In many ways, you serve as the spiritual leader of your organization, the person who holds it all together when times are difficult. You are the person who asks for help from whatever sources are available.

PRINCIPLE 2: THE MORE YOU CARE, THE MORE THEY WILL CARE—CARATOR

"Carator" is the word I am using to describe someone who cares. In nursing, "carative factors" are the behaviors that define caring. Nursing studies have researched caring, and there are at least 20 instruments that assess it.[1] Have you ever thought to *measure* caring? That's what these instruments do. The importance of caring has been long established in the helping professions but hasn't received similar attention in organizational literature. "Mattering" has also been studied, often in school environments. It has not received much attention, either. Still, caring and making people feel they matter are important motivational tools for managers.

I like the categories of caring that Kristen Swanson described in "What's Known about Caring in Nursing Science: A Literary Meta-Analysis" in the *Handbook of Nursing Research.*[2] They are the framework I use here to discuss the responsibilities of a carator. According to Swanson, those categories are maintaining belief, knowing, being with, doing for, and enabling.

Maintain Belief

Swanson says that maintaining belief entails believing in the other person or holding him or her in esteem. Caring leaders view an employee as a whole person, recognize his or her uniqueness, and respect him or her. They help the employee to find meaning in work and to move on when mistakes have been made. Carators go the distance for their employees, have a positive attitude, and offer encouragement.

Know

Swanson defines "knowing" as avoiding assumptions. In this context, carators are open to and accepting of employees. Avoid being judgmental. Be open-minded. A caring manager will carefully assess the skills, abilities, and needs of his or her employees. A carator will be sensitive and keep in touch with employee concerns and emotions. A "knowing" leader will focus on the other person instead of him- or herself and will show a real interest in each employee.

Be With

Have you ever had a boss who had an open-door policy and who kept the door open—but it really wasn't open? A caring manager is available, accessible, and "present" for employees. I have been in too many meetings with supervisors pretending to be listening. Don't do that. Swanson calls this quality "being there," and it requires building trust; being considerate, kind, and patient; and connecting with the other person. It also means sharing feelings with employees, being warm, and laughing together. "Be there" for your employees.

Do For

Swanson divides "doing for" behaviors into comforting, preserving dignity, anticipating, and performing skillfully and competently. For nurses, that entails relieving pain, meeting needs, promoting self-esteem, not being rude or putting someone down, and being ready to meet needs that may arise. For managers, it means supporting employees when they have lost confidence, listening to them when they are in pain or have problems, and having enough knowledge to give guidance or direction when needed. It means protecting your employees' safety, privacy, and emotions and helping them make wise choices. Being an advocate for your employees also demonstrates caring.

Enable

An enabling leader ensures that his or her employees are prepared to move forward. Enabling behavior includes being honest, explaining, coaching, and communicating. Carators teach, model, supervise, and oversee activities when needed. A caring supervisor also provides support and helps employees cope with loss and to feel capable and powerful.

PRINCIPLE 3: THE MORE YOU KNOW ABOUT PEOPLE, THE MORE YOU WILL KNOW WHAT TO DO—STUDENT

Many, upon graduating from school, believe that their student days are over. We know now the importance of lifelong learning. Programs such as Elderhostel, community programs, and company training programs are ways many learn postgraduation. For some, those are the richest learning experiences of their entire lives. For the motivational manager, the role of student is to study human beings. It involves learning about and from his or her employees. The "student" studies what motivates employees.

As discussed in Principle 3, there are two ways to be a student of motivation. One is to study human nature. Learning about motivational theory is one way to study human nature. Another way is to study the human situation. Every employee is different. The responsibilities of the motivator as student are observing, listening, experimenting, inquiring, and being open-minded.

Observe

A student in a laboratory setting observes what happens when various variables are introduced into the environments of molecules, animals, or humans. The same is true for leaders. The department, program, or team is a virtual laboratory. You can observe different motivators or demotivators as they occur. You can see how an employee reacts when she becomes involved in decision making. You can watch firsthand whether she quits or fights when she loses an important contract. What happens to her behavior when the group composition or her role in it changes? The astute observer gains understanding from every situation.

Experiment

Leaders can be proactive and try various tactics to see how employees respond. They become students by experimenting. Leaders have many tools at their disposal to find out what motivates an employee. It could be pay. It could be time off. It could be time with you. It could be time away from you. It could be career development. It could be as simple as being supplied with new equipment. It could be a challenge. You will be completing experiments in your own workplace laboratory and learning what motivates the employee. Remember that each employee will be different, and each will be the same.

Listen

Much has been written about listening. It makes every list of good leadership skills for good reason. It works. Listen not only for what employees *say* motivates them, but also for what they *don't* say. Pay attention to their emotions. What do they get irritated about? What makes them happy? When do they show up with a big smile at work? What makes them surly? Listen for the message underneath the words. *"I like this." "This makes me fearful." "I can't wait to get started." "Here's another meaningless job." "I can't take on one more project." "If I do this, I'll be letting my other clients down."* Unspoken messages are more honest than spoken words. What are the nonverbal messages employees are giving you? Do they slouch and fold their arms, or do they lean forward in anticipation of the assignment? Listening closely requires sensitivity and shelving preconceived notions about what you think the employee should feel or think about the job. Employees are your teachers. They are trying to teach you what motivates them. Be an avid student.

Listen to what others say about employees. Fellow employees, past supervisors, friends, and family members probably have more insight into their personality, drives, and desires than you do.

Inquire

My best students ask questions. They want to explore new ideas. They want to think through concepts in different ways. They question their own thinking for accuracy and comprehensiveness. They wonder if preconceived notions stifle their thinking. Be an inquirer. Ask lots and lots of questions during performance reviews, on the job, and during casual conversations. Test your own assumptions about what drives Joe, Sue, Miguel, or Chandra. Ask others what motivates members of your staff.

PRINCIPLE 4: DO WHAT YOU LOVE, AND THE MOTIVATION WILL FOLLOW—DESIGNER

You must take on the role of work designer if you wish to create work that generates its own motivation. My brother DK Kroth is a lighting designer and a professor at the California Institute of the Arts. I asked him about the responsibilities of an excellent designer, and he gave me an A-to-Z list you can adapt to your own situation. To be an excellent work designer, your responsibilities are the following:

A to know that you are supporting someone else's work or product.
B to respect the genre you are working in. *What kind of work, workplace, and situation are you managing?*

C to let the work come from the piece (of art you are designing). *Don't try to design one-size-fits-all work.*

D to not bring your own aesthetic to the piece. *It's OK to bring your own style, but honor the methods and approaches your employee brings.*

E to communicate in terms others understand. Avoid jargon unique to your craft.

F to let it be personal and then take one step to the side so that it's abstract and meaningful to all. *Start by finding enjoyment in your own work, and then help others find what is enjoyable for them.*

G to use representative language so that collaborators can bring forth their own unique input. *Make sure you are communicating in ways that employees can understand and relate to and that encourage their contribution.*

H to use industry-standard paperwork. *Your work design has to fit company policies and procedure.*

I to make sure everybody gets a "thank you" no matter the end result. Be a pro.

J to know that there is always another show. *There will be another project and goal after this—build on this one and don't burn bridges.*

K to realize that only you care if you are embarrassed; no one else does. Get over it.

L to remember that this is supposed to be fun.

M to let those working for you make some decisions; they'll be designers someday too.

N to let people do their jobs; *don't micromanage.*

O to hope that the end result is much more than your first imaginings.

P to not make surprises—don't change stuff already agreed upon.

Q to be patient and lead the people who can't decide by offering choices and suggestions.

R to let others own the work too.

S to keep in mind that the people who get rehired are those who can be worked with. *Enjoyable work starts with hiring people who like and are good at the work you have to offer.*

T to consider that super-tech uber-designers are awesome but are often jerks and often live in their own world—no one else's. *It doesn't matter how good you are if you can't communicate with your employees.*

U to keep records and documents. Realize every design is for the history books. *Keep a record of what you are doing. Your work design could prove so effective that others may wish to adopt it.*

V to experiment. Miles Davis said, "There are no mistakes in jazz." *Go for it. Try stuff.*

W to make sure that even if the piece is political or strident ranting, you are still entertaining. *The work can be enjoyable even during difficult or disagreeable times.*
X to remember that in the end you call it art, but it's mostly just problem solving.
Y to realize you are never done with a project—opening night just shows how far you got.
Z to be cocky to a degree. People love confidence.

PRINCIPLE 5: BELIEF IN PERSONAL CAPABILITY ENABLES GOAL SETTING AND PURSUIT—EXPECTANCY MANAGER

The effort and amount of persistence your employees dedicate to the job or project is determined by their capability beliefs. What they expect to happen when they do perform also influences their motivation. Your responsibilities as an expectancy manager are training, showing, persuading, promoting wellness, and acting with integrity.

Train

The most powerful way to develop employee capability beliefs is to train them in the skills and knowledge it takes to be successful. The ways to do that on the job are numerous. On-the-job training, moving from easier tasks to more difficult tasks, and practicing what they are expected to do are three ways. Opportunities away from the job are even more numerous. Going to school is one way to learn the skills and competencies related to the job. Skill development will feed employee confidence that she can do what you're asking. The more she believes she can do it, the more motivated she will be.

Show

Modeling behavior builds confidence because your employee learns by watching. How many times have you observed someone completing a task and said to yourself, "Hey, I can do that!" You can be a model, but so can other exemplars, role models, veterans, and master craftspeople in the workplace who can mentor, demonstrate, and help your employees observe what to do and how to do it. Observation will cut learning time and give the employee confidence that he or she can also complete the observed task.

Persuade

Have you had a coach or a teacher who said you would be able to do something you didn't think possible—and then you did it? You have the same opportunity to convince employees to strike beyond what they believe they can do. Your opportunity to persuade employees is high if you have established a close relationship with your employees and if they believe in your competence and authentic interest in them. If you have not done those things, they're not going to believe or give any credibility to what you tell them. The persuader doesn't have to be you. Recruit others to encourage the employee if that would be more effective.

Promote Wellness

Employees are more motivated when they have a healthy physical and psychological work environment. They just feel more personally powerful and optimistic. Your responsibility is to provide a safe, emotionally supportive, aesthetically pleasing work environment. Encourage wellness activities, exercise, and stress-reduction activities. Your employees will be ready to work, and will feel that they can accomplish what you ask them to do.

Act with Integrity

Nothing can destroy your ability to motivate more quickly than to say one thing and do another. If you promise to reward, then do it. If you promise a promotion, give it. Your word is your bond. Then, when you praise an employee, he or she will know it was deserved.

PRINCIPLE 6: GREAT GOALS GET PEOPLE GOING—CHALLENGER

The part you play here is to challenge your employees to stretch and to reach their full potential. The responsibilities of a challenger are to expect excellence, encourage and support risk-taking, turn failure into opportunity, be visionary, and ask for commitment.

Expect Excellence

Doing something in a mediocre way is not motivating. When employees walk into work and see everybody devoting just enough effort to get by, their motivation is undermined. They are then motivated to put in just enough to get by too. Expect excellence and demand 100 percent from your employees. They will be proud of their work and become motivated to sustain high quality.

Support and Encourage Risk-Taking

People who stretch and reach high enough to do their best are going to fail sometimes. Those who take risks are more alive, learn more, and are more enthusiastic about what they're doing. People who don't take risks become "the living dead." Understand what risks are acceptable and what failures can be tolerated. Then you'll have the confidence to take your own risks—this time trusting your employees to succeed, but knowing that sometimes they will not. The minute you punish your stars for trying harder than they ever have before and for stretching further than they thought possible, they won't do it anymore. They'll set their goals much lower and give less effort and motivation. Or they'll leave.

Turn Failure into Opportunity

I've heard that Chuck Yeager once said that you never know how far you can go until you've gone too far. When you demand excellence and ask your employees to stretch, there will be failures. Look for opportunities in those setbacks. When the space shuttle *Challenger* exploded, it renewed instead of defeated our nation's efforts. Two years later, the space shuttle *Discovery* renewed our exploration of space.

Out of tragedy came other opportunities. Families of the crew got together after the accident and committed themselves to carrying on the spirit of the *Challenger* crew's educational mission. They formed the Challenger Center for Space Science Education. Today, more than 500,000 students participate in Challenger Center programs annually, as do thousands of educators. Turn failure into opportunity.

Be a Visionary

The "noncharismatic" leader may not have the legendary foresight or fortune-telling powers that so-called charismatic leaders do. You don't need those talents. You need only to think about what the desired future should be. Take a look at all that is going around you, at all that you can learn about what might occur, and sketch out where you want your organization to be in the future. The more information you have, the better your prediction will be. Knowing the desired future, you can turn the full force of your employees to accomplish it. If employees help to create the vision, they will be even more committed to its success.

Ask for Commitment

A salesperson can go through the pitch, convince the client that the product has merit and is needed, and still walk out the door empty-handed. To be successful, you have to ask for the sale. It is your responsibility to engage your employees' hearts and minds and to gain their commitment to the task at hand. Without that, all you have are words.

PRINCIPLE 7: WILLPOWER IS THE ENGINE FOR GOAL PURSUIT—SUPPORTER

A supporter is something or someone who lifts up. On a building, that could be a scaffold. On a bridge, it is the girders underneath. McKay Christensen, president of Melaleuca International, one of the world's largest catalog consumer-product companies, described the role and responsibilities of leader-as-supporter best for me. The following is excerpted from the Melaleuca case study found in chapter 6:

> At our company we've found [that] a simple leadership formula that works at all levels of the organization is to create a servant mindset with our 2,500 employees. It involves three steps:
>
> Step 1: Clearly set a vision
> Step 2: Help each associate understand their stewardship role in that vision and establish a way for them to regularly account for that stewardship
> Step 3: Focus almost exclusively on helping others reach their full potential
>
> Don't be fooled by the simplicity of the formula. It's extremely challenging to create this type of culture. Once you do, however, your organization, family, or group will never be the same. Imagine being an employee where your manager focused almost exclusively on helping you reach your full potential. Wouldn't that be energizing?

The responsibilities of a supporter are to remove obstacles, track progress, give feedback, and be an encourager.

Remove Obstacles

A cowcatcher, also called a pilot, is the equipment on the front of a train used to move obstructions that could derail it. It is designed to push obstacles up and sideways so that the train will remain on the track. You have a similar job. If you want your employees to remain on track and at full momentum, you must lead the way by clearing the path of obstacles such as burdensome policies, faulty equipment, conflicting priorities, and political maneuvering (see also the section titled "Weed," under the cultivator role). Traveling in front, you can also let your employees know what obstacles are approaching. Motivation gets sapped pretty quickly when people have to take care of paperwork that wastes their time, deal with decision delays, or struggle to get the resources they need. Make it easy for them to do their work.

Give Feedback about Progress

Feedback is the way systems maintain their equilibrium. Darwin thought feedback was the way species evolved. Keeping track of time is a form of feedback. Communication between two people is a continual feedback loop; nonverbal and verbal communication signals are continuously monitored. Thermometers are feedback mechanisms. Satellites receive continual data that allow them to stay on course. Feedback can include guidance in addition to the status of approaching milestones. Without feedback, we don't know if we are on time, ahead of, or behind expected progress. Motivation nosedives without feedback. People who receive feedback perform better. Your role is to give your employee feedback about progress and the quality of the work to date.

Encourage

I was a yell leader in college. Leading cheers from the sideline during a sports event was different for me because previously I'd always been on the field. It was fun and exciting and it felt good. An employee should feel like she has a stadium full of fans cheering her to victory. As she nears the goal, the cheers will come naturally. The time she'll need your encouragement the most, however, will be when the time to project completion seems to stretch out forever. Some people need a slap on the back, some a kick in the rear. A thoughtful leader can find ways to encourage employees from different directions and with different people.

SEVEN PRINCIPLES SUMMARY

You have now read about and completed exercises for all seven of the principles. Before completing your development plan in chapter 6, summarize your learnings in the exercise "Employee Motivation—My Self-Assessment Summary."

Table 5.2
Responsibilities: Seven Principles for Motivating Work

Setting the Environment: Create a Motivating Workplace			
Principle	*Goal*	*Roles*	*Responsibilities*
1. Organizational commitment motivates powerfully.	Develop commitment to your organization.	Cultivator	Preparing, Fertilizing, Planting, Weeding, Harvesting, Praying for rain
2. The more you care, the more they will care.	Develop "beyond-the-call-of-duty" motivation.	Carator	Maintaining belief, Knowing, Being with, Doing for, Enabling
3. The more you know about people, the more you will know what to do.	Understand what motivates employees.	Student	Observing, Listening Experimenting, Inquiring, Being open-minded
4. Do what you love, and the motivation will follow.	Create work that generates its own motivation.	Designer	Responsibilities A-Z
Crossing the Rubicon: Build and Sustain Motivation to Accomplish Goals			
Principle	*Goal*	*Roles*	*Responsibilities*
5. Belief in personal capability enables goal setting and pursuit.	Build self-efficacy.	Expectancy Manager	Teaching, Showing, Persuading, Promoting wellness, Acting with integrity
6. Great goals get people going.	Set challenging goals.	Challenger	Expecting excellence, Encouraging and supporting risk-taking, Turning failure into opportunity, Being visionary, Asking for commitment
7. Willpower is the engine for goal pursuit.	Sustain motivation.	Supporter	Removing obstacles, Tracking progress, Giving feed back, Being an encourager

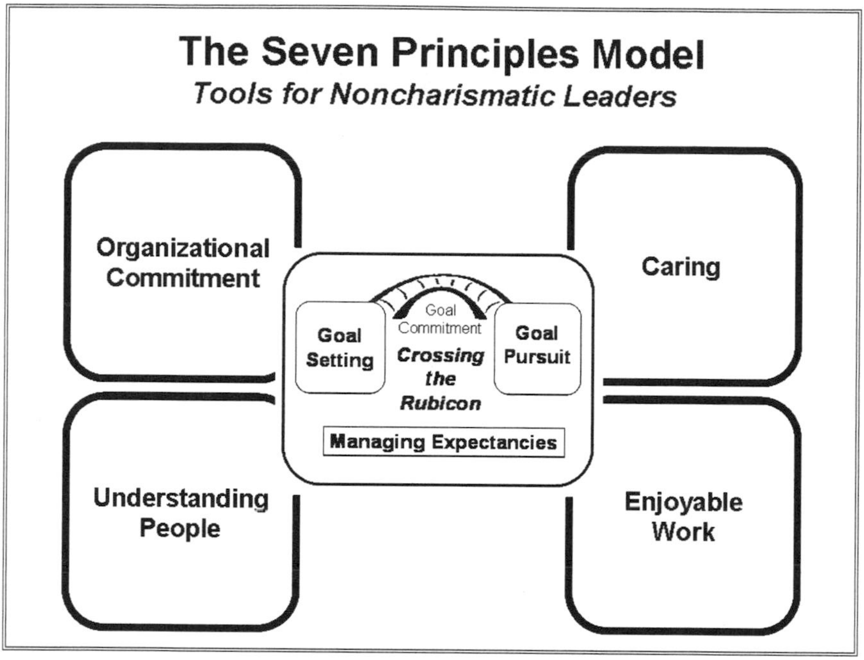

Figure 5.1 The Seven Principles Model

Activity

Complete the exercise "Employee Motivation—My Self-Assessment Summary," found in chapter 6.

SIX

Assessment and Development Tools

WHAT YOU WILL FIND IN THIS CHAPTER

1. A developmental planning process and worksheets
2. A capstone case study
3. Tools for "noncharismatic" leadership skill and knowledge development

In chapter 1, I described ways to get the most out of this book. I am a firm believer that learning occurs most effectively through an iterative process of knowledge acquisition, knowledge application, reflection, revision, and reapplication. Most books are read—or simply scanned—and then reside on bookshelves. The key is learning *transfer*—using new knowledge *on the job* to obtain real results. That is why I included knowledge and skill-development exercises throughout this book rather than waiting until the end. Review the exercises in this chapter if you haven't and get engaged in learning. Don't think having information stuck somewhere in your brain will do you much good. Sure it helps, but the way to make a difference is to apply knowledge regularly.

DEVELOPMENTAL PLANNING

I worked as an internal consultant for years. I have been an external consultant for years. I have developed and run succession-management and leadership-development programs. I have given hundreds of 360-degree feedback results and coached leaders at all organizational levels. I have conducted training for entry-level supervisors up to executive management. I have found the most important factor in leadership development to be the desire of the leader to learn and improve. You can take the horse to water, but you cannot make him drink. People who want to improve don't need fancy development plans—they seek out learning. People who want to have learning magically appear through no effort of their own can have the most supportive, resource-rich organization and will still be thinking the same old thoughts and practicing the same old methods until they are forced to change.

That doesn't mean I don't think a systematic developmental-planning process is important. I do. It also helps to have an excellent human resource development department that is able to provide learning resources and a manager who encourages you and furnishes his or her time and money for learning experiences. That kind of support makes the learning journey so much easier.

What If You Don't Have Support?

Where does the responsibility reside for noncharismatic leaders? It resides with you. It would be nice to have all that support, but guess what? The odds are that you don't. Too many people blame everyone but themselves when they don't progress or succeed. Learning is only limited by your imagination. It doesn't have to cost much. The excellent Center for Creative Leadership, for example, has a publication called *Eighty-Eight Assignments for Development in Place: Enhancing the Developmental Challenge of Existing Jobs.*[1] Learning doesn't have to cost a lot of money. One of your first stops should be your human resource development department, if you have one, because it likely has many ways to support you. After that, use your imagination. Opportunities are everywhere.

Developmental Planning Process

Writing plans down is more powerful and draws more commitment than simply carrying them around in your head. There are seven developmental-planning steps, as shown in Table 6.1.

Table 6.1
Developmental Planning Steps

Step 1	Diagnose learning needs.
Step 2	Identify learning objectives.
Step 3	List strategies required to meet learning objectives.
Step 4	List resources needed to achieve the strategies.
Step 5	Go learn.
Step 6	Demonstrate that you have achieved the learning objectives.
Step 7	Evaluate results and revise the developmental plan.

The exercise "Diagnosing Needs and Developing Learning Objectives" is designed to take all you have discovered (Step 1: Diagnose learning needs) and create learning objectives (Step 2: Identify learning objectives). Objectives should be specific, challenging, and measurable, with a time frame for completion.

Activity

Complete the exercise "Diagnosing Needs and Developing Learning Objectives," found in this chapter.

The exercise "Strategies and Resources for Learning Objectives" is designed to help take the developed learning objectives and identify what is needed to accomplish them (Step 3: List strategies required to meet learning objectives; and Step 4: List resources needed to achieve the strategies).

Activity

Complete the exercise "Strategies and Resources for Learning Objectives," found in this chapter.

I am calling your development plan a "learning contract" because it represents an agreement you are making with yourself to become a more motivating manager. Sharing the plan with employees and your manager if you wish will give you valuable feedback and also help you hold yourself accountable to it. Notice that this plan summarizes everything you wish to accomplish, gives a timeline for completion, notes the status of each objective, and identifies the principle the objective seeks to address. You will be able to pull this document out at any time and easily remind yourself of what you are trying to achieve. It is a way to practice Principles 6 and 7 and a way to show your progress (Step 6: Demonstrate you have achieved the learning objectives; and Step 7: Evaluate results and revise the developmental plan).

Activity

Complete the exercise "Learning Contract," found in this chapter.

MELALEUCA: A CAPSTONE CASE STUDY

Practice all you have learned by reviewing and completing the following case study about Melaleuca, an exceedingly successful company founded just 20 years ago and an example of a highly motivating work environment.

Melaleuca: The Wellness Company[2]

History

Melaleuca was founded in 1985. Today, it is one of America's fastest-growing consumer direct-marketing businesses. The company manufactures high-quality wellness products and distributes them via catalog and Internet shopping. Melaleuca's 350 products are environmentally friendly and include hair and skin care, nutritional, pharmaceutical, and home-cleaning products. The company is headquartered in Idaho Falls, Idaho, and has facilities in Knoxville, Tennessee, and China. It recently began operations in the Netherlands and Singapore. Melaleuca has over 2,500 employees and is privately owned. Revenues exceeded $702 million in 2005. Melaleuca also operates in Hong Kong, Taiwan, China, Japan, Korea, Canada, the United Kingdom, New Zealand, and Australia.

Melaleuca was included in the Inc. 500 list of fastest-growing privately held companies for five consecutive years and was inducted into the magazine's hall of fame because of its continuous growth and profitability. Only 81 companies have received this designation. In 2002 the company was one of the first Idaho companies to be recognized by the American Psychological Association for providing a psychologically friendly workplace. It has set sales records in each of its first 20 years.

Measures of Success

Building and sustaining a highly motivating work environment is a challenge for any company. Melaleuca's operations include manufacturing, order fulfillment, and sales. Their call center is a key part of the sales and customer service functions. Their call center turnover is less than half the industry average. Net company turnover is 60 percent less than the average of similar companies, and almost all of their performance evaluations are completed on time.

Those are examples. By any measure, Melaleuca has been extremely successful in attracting, retaining, and motivating key talent.

The Motivational Work Environment

The company has developed a wide range of strategies to provide a motivating, productive workplace. A number of those follow.

Employee Involvement

Employee Roundtables. Monthly roundtable meetings are held in each facility so that employees have the opportunity to speak openly and honestly about company operations and morale. It's also an opportunity to make suggestions. Personal feedback is given to employees about any suggestions they make.

Employee Opinion Survey. Extensive employee opinion surveys are conducted. The last one resulted in 20 books of information. Melaleuca used the results to make significant changes and to involve employees in the decision-making process. Some of those were adding an overtime premium for working over 45 hours per week, changing the vacation plan, purchasing forklifts, fixing air conditioning, installing bike racks, improving job-posting information, and renovating bathrooms.

Information Kiosk. Confidential employee kiosks were installed at each facility. Each provides access to job postings, e-mail, benefits information, the employee handbook, and information about standard operating procedures.

Suggestion Buttons. Customer service employees have "suggestion buttons" on their computer screens and are encouraged to offer ideas for improvement. Suggestions are forwarded to the person who can address them best. This happens quickly so that employees know their ideas will be acted on speedily.

Family and Personal Support

The company has a number of family-supportive programs. Some examples are listed here. Melaleuca has over 140 shifts. This flexibility gives employees the opportunity to customize their work schedule to fit their life schedule. The company has a day care facility with over 140 children. Company picnics are attended by over

5,000 people. Ten full-time scholarships for higher education are given each year for sons and daughters of company employees. The scholarships cover full tuition for four years. Melaleuca provides a concierge program for employees. Someone is dedicated to helping employees with their needs. The concierge is available to perform a variety of supportive tasks for employees. On any day, he might be running errands for employees, going to the bank for one, getting the car oil changed for another, transporting still another's child, paying a bill, or picking up someone's groceries. Melaleuca's food-service department has healthy, inexpensive food. Lunch costs around $3.00, and employees have a convenient place to eat.

Employee Growth and Development

The company emphasizes giving employees the opportunity to grow. Some examples are listed here. 85 to 90 percent of all promotions are filled internally by the company. Tuition assistance is available for both full-time and part-time employees. Because performance evaluation is so important, managers must have their employees' evaluations completed on time or lose profit sharing for the month. Additional penalties are added if they are completed even later. The company also has an internal career fair. For two days, managers are available to talk to employees about career opportunities in their departments. Employees dress as if they were at an actual external career fair. Melaleuca has developed well-defined career paths for employees. Supervisors have monthly management training that is led by executive leaders.

Employee Health and Safety

Employees and customers are encouraged to set wellness goals and to post them online. Employees receive $80.00 worth of free Melaleuca products each month, and the company's vitamin package is provided through the health insurance plan. The company is focused on safety. A supervisor training program was designed, safety inspections were initiated, the safety bonus was redesigned, and safety was placed at the same priority level as quality, productivity, and profitability.

Rewards and Recognition

Rewards are generous. The company has a profit-sharing plan and an employee stock-ownership plan. Those with 20 years of service receive a $20,000.00 award. Hundreds of gift certificates are given by supervisors to employees to express appreciation for work well done. The Star Performer program provides awards with the recipient's name on a plaque, a picture in the paper with a description of what they have accomplished, and a parking spot next to the building. The Spirit Award is given to two employees a year who epitomize the mission of Melaleuca both inside and outside the company—one employee walked several miles in the snow because her car had broken down. The President's Award is given to 10 employees each year with a check for a thousand dollars. These awards are all for regular employees. The sales force has its own set of rewards and recognition. In the call center, contests are held to meet identified objectives, and thousands of dollars in prizes and gifts are given away.

Employees work hard. Some carry out very routine functions and have been performing them for 10 to 15 years. "They are doing very repetitive jobs, but they love it," HR Director Jann Nielsen says. "They love that they are rewarded, and they love that they are in a safe environment." Every department has measures. "Even janitors have measurements," according to Jann. "They need to check the restrooms a certain amount of times and to clean them at certain intervals."

Corporate Culture

Melaleuca has a powerful culture. Jeff Hill, senior vice president of sales, says about hiring people, "You may be the most talented art designer or director, but if you can't buy into what we do, if you can't fall in love with the people here, if you're not that type of person, please don't come here." Employees have to fit Melaleuca's culture to be successful. "The chemistry is that you've got to be mission-driven." Hill says. "You've got to be a mission-driven type of an individual, and you've got to like people. If you're a lone warrior and want to come in on your horse and slay the world all by yourself and take credit for it, that's a scarcity mentality. If that's the environment you thrive in, this may not be the environment that works well for you."

It's a hard-working, high-performance culture that values and cares for employees, Hill emphasizes. "People feel like they're loved and for the most part love what they do. You know a call center is a call center is a call center. You're on the phone, and it's tough. So then you've got to compensate. We're a mission-driven company in the sense that you're changing people's lives."

Brett Webb, vice president of marketing, says Melaleuca employees connect to the company in multiple ways. "I think you get people both by the heart and the head and that's how you motivate them," he says. "I don't think charisma, at the end of the day, without content goes anywhere." The marketing group has gone to the production plants in Idaho Falls and Knoxville to share goals and the mission with line supervisors. "I think if you engage them, it's amazing how their jobs become more meaningful," Webb says. "They're not just picking up a product to stick in a box to ship to the customer. It just galvanizes that organization."

Motivational Leadership

Jann Nielsen is the company's director of human resources. She believes that motivation begins at the top. "I think motivation is inherent within our culture, and I think that begins with our leaders," she says. "I think that our president and our management team create a good culture; [there is] an excitement and passion for what we do because we buy into our mission. That mission is to enhance the lives of those we touch by helping people reach their goals."

The president and CEO of the company, Frank VanderSloot, still keeps in personal touch with employees. He sets the productivity bar high and is also the person most responsible for the generous rewards and gifts given to employees. "What he does is caring," Jeff Hill says. VanderSloot has been known to take employees and their children with him when he travels to meetings on the company plane so that they can experience different cities, such as Washington, DC.

McKay Christensen, president of Melaleuca International, described the role of leadership in the company. He says,

> At our company we've found a simple leadership formula that works at all levels of the organization is to create a servant mindset with our 2,500 employees. It involves three steps:

Step 1: Clearly set a vision
Step 2: Help each associate understand their stewardship role in that vision and establish a way for them to regularly account for that stewardship
Step 3: Focus almost exclusively on helping others reach their full potential

> Don't be fooled by the simplicity of the formula. It's extremely challenging to create this type of culture. Once you do, however, your organization, family, or group will never be the same. Imagine being an employee where your manager focused almost exclusively on helping you reach your full potential. Wouldn't that be energizing?

Melaleuca leaders don't depend on the magic of charisma to inspire employees. Marketing VP Webb says, "I think at the end of the day, people will follow other people they can believe in. I think, to get down to the bare bones, that you have to believe the leaders are good people, that at the end of the day they want you to succeed, and they're going to make it worth your while to succeed. I've never had someone who I would define as an overly charismatic leader, but I've had a lot of people I believed in, and I felt like giving everything I could give to them—because as people I like them. I felt like they were trustworthy, fair people."

Melaleuca's vision, goals, and work functions are aligned. New employees are given significant training so they feel at ease in their jobs. Managers have face-to-face meetings with their employees to check in, to tell them what they're doing well and what they could be working on, to ask if they are enjoying the job, and to find out what employees want to pursue with their careers. "We find out all the time that employees are really hungry for *feedback.* All they want is feedback," Jann says. Management-development meetings are held each month when topics such as employee feedback, employee development, and taking care of employees are discussed.

Leaders at Melaleuca don't play politics. "We are not political here at all, and that starts at the top," Jann says. "If your leaders are political, your people will be political because they will see that it works. Out managers are respectful, insightful, and give directions—but not for political reasons. Promotions are given because of proven results. That's what is rewarded.

Conclusion

Melaleuca is a highly productive, performance-driven organization, and this has resulted in significant expansion and revenue growth for over 20 years. The company is fueled by highly motivated employees whose managers set and measure goals, reward and recognize performance, and spend priority time supporting their employees.

FUTURE ISSUES FACING MELALEUCA

Describe the issues and opportunities facing Melaleuca's ability to maintain a highly motivating work environment now and in the future.

1. What are Melaleuca's greatest motivational strengths?
2. Does the company have motivational weaknesses that you can identify or assume? What are they?
3. What are potential threats to the company's ability to motivate employees?

4. If you were Frank VanderSloot and McKay Christensen, what would be your biggest concerns relating to employee motivation?

   What alternatives do they have?
   What would you propose?

THE SEVEN PRINCIPLES AND MELALEUCA

In this exercise, describe the ways Melaleuca creates a motivating work environment using the seven principles as an analytical framework.

Setting the Environment

Principle 1: Organizational commitment contributes powerfully to workplace motivation.

Leader's Role: Cultivator

What does Melaleuca do to create organizational commitment?
What are they missing?
How can you apply what they do to your program?

Principle 2: The more you care, the more they will care.

Leader's Role: Carator

What does Melaleuca do to demonstrate care for employees?
What are they missing?
How can you apply what they do to your program?

Principle 3: The more you know about people, the more you will know what to do.

Leader's Role: Student

What does Melaleuca do to develop a deep understanding of employees' needs and desires?
What are they missing?
How can you apply what they do to your program?

Principle 4: Do what you love, and the motivation will follow.

Leader's Role: Designer

What does Melaleuca do to design an enjoyable work environment?
What are they missing?
How can you apply what they do to your program?

Crossing the Rubicon

Principle 5: Belief in personal capability enables goal setting and goal pursuit.

Leader's Role: Expectancy Manager

What does Melaleuca do to develop employees' beliefs in their abilities to perform?
What are they missing?
How can you apply what they do to your program?

Principle 6: Great goals get people going.

Leader's Role: Challenger

What does Melaleuca do to establish and gain commitment to challenging goals?
What are they missing?
How can you apply what they do to your program?

Principle 7: Willpower is the engine for goal pursuit.

Leader's Role: Supporter

What does Melaleuca do to support employees as they pursue demanding goals?
What are they missing?
How can you apply what they do to your program?

CONCLUSIONS

What are the most valuable motivational techniques you have learned from Melaleuca? Which of those would be most useful for you to apply in your own organization?

ACTIVITIES

INITIAL SELF-ASSESSMENT

Directions: Reflect upon yourself and what you want to accomplish. Then complete the worksheet.

My motivational goal(s):

1.

2.

3.

Why working on this is important to me:

Whom I want to motivate:

Why?

Right now, I believe I am (choose one):

A great motivator *A good motivator*

A poor motivator *I demotivate people*

Explain why you chose great, good, poor, or demotivating:

Right now, I get feedback about my motivational skills from:

What I do well as a motivator:

Others who could help me learn more about my motivational skills are:

Until commitment occurs, progress toward goal achievement is limited. You will decide to make commitments to skills or practice development as you read the book and consider what is most important. As you do, write those commitments here. Written commitments generally are completed more steadfastly than those in your head. (Public commitments are even more so!)

Make whatever initial commitments you can now, and add to them as you continue through the book.

Commitments:

MOTIVATING OTHERS STARTS WITH YOU

Directions: Answer the questions below. Before embarking on the task of motivating others, it is helpful to know what motivates you.

Think of a time you were highly motivated at work. It should be a time when work was great—when you couldn't wait to get to work in the morning. Describe that time. Tell a story about what were you doing, what were you feeling, what the qualities of that work were, and why were you so motivated.

What were the factors that made this an exceptionally motivating experience?

What was the role of your manager? How did he or she contribute to this motivational experience?

What motivates you to work to your highest potential?

We are drawn to motivating work environments. They are places where people are excited, accomplish a lot, and enjoy the people they work with and the work they do. Employees want to work there. If you could create such an environment, what would it look like? Describe it physically. What would be going on?

Now think back upon the most motivating leaders, coaches, teachers, parents, or other people you ever knew. What was it about them that motivated you? What did they do to get your best?

Summarize any insights you've gained about what motivates you.

FIELD RESEARCH

What Managers Do to Motivate or Demotivate Employees

Directions: For the next several days (at least a week), gather some data for yourself. In a variety of away-from-work situations, ask people what their bosses do to motivate or demotivate them. This is just casual conversation as you are sitting in a restaurant talking to a waiter, talking in church between services, or waiting in line to buy a ticket.

To these people, you're not a manager looking for data. You just happened to ask what they like or don't like about their work in the middle of another conversation. And then you say something like, "When you've had a great boss, what has he or she done to motivate you?" "What have managers done in the past to demotivate you?"

If you ask it that way, the person doesn't have to openly refer to his or her current supervisor.

Keep a record afterward of what people said their bosses have done to motivate or to demotivate them.

What People Told Me Their Bosses Have Done to Motivate Them	What People Told Me Their Bosses Have Done to Demotivate Them

After you've gathered data (hey, you're now a researcher!) from a few people, ask yourself what your employees would say about you. What do you suppose they would tell someone in the coffee shop *about you?*

What insights about your motivational style, skills, or opportunities have you learned?

MOTIVATIONAL SELF-ASSESSMENT

Directions: Complete this survey based on your self-knowledge. Then ask others—employees, your manager, peers—to complete it as well, and then compare the results. Reflect upon your strengths and opportunities for growth.

Circle or mark the response that most reflects you.

	Strongly Disagree	Disagree	Undecided	Agree	Strongly Agree
Self-Awareness and Growth					
I regularly ask employees and others for feedback about my motivational skills, knowledge, and effectiveness.	1	2	3	4	5
I have a good idea of my motivational strengths and weaknesses.	1	2	3	4	5
I spend time reading, taking classes, or taking part in other developmental activities to become a better motivator.	1	2	3	4	5
Principle 1: Cultivating					
My employees have a strong emotional attachment to our organization.	1	2	3	4	5
I have developed a culture with strong values and expectations.	1	2	3	4	5
I have been able to develop a strong social fabric within our organization.	1	2	3	4	5
I have been able to obtain the compensation, recognition, and other rewards employees deserve.	1	2	3	4	5
Principle 2: Caring					
I care about my work.	1	2	3	4	5
I let my employees know that they matter.	1	2	3	4	5
I practice caring behaviors with my employees.	1	2	3	4	5
I support my employees beyond what the organization expects me to do.	1	2	3	4	5
I treat my employees fairly—the process for making promotion, pay, and other decisions is fair, as are the results.	1	2	3	4	5
My decisions are consistent, are based on good information, and involve employees when possible.	1	2	3	4	5
I treat employees with respect and listen to their concerns and ideas.	1	2	3	4	5

	Strongly Disagree	Disagree	Undecided	Agree	Strongly Agree
Principle 3: Studying					
I keep up-to-date about motivational thinking, research, and techniques.	1	2	3	4	5
I observe behavior and think about why people do what they do.	1	2	3	4	5
I know each of my employees well and have a good understanding of what they are facing in life and work.	1	2	3	4	5
Principle 4: Designing					
Our work environment is fun and enjoyable.	1	2	3	4	5
My employees and I have tried to modify jobs and tasks to suit their interests and what they like doing.	1	2	3	4	5
I find ways to make even the most routine task meaningful for employees.	1	2	3	4	5
I try to help employees move to jobs they enjoy.	1	2	3	4	5
I provide opportunities for continuous learning.	1	2	3	4	5
There are opportunities to socialize both on and off the job. People like each other.	1	2	3	4	5
Principle 5: Managing Expectancies					
I provide training and other opportunities for employees to learn their jobs and tasks well.	1	2	3	4	5
My employees have mentors or other experienced people to learn from.	1	2	3	4	5
I give my employees authentic encouragement when I believe they have the ability to complete difficult assignments.	1	2	3	4	5
I do what I say I will do.	1	2	3	4	5
I know what rewards are important to my employees.	1	2	3	4	5
There are opportunities to relax, reduce stress, and exercise in our workplace.	1	2	3	4	5

	Strongly Disagree	Disagree	Undecided	Agree	Strongly Agree
Principle 6: Challenging					
I set goals that are specific and difficult.	1	2	3	4	5
Employees are involved in goal setting when possible.	1	2	3	4	5
When the goal is beyond the current abilities of my employees, I give them stretch learning goals to support their performance.	1	2	3	4	5
Goals are given to employees with outcomes that are within their ability to control.	1	2	3	4	5
My employees are committed to the goals they are assigned.	1	2	3	4	5
Principle 7: Supporting					
Employees get feedback as they pursue goals.	1	2	3	4	5
I provide emotional support and encourage employees as they pursue goals.	1	2	3	4	5
I remove as many obstacles and distractions as possible that could get in the way of goal accomplishment.	1	2	3	4	5
I help employees plan how they will pursue their goals when needed.	1	2	3	4	5
We prioritize goals so that employees know what is most important.	1	2	3	4	5
We celebrate successes along the way.	1	2	3	4	5
We have a "habit of success" culture. We expect to succeed, not to fail.	1	2	3	4	5

LEARNING ABOUT YOURSELF FROM OTHER PEOPLE

Interview Guide

Directions: Use this worksheet as an outline for interviews or discussions you have with employees, peers, or others to learn more about your motivational skills. Complete one for each person you speak to (or for each group, if you are speaking with a number of people at once). Then summarize what you've learned about yourself.

This interview guide should be followed informally and should fit the occasion (you don't want to ask formal questions that would turn someone off). Adapt it to meet the situation.

Note that the very act of asking questions will raise the expectations and the interest in creating a more motivating work environment. So be prepared to follow up.

Interviewee:

Date:

Welcome

Thank you for spending a few minutes with me. I need your help. I want to learn more about motivating work environments and what I can do to continue to develop one here. I'm going to be asking people this question regularly because I want to continuously improve my skills at creating a motivating work environment here and down the road.

I. The Work We Do Here

First, I'm curious about the work here. Can you think of a time when the work here was great—when you were motivated to do it and you enjoyed it? Tell me about that time. What was happening? What people were involved?

What were the factors that contributed to this being an exceptional motivational experience?

From your experiences or observations of others, what are the obstacles to making our work more motivating here?

II. Motivating Work Environments

Motivating work environments are places we are drawn to. They are places where people are excited, accomplish a lot, and enjoy the people and the work they do. Employees want to work there.

If you were to create a motivating work environment here, what would it look like?

a. Describe it physically. What would the workplace look like?

b. What would be going on?

c. What kind of resources would there be?

d. What would draw people to it?

e. Who would it draw?

f. Now describe what part your boss would play in motivating you during that time. How would he or she contribute to your motivation?

III. My Motivational Skills

Think of a time I did a good job of motivating. What happened? How did you feel? What were the qualities of that experience that made it motivating?

What should I do more of to make this a more motivating work environment for you and others?

IV. Additional Ideas and Recommendations

Are there additional ideas or recommendations you have that would make this a more motivating work environment?

Thank you for your time!

ORGANIZATIONAL CITIZENSHIP BEHAVIORS (OCB)

Types of OCB

Helping behaviors are what employees do voluntarily to help others. They include peacemaking, cheerleading, and preventing or helping solve work problems.

Sportsmanship means keeping a positive attitude even when things don't go the way the employee wants them to, not complaining when inconvenienced, not taking it personally when suggestions aren't adopted, and sacrificing for the good of the group.

Organizational loyalty takes place when employees show concern for others and the organization, support its objectives, speak positively and defend it to outsiders, and stay committed to it even during difficult times.

Organizational compliance means doing what you're supposed to do even when no one is watching and includes following rules and procedures, being on time, and not squandering time or organizational resources.

Individual initiative is what employees do above and beyond the call of duty. These employees stay late, are hard-working and reliable, clean up when they notice trash, build resources instead of wasting them, and help others know what can they do to succeed.

Civic virtue is responsible involvement in the political process of the organization. These folks attend organizational meetings, stay on top of issues affecting the organization, share their ideas, do what they can to keep the environment safe by reporting or preventing dangerous situations, keep on top of larger organizational issues, and are willing to deliver bad news and support unpopular views if needed.

Self-development is what employees do without being asked to improve their knowledge, skills, and abilities. It also means taking an interest in what is happening in their fields of work, expanding knowledge in order to help the organization in different ways, and keeping on top of what is developing in the organization's industry.

Exercise:

1. Identify the employee(s) in your program who go "above and beyond the call of duty." *What* do they do that is above and beyond?

2. If you feel comfortable, ask the person *why* he or she does this. List the reasons. One may simply be personality or the values he or she brings to anything. You are looking for workplace experiences that are causes.

3. What leadership actions could you initiate to provide fertile ground for OCB in your department? What would cause your employees to believe that the organization is fair? What would make them more satisfied with their jobs? Are you supporting them as much as you could?

Source: Podsakoff, Philip M., Scott B. MacKenzie, Julie Beth Paine, and Daniel G. Bachrach. "Organizational Citizenship Behaviors: A Critical Review of the Theoretical and Empirical Literature and Suggestions for Future Research." *Journal of Management* 26, no. 3 (2000): 513.

ASSESSING YOUR ORGANIZATIONAL COMMITMENT STRATEGIES

Tapping the Heart, Strengthening the Connection, and Making Your Organization Hard to Leave

Directions: Review the ways you currently create organizational commitment in your area. Assess your own organization.

1. What commitment strategies are you already using in each of the three areas—adoring, choring, and storing?
2. How effective are they? What could you add to increase organizational commitment?
3. How can you involve your employees in assessing and developing their own commitment to your program?
4. How can you *tap their hearts, strengthen their connection, and make it hard to leave* your organization?

Current Strategies (List What You Are Doing in These Areas):

Adoring (How are you tapping their hearts?)	Choring (How are you strengthening their connection to the program?)	Storing (How are you making it hard for them to leave?)
1.	1.	1.
2.	2.	2.
3.	3.	3.
4.	4.	4.
What are your most effective strategies in this area?	What are your most effective strategies in this area?	What are your most effective strategies in this area?
What are possible strategies in this area you might start?	What are possible strategies in this area you might start?	What are possible strategies in this area you might start?

Action Plan—What Strategies Will You Pursue?

Strategy	Who Will Be Responsible?	When Will It Be Due?

How will you involve your employees in developing these strategies? (If you were paying attention earlier, you would have included them from the start of this exercise!)

DO YOUR EMPLOYEES MATTER TO YOU?

(*Manager Instructions*)

Directions (Manager): Make a copy of the employee portion of this activity and give it to employees. Type in your name and who it should be returned to. Find a way to have the surveys returned anonymously (perhaps have them sent in a sealed envelope to an assistant or to your HR consultant). Fill out one of your own. Compare the results. (Note that for some answers, "Strongly Disagree" is the response you want.)

Managerial Survey (*Employee Instructions*)

Directions: Please circle or mark the correct answer for each question. Please respond according to how you normally feel about your manager.

Please respond concerning: [Manager's name]

Complete anonymously and return to: ___________ no later than:___________

	Strongly Disagree	Disagree	Undecided	Agree	Strongly Agree
Awareness*—Do you feel your manager notices or is interested in your work?*					
My manager seems to notice what I do.	1	2	3	4	5
My manager probably doesn't know my name.	1	2	3	4	5
I can get my manager's attention when I need to.	1	2	3	4	5
I feel like my manager ignores me.	1	2	3	4	5
Importance*—Do you feel your manager seems to care about what you want, think, or do?*					
My manager doesn't care what happens to me.	1	2	3	4	5
My manager is proud when I succeed.	1	2	3	4	5
My manager will go out of his/her way to help me even if it is inconvenient.	1	2	3	4	5
My manager is willing to listen to me and help me when I have a problem.	1	2	3	4	5
My manager cares enough about me to give me helpful feedback if I need it.	1	2	3	4	5
My manager needs me.	1	2	3	4	5
My manager thinks I'm important enough to invest in me.	1	2	3	4	5
My manager listens to me.	1	2	3	4	5

Reliance*—Do you feel your manager relies on you?*

My manager asks my advice on important matters.	1	2	3	4	5
My manager turns to me when he/she needs help.	1	2	3	4	5
My manager trusts me with important information and tasks	1	2	3	4	5
My manager believes he/she can count on me.	1	2	3	4	5
My manager thinks I make a valuable contribution to our program.	1	2	3	4	5

Source: Adapted from Elliott, Gregory, Suzanne Kao, and Ann-Marie Grant. "Mattering: Empirical Validation of a Social-Psychological Concept." *Self & Identity* 3, no. 4 (2004): 339.

HOW TO CARE WHEN YOU *DO* CARE

Directions: If you do care, how do you show you care? Take each category of caring that Wilkes and Wallace identified (listed below) and give examples of how you have demonstrated them in your work place. Then develop ideas for doing it better.

Qualities of Caring	Examples of What I Do Now	Ideas for What I Could Do
Compassion		
Communication		
Concern		
Competence		
Commitment		
Confidence		
Conscience		
Courage		

Qualities listed are from the following source: Wilkes, Lesley M., and Marianne C. Wallis. "A Model of Professional Nurse Caring: Nursing Students' Experience." *Journal of Advanced Nursing* 27, no. 3 (1998): 582–89. For descriptions, see the section on Principle 2, "The More You Care, the More They Will Care," in chapter 3.

HOW TO CARE WHEN YOU *DON'T* CARE

Directions: Consider areas to develop care in your organization. List ideas for each program area.

Learning to Care Strategies	Caring Opportunities—Ideas
What problems need solving around here?	
How can I develop deeper but appropriate relationships with my employees? Who is someone I'd like to know more about?	
What standards of excellence can I identify that would be important?	
What goals can I make more meaningful? What subgoals with deadlines could I set?	
Who is affected by the work of our organization? What is the impact of excellent or poor work?	
On whom do we depend in our organization? What are ways to make their work more productive, easy, and fun?	
What work processes could be accomplished more quickly, more inexpensively, and at a higher quality?	
What are the learning opportunities from my work? Where could I go to learn them? Be creative—there are many opportunities to learn and not just in classrooms or on the job.	
What provides deeper sources of meaningful work? Look inside and to what you value.	

Do I act like I care at work? Do people perceive me as someone who is there because I have to be or there because I want to do something important? What could I do to act more like I care about the work we are doing?

If you can't find anything to care about in the previous strategies, what work would you care about? What plans could you start to make to move to the kinds of jobs that provide that opportunity?

Prioritize

Choose the five most promising ideas, and plan how you will follow up.

Top Five Activities	Action Steps
1.	
2.	
3.	
4.	
5.	

WHAT MOTIVATES EVERYONE

Directions: All human beings are motivated similarly and also differently. The purpose of this worksheet is to start thinking about what motivates you and others. Create as many ideas as you can.

First, list things that motivate you to do something or that have motivated you during your life. List everything that comes to mind.

Now, list things that you have seen motivate others. List everything that comes to mind.

Finally, list things that motivate *everyone* to some degree.

FINDING THE DIFFERENCES

Directions: People are motivated differently depending on their personalities and circumstances. Read the short profiles of Beth, Peter, and Bill and then list what might motivate them in the workplace.

Beth is a 26-year-old computer programmer. She has many friends and is involved in many activities outside work. She is single. Unknown to nearly all her friends or anyone at work, she recently discovered that she has cancer. She went to a technical-vocational school in town and worries that her parents are beginning to age.

What might be strong motivators for Beth?

Peter is 58 years old and was recently moved from a management position to an internal consulting job. He is seven years from retirement. His wife is already retired, and their children have moved on. He likes a good game of golf on Saturday mornings. He recently received a poor performance review for the first time anyone can remember.

What might be strong motivators for Peter?

Bill plays all kinds of sports, and at work, he is the best at moving the inventory to where it needs to be stored. He is 46 and has always been physically active. Recently, the company moved him to a "desk" job. He graduated high school and went right to work. His wife stays at home and takes care of their two young children.

What might be strong motivators for Bill?

How might these three be motivated similarly?

What would you plan to do for each?

HOW WELL DO YOU KNOW YOUR EMPLOYEES?

Directions: You can work next to someone for 25 years and not know whether they have children or what they really care about. The purpose of this worksheet is to help you reflect upon how deeply you really know and understand what is important to the people who work for you every day.

How would your employees answer these questions? Check one response for each item.

Yes	No	Doesn't Care	My Manager ...
—	—	—	**People**
—	—	—	... knows the name of my spouse/significant other.
—	—	—	... knows what my spouse/significant other does for a living.
—	—	—	... knows the names and ages of my children.
—	—	—	... knows the name of my best friend, what he/she does for a living, and why we're buddies.
—	—	—	... knows who I am, or worry about being, a caregiver for.
—	—	—	**Activities**
—	—	—	... knows what I like to do when I'm not working.
—	—	—	... knows my favorite hobbies and what I'm really good at doing away from the job.
—	—	—	... knows where I take vacations and like to travel.
—	—	—	... knows what my children are involved in doing and about their progress in school.
—	—	—	**Investments**
—	—	—	... knows where I live and what kind of house I have.
—	—	—	... knows if I feel financially stable or am in trouble.
—	—	—	**Work**
—	—	—	... knows my career aspirations.
—	—	—	... knows what I think my biggest accomplishment is and what I am most proud of.
—	—	—	... knows what I really enjoy doing at work and what I really don't like doing.
—	—	—	... knows what kind of rewards and recognition I like.
—	—	—	... knows how I feel about the organization and its future.
—	—	—	... knows what I think are great opportunities for our program.
—	—	—	**Me**
—	—	—	... knows what I fear and what makes me insecure.
—	—	—	... knows my spiritual, political, and moral beliefs and values.
—	—	—	... knows the dreams I have for my life and what is important to me.
—	—	—	... what brings me great happiness.

Adapted from Coonradt, Charles A., and Lee Nelson. "Employee Awareness Questionnaire." In *The Game of Work,* Park City, UT: 3rd ed., 1997.

EMPLOYEE WORK ENJOYMENT

Directions: Complete a worksheet for each of your employees.

Category	Current Situation	Employee Interests	Opportunities for Improvement
Is this a pleasurable physical environment for *this employee?*			
What relationship-building activities would be meaningful for *this employee?*			
How challenging is the job or task for *this employee?*			
How can this task or job provide opportunities to learn and also build competence for *this employee?*			
How much ability does *this employee* have to exercise choice and creativity and to self-manage in this job or task?			
What makes this job interesting for *this employee*?			

Overall Approach

Given where this employee is in her or his career and the type of work and work environment that is enjoyable for him or her, what will you plan to do? Will you modify the job or task, suggest a career change or move, or give other opportunities outside the specific job to make the work more enjoyable? What is within your power to do over time, using your imagination and creativity?

DOING WORK FOR THE FUN AND REWARD OF IT

Directions:

1. Select a job or task that one of your employees is engaged in or one of your own tasks. Write as many ways as you can think of that you currently motivate in each of the categories. Contrast intrinsic motivators, which come from within and are the joy of doing the work, with extrinsic motivators, which come from external consequences of doing or not doing the work.
2. Think of what you could do to make it more motivating in each of the categories.
3. Brainstorm (perhaps you want to involve your employees in this exercise) ways you could make the job more intrinsically motivating in each of the categories.

Doing Work for the Fun of It

Qualities of Intrinsic Work—Enjoyment in Doing Something

Job/Task: ____________

Qualities	**Current Motivators**	**Potential Motivators**
Ability to make choices		
Challenge, stretching		
Enjoyment and fun		
Curiosity		
Creativity		
Relationships		
Complexity		
Competence		
Novelty, new experiences		
Problem solving		
Opportunity to learn		
Meaningfulness		
Self-expression		
Determining my own goals		

Doing Work for the Reward of It

Qualities of Extrinsic Work—Rewards for Doing Something

Job/Task: ____________

Qualities	**Current Motivators**	**Potential Motivators**
Opportunities for recognition		
Competition		
Incentives (e.g., money, grades, promotions) for performance		
Avoiding punishment (e.g., being fired, social embarrassment)		
Being well thought of, respected		
Winning, being better than others		

DOING WORK FOR THE FUN OF IT—OUR DEPARTMENT

Directions: Now think beyond a specific job or task and consider your entire department. What policies, programs, events, and activities currently provide intrinsic motivation for your entire work group? Think of ways to make your work area more intrinsically motivating. What could you and your employees create to make the work more enjoyable overall?

Qualities	Our Department *Current Motivators*	Our Department *Potential Motivators*
Ability to make choices		
Challenge, stretching		
Enjoyment and fun		
Curiosity		
Creativity		
Complexity		
Competence		
Relationships		
Meaningfulness		
Novelty, new experiences		
Problem solving		
Opportunity to learn		
Self-expression		
Determining our own goals		

SUPERVISOR SUPPORT TO INCREASE EMPLOYEE OPTIMISM

Directions: Read through the example, which shows how sales managers can help change customer rejection to an optimistic view. Then give examples of how you might do the same with your employees.

Sales Person Response to Customer Rejection	Sales Manager Response	Desired Change
I'm a totally incompetent salesperson.	You are still learning how to be an effective salesperson. Training will help you significantly.	Salesperson's belief to change from permanent (I'm inept) to temporary (I can learn how to do this).
No one likes our products.	Some people need our products more and some less. Let's figure out how to find those who need it.	Salesperson's belief to change from pervasive (everyone) to specific (some people).
Customers don't relate to me.	Customers don't like the way you present our product, but we can change that.	Salesperson's belief to change from personal (me) to impersonal (the presentation effectiveness).
Your Employee's Response to Difficulty	**Your Response**	**Desired Change**

Sales example adapted from: Rich, Gregory A. "Salesperson Optimism: Can Sales Managers Enhance It and So What If They Do?" *Journal of Marketing Theory & Practice* 7, no. 1 (1999): 53.

PRACTICING THE ABCDE METHOD

Directions: The ABCDE model can help employees who doubt their abilities when problems strike. Read the definitions of ABCDE. Complete steps I through V. Practice this anytime you or your employees engage in self-defeating beliefs about your work or workplace.

Adversity—Problems cause some people to give up. Optimistic people view them as opportunities for learning and growth. We run into adversities every day in work and in life.

Beliefs—Adversities lead to beliefs about the situation. How we explain adversity to ourselves will determine whether it motivates us or defeats us. Beware of phrases such as "It's my fault," "Nothing ever changes," or "Whenever I try something, this is always the result."

Consequences—Beliefs lead to consequences. When I believe the problem is my lack of intelligence, I may give up. If, on the other hand, I believe the problem is that I didn't have the right information, I may work harder to get it next time.

Disputation—This is challenging self-defeating beliefs. Instead of accepting your first thought ("I'm never good enough"), take another look and think of alternative explanations ("What a fluke that she got the contract instead of us"). Many times, our first thoughts are engrained and come from years of socialization, including what our parents may have told us as children, so disputing them may be difficult.

Energization—The result of more healthy beliefs is greater energy and more resilience. Motivation stays high!

Practice with Real Employee Examples

I. List a work adversity. (This could be anything—"I didn't get the job." "We missed the deadline." "The competition got the contract.")

II. List initial beliefs for each adversity. ("I'm not talented enough." "With a little more effort, I could have had this job." "I've always been a quitter." "I think they got lucky this time.")

1.

2.

3.

III. Consequences. What would be the result of each belief? How would you feel? Act?

1.

2.

3.

IV. Disputation. List alternative, healthier explanations for the adversity.

1.

2.

3.

Energization: What would be the differences between the first and alternative beliefs?

Source: Seligman, Martin E. P. *Learned Optimism.* New York: Pocket Books, 1998.

DEVELOPING SELF-CONFIDENCE

Directions: Complete the worksheet below. Consider ways you or others have developed confidence in the past. What can you learn from those experiences?

Think of a time you worked with one of your employees to help develop confidence.

1. What was the task?

2. Where did your employee start out? Were his or her fears based on reality? Imagined?

3. How did the lack of confidence affect performance? Why?

4. What did you do to help develop confidence? List what happened.

5. Has there been a time when you moved from insecurity to confidence in your own abilities? How did it happen?

6. What were the results? Did productivity change?

7. How can you apply what you learned to your employees today?

DEVELOPING "I CAN" EMPLOYEES— FUND-RAISING VOLUNTEER

Case Study

Directions: Reread the section in chapter 4 about developing fund-raising volunteers. Answer the questions under "Potential Experiences."

Employee name: Fund-raising Volunteer
Current Job: New Volunteer *Task to be assigned:* Ask a potential donor for a contribution.
Current Competency level: Extensive community volunteer experience. No experience directly asking for money.

Competencies required to succeed:

(1) able to describe the "case for support"; (2) able to obtain appointments with potential donors; (3) has the ability to conduct a face-to-face meeting with the donor, assess their potential interests in the organization, move the donor to a closer relationship with the organization, and creatively codesign giving alternatives with the donor that are related to those interests; and (4) can ask, in a productive, professional way, for a contribution at a level that fits the donor's giving capacity.

	Potential Experiences
Train them how to do it.	How were volunteers taught the competencies needed? Did they gain progressive mastery of the competencies required? How did they do that?
Show them how to do it.	Who modeled the correct behavior? How was it done?
Tell them they can do it.	Were volunteers given verbal assurances that they could successfully complete this activity? In what ways?
Get them in physical and emotional shape to do it	In what ways were volunteers given a positive emotional or physical environment?

DEVELOPING "I CAN" EMPLOYEES

Directions: Complete a worksheet when assigning a task to an employee.

Employee name:

Current Job:

Current Competency level:

Task to be assigned:

Competencies required to succeed:

	List Ways Your Employee May Experience This	**My Plan for This Employee**
Train them how to do it. What learning experiences will give them the competencies needed to succeed in this task?		
Show them how to do it. Who can model the behavior that is required for this task to be successfully completed? What situations are similar enough to enhance learning transfer to this employee?		
Tell them they can do it. Whom does this employee trust to give feedback and to assess ability to complete this task? In what ways can I be intentional about getting the right people to give useful feedback to this employee?		
Get them in physical and emotional shape to do it. Assess your work environment. What is emotionally or physically draining? What is overly or unnecessarily stressful? What can I do to provide a confidence-building, enthusiastic work environment?		

SETTING SPECIFIC GOALS

Directions: Highly motivating goals are specific and difficult. Too many goals are vague and used as excuses for underperformance. Use this worksheet to make goals crystal clear.

Be Specific. To be most effective, goals should describe behavior that can be observed. An outside person should be able to tell when the goals have been successfully completed. Goals should describe a standard of performance (quality/quantity—how well/how much) and a time (when it will be completed) that can be measured.

Unclear Goals	Better
To work with the legislature (what does "work with" mean?)	To pass three bills we favor and to kill the one we don't in this upcoming legislative session.
To improve communications (how will you know you've done it?)	To improve our employee communication survey rating by 10% this quarter.
To understand our competitors better ("to understand" is one of the vaguest verbs).	To complete a comprehensive competitor analysis, listing strengths and weaknesses of our three main rivals, by the end of the month.
To know our customer referral procedures (How would you know when he/she "knows?")	To demonstrate our three referral procedures when observed interacting with customers during the week of June 1, 2006.
To create an attractive brochure (how do you define "attractive'?)	To create a new brochure by the end of the year, tested by customer focus groups on the following attributes: (1) Would positively influence my purchase decision, and (2) Would cause me to visit the store location.
To increase our output (how much and by when?)	To produce at least 10 reports a day.
To reduce our costs (again, how much, and where will you do it?)	Reduce the cost of producing each XXX, by 10% this year. Improve quality production standards so that rework costs are reduced by $500,000 within two years.
Develop a succession plan (by when, what quality)	Develop a succession-planning process such that within two years, 90% of our leadership positions are filled internally.

Practice: Write workplace goals that are unclear and make them into performance goals. Be sure to include a time it's due and performance you can observe. Then ask your employees to do the same.

Unclear Goals	Improved Goals

PROCESS, PERFORMANCE, AND OUTCOME GOALS

Directions: Sometimes it is easy to confuse performance with outcomes. It is also better to focus on process and performance goals, which are the goals most under our control, than on outcome goals, which may not be within our influence.

Practice setting goals in your workplace. List the processes that lead to performance that lead to desired outcomes.

Example 1

Desired Outcome: Reduce customer complaints by 10 percent

Performance Goal(s):

1. Improve on-time deliveries by 25 percent
2. Reduce broken product by 14 percent

Process Goal(s):

1a. Develop just-in-time dispatch service

1b. Install GPS systems in each delivery truck

2a. Integrate quality-improvement measures in the manufacturing process

2b. Develop improved product packaging

Example 2

Desired Outcome: Signed contract with new client

Performance Goal(s):

1. Effective sales presentation
2. Flawless execution of follow-up contact plan

Process Goal(s):

1a. Collect market and client data

1b. Produce high-quality sales brochure

2a. Identify key decision makers in the company

2b. Create telephone, meeting, and e-mail schedule for client contact

Desired Outcome:

Performance Goal(s):

1.

2.

3.

Process Goal(s):

1a.

1b.

1c.

2a.

2b.

2c.

Desired Outcome:

Performance Goal(s):

1.

2.

3.

Process Goal(s):

1a.

1b.

1c.

2a.

2b.

2c.

SMARTER GOALS

Directions: SMART goals (specific, measurable, achievable, relevant, and time-specific) are commonly used to help develop effective goals in the workplace and beyond. SMARTer goals focus on increasing motivation by adding challenge and asking whether the goal should be for learning or performance. Practice setting difficult, specific goals using this worksheet.

Goal 1: **Plan to Achieve:**

Is this challenging enough?

Should this be a learning or a performance goal?

Is this the most appropriate, manageable "chunk"?
Does it need further subgoals?

What are they?

Specific (What is to be accomplished?):

Measurable (How will we know when it's complete?);

Achievable (Can it be done?):

Evaluation: How will success be determined/measured?

Relevant (Does it make a difference?):

Time-specific (When should it be completed?):

BREAKING LONG-TERM GOALS INTO SHORT-TERM GOALS

Directions: Using shorter-term goals increases confidence, focuses attention, provides better strategies, and boosts effort.

1. Use this worksheet to break longer-term goals into more manageable ones.
2. Sit down with one of your employees with a difficult, long-term goal. Work together to develop subgoals with separate strategies that are accomplishable.
3. Survey the most difficult program goals you have. Identify ones that could benefit from breaking the goals into parts. When possible, engage your employees (that way you are not only involving them but also teaching them how to do it) in taking program goals and developing subgoals and strategies with deadlines and feedback processes.

Long-term goal:

Strategy for accomplishing it:

Subgoals

1.

2.

Subgoal 1:

Deadline:

Strategy:

How will feedback be sought?

Subgoal 2:

Deadline:

Strategy:

How will feedback be sought?

SELF-REGULATION TRAINING CHECKLIST

Directions: Self-regulation training can improve performance. Such training usually involves learning goal setting, visualizing obstacles to success, planning to overcome obstacles, self-monitoring progress, and self-reinforcement techniques. The purpose of this worksheet is to help you think about what learning your employees should pursue.

Check how well each of your employees performs each activity. Give each employee a 1, 2, or 3 for each activity. 1 = Needs Improvement, 2 = Performs Adequately, and 3 = Does Well.

Based on the results, list priority learning opportunities for each employee.

Activities Checklist	**Employee:** ________	**Employee:** ________	**Employee:** ________	**Employee:** ________
Overcomes obstacles to goals	___	___	___	___
Motivates him/herself day-to-day	___	___	___	___
Manages time	___	___	___	___
Doesn't allow adversities to affect future performance	___	___	___	___
Handles criticism productively	___	___	___	___
Exhibits persistence	___	___	___	___
Can self-reward for accomplishments	___	___	___	___
Becomes distracted from goal pursuit	___	___	___	___
Monitors own goal progress and quality	___	___	___	___
Learns skills required to complete goals	___	___	___	___
Handles feedback from others productively	___	___	___	___
Seeks feedback about performance	___	___	___	___
Sets challenging, specific, measurable goals	___	___	___	___
Prioritizes goals	___	___	___	___
Learns from mistakes	___	___	___	___
Controls impulses—avoids temptations	___	___	___	___
Thinks ahead, plans how to pursue goals	___	___	___	___
Gets started on pursuing goals—thinks of first steps to begin	___	___	___	___
Cheers him/herself up, thinks positively	___	___	___	___
Arranges environment to help focus on goal pursuit	___	___	___	___

Finds ways to make goal pursuit fun, interesting, challenging	—	—	—	—
Controls emotions such as anger	—	—	—	—
Reduces unhealthy anxiety	—	—	—	—
Visualizes success, imagines positive outcomes	—	—	—	—
Exercises patience while pursuing goals	—	—	—	—
Gathers materials and resources needed to pursue goals	—	—	—	—
Looks for the most efficient way to accomplish tasks	—	—	—	—
Asks for help when needed	—	—	—	—
Shares feelings when needed	—	—	—	—
Exercises, participates in wellness activities	—	—	—	—
Thinks about the rewards from successes	—	—	—	—

Learning Priorities

Employee:

Employee:

Employee:

Employee:

GIVING EFFECTIVE FEEDBACK

Directions: (1) Review the checklist below, (2) practice, and (3) assess the results.

Checklist

Providing effective feedback is one of the most important yet difficult jobs you perform. Doing it well is a key for sustaining motivation. It helps the employee know whether he or she is on track and performing at the quality level desired. Doing it poorly will deflate motivation.

Be sure your employee knows you care about him or her. High trust and the knowledge you want him or her to succeed makes feedback more effective.

Focus on the behavior, not the person. Make sure you are clear about the behavior you desire. Asking them to "bring you a rock" creates unrealistic and unfair expectations. Expectations should be simple and easy to understand.

Be consistent. When employees have to guess at what you want, they will spend their time trying to figure you out rather than performing at their highest level.

Set the example. Ask for feedback on your performance regularly. Act upon it.

Be clear that feedback is not punishment, but intended to help the employee succeed.

Catch employees doing well, and make sure they know you know. Regular positive feedback is just as important and maybe more so than negative feedback.

Start by asking how they think they're doing. Many times, they will tell you what you had intended to tell them. Then the whole approach is more positive because you are working with their concerns, helping them to succeed as their supporter.

Ask what they would do differently. Many times, they have the answers already. Then, rather than offering your advice, you are supporting and improving their ideas.

Don't wait. If you see a problem, give feedback before the employee digs a hole he can't get out of or will have to spend considerable energy to overcome.

Don't mince words. Showing concern is helpful, but employees know there may be a problem and want you to get to the point.

Offer suggestions for improvement if needed. Don't criticize and leave them hanging. Sometimes it will be more helpful to explore ideas together. Sometimes the employee has enough experience and knowledge to figure it out without your help. Sometimes they won't know what to do and will need your guidance.

Listen. There may be obstacles or issues that your employees are embarrassed to share with you. You need to know those. Ask questions. Check for understanding. Observe feelings. Show that you really are there to help and need to know what they are facing.

Make sure the next steps are clear.

Offer your support. Ask what help they need from you to be successful.

Reassure and encourage.

LISTENING FOR SUCCESS

Directions: (1) Review the tips and techniques below, (2) practice, and (3) assess the results.

Listening Skills—Tips and Techniques

Listening is a key motivational skill. It can be learned. Here are some tips to help develop your own ability to do this important activity well.

Don'ts

Listening can get sidetracked. Be careful when you are:

Emotional—it will be too easy to react negatively.

Tired—listening takes effort. You have to be able to give energy to doing it.

In a noisy, busy room—have you ever tried to have a serious conversation with your spouse or significant other with children roaming the hallways?

Tempted to impress—don't use big words or drop names; those are doomed to lose your employee.

Trying to do two or more things at once—avoid distractions. How did you feel when your own boss answered the phone continually during your important meeting with her?

Do's

Listening well takes practice and can take a lifetime to master. Try these simple-to-understand, but harder-to-execute, practices:

Be sincere. Nothing is more important than deeply wanting to understand and learn from another person. Sincerity makes the other person feel heard even if your other skills are weak, and it builds trust.

Listen for what is not said. Many times, the other person is telling you much more by his nonverbal behavior. Pay attention to his emotions. Is he saying one thing verbally but telling you something completely different by his actions?

Ask open-ended questions. Yes or no questions often make people feel on the spot and therefore defensive. Questions such as "Tell me … " "What do you think about … ?" and "What would make you feel better about … ?" open up the conversation.

Avoid weighing in too early and too much. You are, after all, trying to learn from them. Listening is not an excuse for speaking, expressing your opinion, or trying to persuade. Yes, there are times for that. Yes, your employee will want your opinion at some point. Wait. Listen. Be thankful. Offer your thoughts if requested.

Signal your understanding. A friend of mine sometimes says, "Would you nod your head if you heard me?!" Sometimes I get so deep into thought that I don't communicate back that I received the message (though I usually get *that* message!). Listening, though an act of receptivity, is collaborative. Let your employee know you are understanding by nodding your head, giving verbal affirmation, and checking for understanding ("Are you telling me … ?").

EMPLOYEE MOTIVATION—
MY SELF-ASSESSMENT SUMMARY

Directions: Summarize what you believe you do well or poorly to motivate your employees today.

What I Do Well to Motivate Employees	What I Do Poorly in Motivating Employees
Principle 1: Cultivator	*Principle 1: Cultivator*
Principle 2: Carator	*Principle 2: Carator*
Principle 3: Student	*Principle 3: Student*
Principle 4: Designer	*Principle 4: Designer*
Principle 5: Expectancy Manager	*Principle 5: Expectancy Manager*
Principle 6: Challenger	*Principle 6: Challenger*
Principle 7: Supporter	*Principle 7: Supporter*

DIAGNOSING NEEDS AND DEVELOPING LEARNING OBJECTIVES

Directions: Use this worksheet to create learning objectives to help increase your ability to motivate employees. We discussed the importance of giving your employees specific, measurable, challenging goals in Principle 6. The same holds true for you. This worksheet will get you started as you begin to think about developing your skills and knowledge.

1. Review the seven principles and your self-assessments. Identify your greatest learning needs. List them under the first column.
2. Write a specific, measurable, time-limited objective for each learning need. The best learning objectives are behavioral—you should be able to demonstrate mastery of knowledge or skill of what you have learned.
3. Identify the importance that this learning objective has for your growth. Then identify the one to three objectives that are your top priorities. A = Vitally important, B = Important, and C= Helpful but not critical.

Skills and Knowledge Important for My Future Success	Learning Objective—measurable and time-specific. Must answer the question "How would I be able to show others I have accomplished it?"	Importance (A, B, C)
1.		
2.		
3.		
4.		
5.		
6.		
7.		

STRATEGIES AND RESOURCES FOR LEARNING OBJECTIVES

Directions: Use this worksheet to identify strategies for each learning objective and the resources you will need to accomplish it.

1. List strategies describing how you will accomplish each learning objective you have identified.
2. List the resources you will need in order to pursue each strategy. Resources could include time, information, money, personnel, equipment, software, and more.

Learning Objective	Developmental Strategy—How will I accomplish this objective?	Resources—What will I need to have in order to pursue this strategy?

LEARNING CONTRACT

Your Seven Principles Development Plan

Directions: This worksheet is a summary of the learning objectives you have identified, the developmental activities you chose to accomplish them, the time frame in which you plan to accomplish them, their status, and the principle to which they apply. *This is a contract you are making with yourself!*

Date Revised:

Learning Objective	Developmental Activities to Meet Identified Needs (assignments, training, certifications, education, projects)	Projected Time Frame (estimated time this will be completed)	Status*	Principle (1–7)
1.				
2.				
3.				
4.				
5.				

* Status: O = On hold, A = Current Action Item, P = Planned, C = Completed

SEVEN

Resources

This book summarizes a vast field of research and practice. It is intended to provide useful information for practicing managers. I have included additional information here for those interested in going deeper. It is also a resource list that can be drawn upon as issues need attention. This is just a starting place. No one book can include the voluminous scholarly research that has occurred and is vigorously continuing or the vast number of organizations and other sources of practical information available. The learning process is a continuously interesting lifelong journey. For the noncharismatic leader, that means an opportunity for daily growth and insight.

The "Books and Articles" section includes a selection of materials I found particularly useful when preparing this book, broken into interest categories. The list of organizations and journals is a representative list to tap into for a continuing stream of related information. Notes are listed by chapter. I found these sources to be a wealth of insight, information, and wisdom as I prepared this manuscript. I encourage you to draw from these and the many others that exist.

BOOKS AND ARTICLES

Items are categorized for simplicity. Some articles and books could be placed in more than one category.

Caring/Mattering

Amundson, Norman E., "Mattering: A Foundation for Employment Counseling and Training." *Journal of Employment Counseling* 30 (1993): 146–52

Boykin, Anne, Nancy Smith, and Dianne Aleman. "Transforming Practice Using a Caring-Based Nursing Model." *Nursing Administration Quarterly* 27, no. 3 (2003): 223.

Coonradt, Charles A., and Lee Nelson. "Employee Awareness Questionnaire." In *The Game of Work*, Park City, UT: 3rd ed. (1997).

Elliott, Gregory, Suzanne Kao, and Ann-Marie Grant. "Mattering: Empirical Validation of a Social-Psychological Concept." *Self & Identity* 3, no. 4 (2004): 339.

Galt, Kimberly A., and Ronald Markert. "Description and Assessment of an Early Curriculum to Teach Pharmacy Students Caring Behaviours." *Pharmacy Education* 2, no. 1 (2002): 23.

Hanson, M. Dave. "Using Data from Critical Care Nurses to Validate Swanson's Phenomenological Derived Middle Range Caring Theory." *Journal of Theory Construction & Testing* 8, no. 1 (2004): 21.

Rosenberg, Morris, and Claire McCullough. "Mattering: Inferred Significance and Mental Health among Adolescents." *Research in Community Mental Health* 2 (1981): 163–82.

Schlossberg, Nancy K., et al. "The Mattering Scales for Adult Students in Postsecondary Education" *American Council on Education,* Washington DC: Center for Adult Learning and Educational Credientials, 1990. (ED341772).

Skovholt, Thomas M. "The Cycle of Caring: A Model of Expertise in the Helping Professions." *Journal of Mental Health Counseling* 27, no. 1 (2005): 82.

Smith, Marlaine. "Review of Research Related to Watson's Theory of Caring." *Nursing Science Quarterly* 17, no. 1 (2004): 13.

Swanson, Kristen. "Empirical Development of a Middle Range Theory of Caring." *Nursing Research* 40, no. 3 (1991): 161–66.

——. "What's Known about Caring in Nursing Science: A Literary Meta-Analysis." In *Handbook of Clinical Nursing Research,* ed. A. S. Hinshaw, S. Feetham, and J.L.F. Shaver, 31–60. Thousand Oaks, CA: Sage, 1999.

Thornton, Lucia. "The Model of Whole-Person Caring." *Holistic Nursing Practice* 19, no. 3 (2005): 106.

Watson, Jean. *Assessing and Measuring Caring in Nursing and Health Science.* New York: Springer, 2002.

Watson, Jean, and Roxie Foster. "The Attending Nurse Caring Model: Integrating Theory, Evidence and Advanced Caring-Healing Therapeutics for Transforming Professional Practice." *Journal of Clinical Nursing* 12, no. 3 (2003): 360.

Wilkes, Lesley M., and Marianne C. Wallis. "A Model of Professional Nurse Caring: Nursing Students' Experience." *Journal of Advanced Nursing* 27, no. 3 (1998): 582–89.

Wooden, John R., and Steve Jamison. *My Personal Best: Life Lessons from an All-American Journey.* (New York: McGraw-Hill, 2004)

Exchange Theory

Cropanzano, Russell, and Marie S. Mitchell. "Social Exchange Theory: An Interdisciplinary Review." *Journal of Management* 31, no. 6 (2005): 874.

Cropanzano, Russell, and Thomas A. Wright. "When a 'Happy' Worker is Really a 'Productive' Worker: A Review and Further Refinement of the Happy-productive Worker Thesis." *Consulting Psychology Journal: Practice and Research.* 53, no. 3 (2001): 182-199

Foa, Uriel G. *Resource Theory: Explorations and Applications.* San Diego: Academic Press, 1993.

Foa, Uriel G., and Edna B. Foa. *Societal Structures of the Mind.* Springfield, IL: Thomas, 1974.

Gerstner, Charlotte R., and David V. Day. "Meta-Analytic Review of Leader-Member Exchange Theory: Correlates and Construct Issues." *Journal of Applied Psychology* 82, no. 6 (1997): 827–44.

Graen, George Bearnard, and Terri A. Scandura. "Toward a Psychology of Dyadic Organizing." *Research in Organizational Behavior* 9 (1987): 175.

Graen, George B., and Mary Uhl-Bien. "Relationship-Based Approach to Leadership: Development of Leader–Member Exchange (LMX) Theory of Leadership over 25 Years: Applying a Multi-Level Multi-Domain Perspective." *The Leadership Quarterly* 6, no. 2 (1995): 219.

Janssen, Onne, and Nico W. Van Yperen. "Employees' Goal Orientations, the Quality of Leader–Member Exchange, and the Outcomes of Job Performance and Job Satisfaction." *Academy of Management Journal* 47, no. 3 (2004): 368.

Molm, Linda D. "Theoretical Comparisons of Forms of Exchange." *Sociological Theory* 21, no. 1 (2003): 1–17.

Teichman, Meir, and Uriel G. Foa. "Effect of Resources Similarity on Satisfaction with Exchange." *Social Behavior & Personality: An International Journal* 3, no. 2 (1975): 213.

Expectancy

Cady, Steven H., Debra G. Boyd, and Mitchell J. Neubert. "Multilevel Performance Probability: A Meta-Analytic Integration of Expectancy and Self-Efficacy." *Psychological Reports* 88, no. 3 (2001): 1077.

Lawler, Edward E. *Motivation in Work Organizations,* 1st ed. The Jossey-Bass Management Series. San Francisco: Jossey-Bass, 1994.

Vroom, Victor Harold. *Work and Motivation.* Malabar, FL: Krieger, 1982.

Feedback

Audia, Pino G., and Edwin A. Locke. "Benefiting from Negative Feedback." *Human Resource Management Review* 13, no. 4 (2003): 631.

Ilies, Remus, and Timothy A. Judge. "Goal Regulation across Time: The Effects of Feedback and Affect." *Journal of Applied Psychology* 90, no. 3 (2005): 453–67.

Kluger, Avraham N., and Angelo DeNisi. "The Effects of Feedback Interventions on Performance." *Psychological Bulletin* 119, no. 2 (1996): 254.

Korsgaard, M. Audrey, and Margaret Diddams. "The Effect of Process Feedback and Task Complexity on Personal Goals, Information Searching, and Performance Improvement." *Journal of Applied Social Psychology* 26, no. 21 (1996): 1889.

Neubert, Mitchell J. "The Value of Feedback and Goal Setting over Goal Setting Alone and Potential Moderators of This Effect: A Meta-Analysis." *Human Performance* 11, no. 4 (1998): 321.

Paswan, Audhesh K., Lou E. Pelton, and Sheb L. True. "Perceived Managerial Sincerity, Feedback-Seeking Orientation and Motivation among Front-Line Employees of a Service Organization." *Journal of Services Marketing* 19, no. 1 (2005): 3.

Renn, Robert W. "Moderation by Goal Commitment of the Feedback–Performance Relationship: Theoretical Explanation and Preliminary Study." *Human Resource Management Review* 13, no. 4 (2003): 561.

Renn, Robert W., and Donald B. Fedor. "Development and Field Test of a Feedback Seeking, Self-Efficacy, and Goal Setting Model of Work Performance." *Journal of Management* 27, no. 5 (2001): 563.

Goals

Austin, James T., and Jeffrey B. Vancouver. "Goal Constructs in Psychology: Structure, Process, and Content." *Psychological Bulletin* 120, no. 3 (1996): 338–75.

Burton, D., & Raedeke, T. *Sport Psychology for Coaches.* Champaign, IL: Human Kinetics, in press.

Deci, Edward L., and Richard M. Ryan. "The 'What' and 'Why' of Goal Pursuits: Human Needs and the Self-Determination of Behavior." *Psychological Inquiry* 11, no. 4 (2000): 227.

Dweck, Carol S. *Self-Theories: Their Role in Motivation, Personality, and Development, Essays in Social Psychology.* Philadelphia, PA: Psychology Press, 1999.

Higgins, E. Tory. "Beyond Pleasure and Pain." *American Psychologist* 52, no. 12 (1997): 1280–1300.

———. "Promotion and Prevention: Regulatory Focus as a Motivational Principle." In *Advances in Experimental Social Psychology,* ed. M. P. Zanna, 1–46. New York: Academic Press, 1998.

Kerr, Steven, and Steffen Landauer. "Using Stretch Goals to Promote Organizational Effectiveness and Personal Growth: General Electric and Goldman Sachs." *Academy of Management Executive* 18, no. 4 (2004): 134.

Latham, Gary P. "Goal Setting: A Five-Step Approach to Behavior Change." *Organizational Dynamics* 32, no. 3 (2003): 309.

——. "The Motivational Benefits of Goal Setting." *Academy of Management Executive* 18, no. 4 (2004): 126.

Latham, Gary P., and Craig C. Pinder. "Work Motivation Theory and Research at the Dawn of the Twenty-First Century." *Annual Review of Psychology* 56, no. 1 (2005): 485.

Latham, Gary P., and Gerard H. Seijts. "The Effects of Proximal and Distal Goals on Performance on a Moderately Complex Task." *Journal of Organizational Behavior* 20, no. 4 (1999): 421.

Locke, Edwin A. "Guest Editor's Introduction: Goal Setting Theory and Its Applications to the World of Business." *Academy of Management Executive* 18, no. 4 (2004): 124.

——. "Linking Goals to Monetary Incentives." *Academy of Management Executive* 18, no. 4 (2004): 130.

Locke, Edwin A., Gary P. Latham, and Miriam Erez. "The Determinants of Goal Commitment." *Academy of Management Review* 13, no. 1 (1988): 23.

Locke, Edwin A., and Gary P. Latham. *Goal Setting: A Motivational Technique That Works!* Englewood Cliffs, NJ: Prentice-Hall, 1984.

———. *A Theory of Goal Setting & Task Performance.* Englewood Cliffs, NJ: Prentice Hall, 1990.

———. "Building a Practically Useful Theory of Goal Setting and Task Motivation." *American Psychologist* 57, no. 9 (2002): 705.

Seijts, Gerard H., and Gary P. Latham. "Learning versus Performance Goals: When Should Each Be Used?" *Academy of Management Executive* 19, no. 1 (2005): 124.

Seijts, Gerard H., Gary P. Latham, Kevin Tasa, and Brandon W. Latham. "Goal Setting and Goal Orientation: An Integration of Two Different yet Related Literatures." *Academy of Management Journal* 47, no. 2 (2004): 227.

Shaw, Karyll N. "Changing the Goal-Setting Process at Microsoft." *Academy of Management Executive* 18, no. 4 (2004): 139.

Intrinsic Motivation—Enjoyable Work

Amabile, Teresa M., Elizabeth M. Tighe, Karl G. Hill, and Beth A. Hennessey. "The Work Preference Inventory: Assessing Intrinsic and Extrinsic Motivational Orientations." *Journal of Personality & Social Psychology* 66, no. 5 (1994): 950.

Berns, Gregory. *Satisfaction,* 1st ed. New York: Holt, 2005.

Csikszentmihalyi, Mihaly, and Isabella Selega Csikszentmihalyi. *Optimal Experience: Psychological Studies of Flow in Consciousness.* Cambridge/ New York: Cambridge University Press, 1988.

Deci, Edward L., and Richard Flaste. *Why We Do What We Do: The Dynamics of Personal Autonomy.* New York: Putnam's Sons, 1995.

Deci, Edward L., and Richard Koestner. "A Meta-Analytic Review of Experiments Examining the Effects of Extrinsic Rewards on Intrinsic." *Psychological Bulletin* 125, no. 6 (1999): 627.

Deci, Edward L., and Richard M. Ryan. "The 'What' and 'Why' of Goal Pursuits: Human Needs and the Self-Determination of Behavior." *Psychological Inquiry* 11, no. 4 (2000): 227.

Frankl, Viktor Emil. *Man's Search for Meaning: An Introduction to Logotherapy.* Boston: Beacon Press, 1963.

Gagne, Marylene, and Edward L. Deci. "Self-Determination Theory and Work Motivation." *Journal of Organizational Behavior* 26, no. 4 (2005): 331.

Jamison, Kay R. *Exuberance: The Passion for Life,* 1st ed. New York: Knopf, 2004.

Sinetar, Marsha. *Do What You Love, the Money Will Follow: Discovering Your Right Livelihood.* New York: Dell, 1989.

Thomas, Kenneth Wayne. *Intrinsic Motivation at Work: Building Energy & Commitment,* 1st ed. San Francisco: Berrett-Koehler, 2000.

Thoreau, Henry David. *Walden.* New York: AMS Press, 1982.
Vansteenkiste, Maarten, Joke Simons, Willy Lens, Kennon M. Sheldon, and Edward L. Deci. "Motivating Learning, Performance, and Persistence: The Synergistic Effects of Intrinsic Goal Contents and Autonomy-Supportive Contexts." *Journal of Personality and Social Psychology* 87, no. 2 (2004): 246–60.
Vansteenkiste, Maarten, Willy Lens, and Edward L. Deci. "Intrinsic versus Extrinsic Goal Contents in Self-Determination Theory: Another Look at the Quality of Academic Motivation." *Educational Psychologist* 41, no. 1 (2006): 19.
Wooden, John R., and Steve Jamison, *My Personal Best: Life Lessons from an All-American Journey.* New York: McGraw-Hill, 2004.

Job Satisfaction

Harter, James K., Frank L. Schmidt, and Theodore L. Hayes. "Business-Unit-Level Relationship between Employee Satisfaction, Employee Engagement, and Business Outcomes: A Meta-Analysis." *Journal of Applied Psychology* 87, no. 2 (2002): 268–79.
Hegney, Desley, Ashley Plank, and Victoria Parker. "Extrinsic and Intrinsic Work Values: Their Impact on Job Satisfaction in Nursing." *Journal of Nursing Management* 14, no. 4 (2006): 271.
Judge, Timothy A., and Joyce E. Bono. "Relationship of Core Self-Evaluations Traits—Self-Esteem, Generalized Self-Efficacy, Locus of Control, and Emotional Stability—with Job Satisfaction and Job Performance: A Meta-Analysis." *Journal of Applied Psychology* 86, no. 1 (2001): 80–92.
Judge, Timothy A., Joyce E. Bono, Carl J. Thoresen, and Gregory K. Patton. "The Job Satisfaction–Job Performance Relationship: A Qualitative and Quantitative Review." *Psychological Bulletin* 127, no. 3 (2001): 376.

Learned Helplessness and Optimism—Positive Psychology

Peterson, C., S. F. Maier, and M.E.P. Seligman. *Learned Helplessness: A Theory for the Age of Personal Control.* New York: Oxford University Press, 1993.
Rich, Gregory A. "Salesperson Optimism: Can Sales Managers Enhance It and So What If They Do?" *Journal of Marketing Theory & Practice* 7, no. 1 (1999): 53.
Schulman, Peter. "Applying Learned Optimism to Increase Sales Productivity." *Journal of Personal Selling & Sales Management* 19, no. 1 (1999): 31.
Seligman, Martin E. P. *Learned Optimism.* New York: Pocket Books, 1998.

Seligman, Martin E. P., Tracy A. Steen, Nansook Park, and Christopher Peterson. "Positive Psychology Progress." *American Psychologist* 60, no. 5 (2005): 410.

Motivational Theory and Practice—General

Blanchard, Kenneth H., Drea Zigarmi, and Patricia Zigarmi, *Situational Leadership II*. San Diego: Blanchard Training and Development, Inc, 1994.

Boverie, Patricia Eileen, and Michael S. Kroth. *Transforming Work: The Five Keys to Achieving Trust, Commitment, and Passion in the Workplace. New Perspectives in Organizational Learning, Performance, and Change.* Cambridge, MA: Perseus, 2001.

Buckingham, Marcus., and Curt Coffman. *First Break All the Rules: What the World's Greatest Managers Do Differently.* New York: Simon and Schuster, 1999.

Collins, James C. *Good to Great: Why Some Companies Make the Leap—and Others Don't*, 1st ed. New York: HarperBusiness, 2001.

Collins, James C., and Jerry I. Porras. *Built to Last: Successful Habits of Visionary Companies*, 1st ed. New York: HarperBusiness, 1994.

Goleman, D., R. Boyatzis, and A. McKee. *Primal Leadership: Recognizing the Power of Emotional Intelligence.* Boston, MA: Harvard Business School Press, 2002.

Goodwin, Doris Kearns. *Team of Rivals: The Political Genius of Abraham Lincoln*. New York: Simon & Schuster, 2005.

Hilgard, Ernest. "The Trilogy of Mind: Cognition, Affection, and Conation." *Journal of the History of the Behavioral Sciences* 16 (1980): 107–17.

Hughes, Richard L., Robert C. Ginnett, and Gordon J. Curphy. *Leadership: Enhancing the Lessons of Experience*, 5th ed. Boston: McGraw-Hill/Irwin, 2006.

Latham, Gary P., and Craig C. Pinder. "Work Motivation Theory and Research at the Dawn of the Twenty-First Century." *Annual Review of Psychology* 56, no. 1 (2005): 485.

Locke, Edwin A., and Gary P. Latham. "What Should We Do about Motivation Theory? Six Recommendations for the Twenty-First Century." *Academy of Management Review* 29, no. 3 (2004): 388.

Lombardo, Michael M., Robert W. Eichinger, and Center for Creative Leadership. *Eighty-Eight Assignments for Development in Place: Enhancing the Developmental Challenge of Existing Jobs* Greensboro, NC: Center for Creative Leadership, 1989.

"Melaleuca Continues 20 Year Streak, Sales Top $702 million." *Idaho Business Review* (10 April 2006), p. 7A.

Peters, Tom. "Rule #3: Leadership Is Confusing as Hell" [cover story], *Fast Company*, no. 44 (2001).

Pfeffer, Jeffrey. *The Human Equation: Building Profits by Putting People First.* Boston: Harvard Business School Press, 1998.

Porter, Lyman W., Gregory A. Bigley, and Richard M. Steers. *Motivation and Work Behavior*, 7th ed. Boston: McGraw-Hill/Irwin, 2003.

Reeve, John Marshall. *Understanding Motivation and Emotion*, 4th ed. Hoboken, NJ: Wiley, 2005.

Snow, Richard E. "Toward Assessment of Cognitive and Conative Structures in Learning." *Educational Researcher* (1989).

Wooden, John R., and Steve Jamison. *My Personal Best: Life Lessons from an All-American Journey.* New York: McGraw-Hill, 2004

Organizational Citizenship Behavior (OCB)

Dalal, Reeshad S. "A Meta-Analysis of the Relationship between Organizational Citizenship Behavior and Counterproductive Work Behavior." *Journal of Applied Psychology* 90, no. 6 (2005): 1241.

LePine, Jeffrey A., Amir Erez, and Diane E. Johnson. "The Nature and Dimensionality of Organizational Citizenship Behavior: A Critical Review and Meta-Analysis." *Journal of Applied Psychology* 87, no. 1 (2002): 52.

Mackenzie, Scott B., Philip M. Podsakoff, and Gregory A. Rich. "Transformational and Transactional Leadership and Salesperson Performance." *Journal of the Academy of Marketing Science* 29, no. 2 (2001): 115.

Podsakoff, Philip M., Scott B. MacKenzie, Julie Beth Paine, and Daniel G. Bachrach. "Organizational Citizenship Behaviors: A Critical Review of the Theoretical and Empirical Literature and Suggestions for Future Research." *Journal of Management* 26, no. 3 (2000): 513.

Organizational Justice

Colquitt, Jason A., Donald E. Conlon, Michael J. Wesson, Christopher O. L.H. Porter, and K. Yee Ng. "Justice at the Millenium: A Meta-Analytic Review of 25 Years of Organizational Justice Research." *Journal of Applied Psychology* 86, no. 3 (2001): 425–45.

Colquitt, Jason A., Jerald Greenberg, and Cindy Zapata-Phelan. "What Is Organizational Justice: A Historical Overview." In *Handbook of Organizational Justice,* 3–56. Mahway, NJ: Erlbaum, 2005.

Cropanzano, Russell, and Deborah Rupp, "An Overview of Organizational Justice: Implications for Work Motivation," in *Motivation and*

Work Behavior, ed. Lyman W. Porter, Gregory A. Bigley, and Richard M. Steers. Boston: McGraw-Hill Irwin, 2003.

Organizational Commitment

Allen, Natalie J., and John P. Meyer. "Affective, Continuance, and Normative Commitment to the Organization: An Examination of Construct Validity." *Journal of Vocational Behavior* 49, no. 3 (1996): 252.

"Introduction to Naval Special Warfare." *Navy SEALs.* http://www.sealchallenge.navy.mil/seal/introduction.aspx (accessed September 21, 2006).

Jaramillo, Fernando, Jay Prakash Mulki, and Greg W. Marshall. "A Meta-Analysis of the Relationship between Organizational Commitment and Salesperson Job Performance: 25 Years of Research." *Journal of Business Research* 58, no. 6 (2005): 705.

Meyer, John P., and Natalie Jean Allen. *Commitment in the Workplace: Theory, Research, and Application, Advanced Topics in Organizational Behavior.* Thousand Oaks, CA: Sage, 1997.

Meyer, John P., Thomas E. Becker, and Christian Vandenberghe. "Employee Commitment and Motivation: A Conceptual Analysis and Integrative Model." *Journal of Applied Psychology* 89, no. 6 (2004): 991.

Meyer, John P., and Lynne Herscovitch. "Commitment in the Workplace: Toward a General Model." *Human Resource Management Review* 11, no. 3 (2001): 299.

Meyer, John P., David J. Stanley, Lynne Herscovitch, and Laryssa Topolnytsky. "Affective, Continuance, and Normative Commitment to the Organization: A Meta-Analysis of Antecedents, Correlates, and Consequences." *Journal of Vocational Behavior* 61, no. 1 (2002): 20.

Rhoades, Linda, Robert Eisenberger, and Stephen Armeli. "Affective Commitment of the Organization: The Contribution of Perceived Organizational Support." *Journal of Applied Psychology* 86, no. 5 (2001): 825.

Perceived Organizational/Supervisor Support (POS/PSS)

Bishop, James W., K. Dow Scott, Michael G. Goldsby, and Russell Cropanzano. "A Construct Validity Study of Commitment and Perceived Support Variables: A Multifoci Approach across Different Team Environments." *Group & Organization Management* 30, no. 2 (2005): 153.

Eisenberger, Robert, Stephen Armeli, Barbara Rexwinkel, Patrick D. Lynch, and Linda Rhoades. "Reciprocation of Perceived Organizational Support." *Journal of Applied Psychology* 86, no. 1 (2001): 42.

Eisenberger, Robert, Jim Cummings, Stephen Armeli, and Patrick Lynch. "Perceived Organizational Support, Discretionary Treatment, and Job Satisfaction." *Journal of Applied Psychology* 82, no. 5 (1997): 812–20.

Eisenberger, Robert, Robin Huntington, Steven Hutchison, and Debora Sowa. "Perceived Organizational Support." *Journal of Applied Psychology* 71, no. 3 (1986): 500–507.

Eisenberger, Robert, Florence Stinglhamber, Christian Vandenberghe, Ivan L. Sucharski, and Linda Rhoades. "Perceived Supervisor Support: Contributions to Perceived Organizational Support and Employee Retention." *Journal of Applied Psychology* 87, no. 3 (2002): 565–73.

Gagnon, Mark A., and Judd H. Michael. "Outcomes of Perceived Supervisor Support for Wood Production Employees." *Forest Products Journal* 54, no. 12 (2004): 172.

Lynch, Patrick D., Robert Eisenberger, and Stephen Armeli. "Perceived Organizational Support: Inferior versus Superior Performance by Wary Employees." *Journal of Applied Psychology* 84, no. 4 (1999): 467.

Rhoades, Linda, and Robert Eisenberger, "Perceived Organizational Support: A Review of the Literature." *Journal of Applied Psychology* 87 (2002): 698–714.

Rhoades, Linda, Robert Eisenberger, and Stephen Armeli. "Affective Commitment of the Organization: The Contribution of Perceived Organizational Support. *Journal of Applied Psychology* 86, no. 5 (2001): 825.

Rewards

Bård, Kuvaas. "Work Performance, Affective Commitment, and Work Motivation: The Roles of Pay Administration and Pay Level." *Journal of Organizational Behavior* 27, no. 3 (2006): 365–85.

Herpen, Marco, Mirjam Praag, and Kees Cools. "The Effects of Performance Measurement and Compensation on Motivation: An Empirical Study." *De Economist (Kluwer)* 153, no. 3 (2005): 303.

Kerr, Steven. "On the Folly of Rewarding A, While Hoping for B." *Academy of Management Executive* 9, no. 1 (1995): 7.

Locke, Edwin A. "Linking Goals to Monetary Incentives." *Academy of Management Executive* 18, no. 4 (2004): 130.

Pfeffer, Jeffrey. "Put the Spotlight on Personnel." *Security Management* 43, no. 8 (1999): 31–35.

Sisk, Michael. "Reward Systems That Really Work." *Harvard Management Update* 10, no. 9 (2005): 1.

Williams, Margaret L., Michael A. McDaniel, and Nhung T. Nguyen. "A Meta-Analysis of the Antecedents and Consequences of Pay Level Satisfaction." *The Journal of Applied Psychology* 91, no. 2 (2006): 392.

Self-Efficacy

Bandura, Albert. "Human Agency in Social Cognitive Theory." *American Psychologist* 44, no. 9 (1989): 1175–84.

——. *Self-Efficacy: The Exercise of Control.* New York: Freeman, 1997.

Bandura, Albert, and Edwin A. Locke. "Negative Self-Efficacy and Goal Effects Revisited." *Journal of Applied Psychology* 88, no. 1 (2003): 87.

Heggestad, Eric D., and Ruth Kanfer. "The Predictive Validity of Self-Efficacy in Training Performance: Little More Than Past Performance." *Journal of Experimental Psychology/Applied* 11, no. 2 (2005): 84.

Stajkovic, Alexander D., and Fred Luthans. "Self-Efficacy and Work-Related Performance: A Meta-Analysis." *Psychological Bulletin* 124, no. 2 (1998): 240.

Vancouver, Jeffrey B., Charles M. Thompson, E. Casey Tischner, and Dan J. Putka. "Two Studies Examining the Negative Effect of Self-Efficacy on Performance." *Journal of Applied Psychology* 87, no. 3 (2002): 506–16.

Volition and Self-Regulation

Aarts, Henk, and Ap Dijksterhuis. "Habits as Knowledge Structures: Automaticity in Goal-Directed Behavior." *Journal of Personality and Social Psychology* 78, no. 1 (2000): 53–63.

Ackerman, Phillip L., and Ruth Kanfer. "Integrating Laboratory and Field Study for Improving Selection: Development of a Battery for Predicting Air Traffic Controller Success." *Journal of Applied Psychology* 78, no. 3 (1993): 413.

Bargh, John A. "The Ecology of Automaticity: Toward Establishing the Conditions Needed to Produce Automatic Processing Effects." *American Journal of Psychology. Special Issue: Views and varieties of automaticity* 105, no. 2 (1992): 181–99.

Bargh, John A., Peter M. Gollwitzer, Annette Lee-Chai, Kimberly Barndollar, and Roman Trotschel. "The Automated Will: Nonconscious Activation and Pursuit of Behavioral Goals." *Journal of Personality and Social Psychology* 81, no. 6 (2001): 1014–27.

Boekaerts, Monique, and Lyn Corno. "Self-Regulation in the Classroom: A Perspective on Assessment and Intervention." *Applied Psychology* 54, no. 2 (2005): 199–231.

Corno, Lyn. "The Best-Laid Plans: Modern Conceptions of Volition and Educational Research." *Educational Researcher* 22, no. 2 (1993): 14–22.

Corno, Lyn, and Ruth Kanfer. "The Role of Volition in Learning and Performance." In *Review of Research in Education*, edited by Darling-Hammond,

301–41. Washington, D.C.: American Educational Research Association, 1993.

Ghoshal, Sumantra, and Heike Bruch. "Going Beyond Motivation to the Power of Volition." *MIT Sloan Management Review* 44, no. 3 (2003): 51.

Gollwitzer, Peter M. "Implementation Intentions." *American Psychologist* 54, no. 7 (1999): 493.

Gollwitzer, Peter M., Heinz Heckhausen, and Heike Ratajczak. "From Weighing to Willing: Approaching a Change Decision through Pre- or Postdecisional Mentation." *Organizational Behavior & Human Decision Processes* 45, no. 1 (1990): 41.

Gollwitzer, Peter M., and Bernd Schaal. "Metacognition in Action: The Importance of Implementation Intentions." *Personality & Social Psychology Review* 2, no. 2 (1998): 124.

Heckhausen, Heinz, and Julius Kuhl. "From Wishes to Action: The Dead Ends and Short Cuts on the Long Way to Action." In *Goal Directed Behavior: The Concept of Action in Psychology,* ed. M. Frese and J. Sabini, 134–60. Hillsdale, NJ: Erlbaum, 1985.

Kanfer, Ruth. "Self-Regulation Research in Work and I/O Psychology." *Applied Psychology: An International Review* 54, no. 2 (2005): 186.

Kanfer, Ruth, and Phillip L. Ackerman, "Motivational Skills and Self-Regulation for Learning: A Trait," *Learning & Individual Differences* 8, no. 3 (1996).

Kuhl, Julius, and A. Fuhrmann. "Decomposing Self-Regulation and Self-Control: The Volitional Components Inventory." In *Motivation and Self-Regulation across the Life-Span,* edited by J. Heckhausen and Carol S. Dweck, New York: Cambridge University Press, 1998.

Leach, Mark P., Annie H. Liu, and Wesley J. Johnston. "The Role of Self-Regulation Training in Developing the Motivation Management Capabilities of Salespeople." *Journal of Personal Selling & Sales Management* 25, no. 3 (2005): 269.

McCann, Erin J., and Teresa Garcia. "Maintaining Motivation and Regulating Emotion: Measuring Individual Differences in Academic Volitional Strategies." *Learning & Individual Differences* 11, no. 3 (1999): 259.

Oettingen, Gabriele, Gaby Honig, and Peter M. Gollwitzer. "Effective Self-Regulation of Goal Attainment." *International Journal of Educational Research* 33, no. 7–8 (2000): 705.

Pintrich, Paul R. "Taking Control of Research on Volitional Control: Challenges for Future Theory and Research." *Learning & Individual Differences* 11, no. 3 (1999): 335.

"Rubicon." *Wikipedia: The Free Encyclopedia.* http://en.wikipedia.org/wiki/Rubicon (accessed September 21, 2006).

Scott, Karen Wilson. "Congruous Autonomy: The 'Pull' of Personal Commitment to Extraordinary Involvement in a Pursuit," *MPAEA Journal of Adult Education* 33, no. 1 (2004).

Vancouver, Jeffrey B., and David V. Day. "Industrial and Organisation Research on Self-Regulation: From Constructs to Applications." *Applied Psychology: An International Review* 54, no. 2 (2005): 155.

Work Redesign

Butler, Timothy, and James Waldroop. "Job Sculpting." *Harvard Business Review* 77, no. 5 (1999): 144.

Fomaciari, Charles J., and Kathy Lund Dean. "Experiencing Organizational Work Design: Beyond Hackman and Oldham." *Journal of Management Education* 29, no. 4 (2005): 631.

Hackman, J. Richard, and Greg R. Oldham. "Motivation through the Design of Work: Test of a Theory." *Organizational Behavior & Human Performance* 16, no. 2 (1976): 250.

Hackman, J. Richard, Jone L. Pearce, and Jane Caminis Wolfe. "Effects of Changes in Job Characteristics on Work Attitudes and Behaviors: A Naturally Occurring Quasi-Experiment." *Organizational Behavior & Human Performance* 21, no. 3 (1978): 289.

Wrzesniewski, Amy, and Jane E. Dutton. "Crafting a Job: Revisioning Employees as Active Crafters of Their Work." *Academy of Management Review* 26, no. 2 (2001): 179.

Workplace Environment/Organizational Climate

Amburgey, Terry L., and Hayagreeva Rao. "Organizational Ecology: Past, Present, and Future Directions." *Academy of Management Journal* 39, no. 5 (1996): 1265.

Arthur, Michelle, "Share Price Reactions to Work-Family Initiatives: An Institutional Perspective," *Academy of Management Journal* 46, no. 4 (2003).

Ballou, Brian, Norman H. Godwin, and Rebecca Toppe Shortridge, "Firm Value and Employee Attitudes on Workplace Quality," *Accounting Horizons* 17, no. 4 (2003).

Bednar, Susan G. "Elements of Satisfying Organizational Climates in Child Welfare Agencies." *Families in Society* 84, no. 1 (2003): 7.

Boyle, Matthew, "Happy People, Happy Returns," *Fortune* 153, no. 1 (2006).

Colvin, Geoff. "The 100 Best Companies to Work for 2006" [cover story]. *Fortune* 153, no. 1 (2006): 71.

Dickson, Marcus W., Christian J. Resick, and Paul J. Hanges. "When Organizational Climate Is Unambiguous, It Is Also Strong." *Journal of Applied Psychology* 91, no. 2 (2006): 351–64.

Ehrenreich, Barbara. *Nickel and Dimed: On (Not) Getting by in America.* New York: Metropolitan Books, 2001.

Kroth, Michael and Patricia Boverie. "Poudre Valley Health System: A Transformational Work Environment." Presentation, Sixth International Transformative Learning Conference, East Lansing, MI, October 6–9, 2005.

Krueger, Jerry, and Emily Killham, "Why Dilbert Is Right: Uncomfortable Work Environments Make for Disgruntled Employees—Just Like the Cartoon Says," *Gallup Management Journal Online* (2006). http://gmj.gallup.com/content/default.asp?ci=21802.

Levering, Robert. "Creating a Great Place to Work: Why It Is Important and How It Is Done." *Corrections Today* 66, no. 5 (2004): 86–88.

Levering, Robert, Milton Moskowitz, Eugenia Levenson, Jenny Mero, Christopher Tkaczyk, and Matthew Boyle. "And the Winners Are … " *Fortune* 153, no. 1 (2006): 89–108.

Lipman-Blumen, Jean. "The Allure of Toxic Leaders: Why Followers Rarely Escape Their Clutches." *Ivey Business Journal* 69, no. 3 (2005): 1–8.

May, Bruce E., R.S.M. Lau, and Stephen Johnson, "A Longitudinal Study of Quality of Work Life and Business Performance," *South Dakota Business Review* 58, no. 2 (1999).

Patterson, Malcolm, Peter Warr, and Michael West. "Organizational Climate and Company Productivity: The Role of Employee Affect and Employee Level." *Journal of Occupational & Organizational Psychology* 77, no. 2 (2004): 193.

Rivera, Michelle. "Corporate Spotlight: Poudre Valley Health System." *Health Executive.* March, 2006. http://www.healthexecutive.com/spotlights/mar_2006/sl_Poudre.asp (Accessed September 28, 2006).

Sinclair, Upton, *The Jungle* [Copyright Paperback Collection, Library of Congress] New York: Signet Classic, 2001.

Terkel, Studs. *Working.* New York: Pantheon Books, 1974.

Wielkiewicz, Richard M., and Stephen P. Stelzner. "An Ecological Perspective on Leadership Theory, Research, and Practice." *Review of General Psychology* 9, no. 4 (2005): 326–41.

ORGANIZATIONS AND THEIR JOURNALS

Organizations

Academy of Human Resource Development
College of Technology
Bowling Green State University
Bowling Green, OH 43403-0301

Phone: (419) 372-9155
Fax: (419) 372-8385
http://www.ahrd.org

Journals
Advances in Developing Human Resources
Human Resource Development International
Human Resource Development Quarterly
Human Resource Development Review

Academy of Management
PO Box 3020
Briarcliff Manor, NY 10510-8020 (USA)
Phone: 1 + (914) 923-2607
Fax: 1 + (914) 923-2615
http://aomonline.org

Journals
Academy of Management Review
Academy of Management Journal
Academy of Management Learning & Education
Academy of Management Perspectives

American Society for Training and Development
1640 King Street, Box 1443
Alexandria, Virginia, 22313-2043, USA
Phone: (703) 683-8100
Fax: (703) 683-8103
http://www.astd.org

Journals
T+D
Learning Circuits

Center for Creative Leadership
Headquartered in Greensboro, North Carolina
with campuses in Colorado Springs, Colorado, and San Diego, California.
Phone: (336) 545-2810
http://www.ccl.org

Journals
Leadership in Action
Leading Effectively—e-newsletter
Many leadership development publications

International Society for Performance Improvement
1400 Spring Street, Suite 260
Silver Spring, Maryland USA 20910
Phone: (301) 587-8570
Fax: (301) 587-8573
http://www.ispi.org

Journals
Performance Improvement
Performance Improvement Quarterly

Organization Development Network
71 Valley Street, Suite 301
South Orange, NJ 07079-2825
Phone: (973) 763-7337
Fax: (973) 763-7488
odnetwork@ODNetwork.org
http://www.ODNetwork.org

Journals
OD Practitioner
Practicing
Seasonings

Society for Human Resource Management
1800 Duke Street
Alexandria, Virginia 22314 USA
Phone U.S. Only: (800) 283-SHRM
Phone International: +1 (703) 548-3440
TTY/TDD (703) 548-6999
Fax: (703) 535-6490
http://www.shrm.org

Journals
HR Magazine
Staffing Management

JOURNALS

American Psychologist
Applied Psychology
California Management Review
Gallup Management Journal

Harvard Business Review
Human Performance
Journal of Applied Psychology
Journal of Management
Journal of Management Development
Journal of Management Studies
Journal of Managerial Psychology
Journal of Organizational Excellence
Journal of Vocational Behavior
Journal of Workplace Learning
Leader To Leader
Leadership & Organization Development Journal
Leadership Quarterly
Mckinsey Quarterly
Motivation and Emotion
Organizational Dynamics
Sloan Management Review

Notes

Acknowledgments

1. Patricia Eileen Boverie and Michael S. Kroth, *Transforming Work: The Five Keys to Achieving Trust, Commitment, and Passion in the Workplace. New Perspectives in Organizational Learning, Performance, and Change* (Cambridge, MA: Perseus, 2001).

Chapter 1

1. James C. Collins, *Good to Great: Why Some Companies Make the Leap—and Others Don't,* 1st ed. (New York: HarperBusiness, 2001).
2. Philip M. Podsakoff et al., "Organizational Citizenship Behaviors: A Critical Review of the Theoretical and Empirical Literature and Suggestions for Future Research," *Journal of Management* 26, no. 3 (2000).
3. Malcolm Patterson, Peter Warr, and Michael West, "Organizational Climate and Company Productivity: The Role of Employee Affect and Employee Level," *Journal of Occupational & Organizational Psychology* 77, no. 2 (2004).

4. Edwin A. Locke, "Guest Editor's Introduction: Goal-Setting Theory and Its Applications to the World of Business," *Academy of Management Executive* 18, no. 4 (2004).

5. Edwin A. Locke and Gary P. Latham, "Building a Practically Useful Theory of Goal Setting and Task Motivation," *American Psychologist* 57, no. 9 (2002).

6. Gary P. Latham and Craig C. Pinder, "Work Motivation Theory and Research at the Dawn of the Twenty-First Century," *Annual Review of Psychology* 56, no. 1 (2005).

7. Robert Eisenberger et al., "Perceived Organizational Support: A Review of the Literature," *Journal of Applied Psychology* 87, no. 4 (2002); Robert Eisenberger et al., "Perceived Supervisor Support: Contributions to Perceived Organizational Support and Employee Retention," *Journal of Applied Psychology* 87, no. 3 (2002).

8. Doris Kearns Goodwin, *Team of Rivals: The Political Genius of Abraham Lincoln* (New York: Simon & Schuster, 2005).

Chapter 2

1. E. Tory Higgins, "Beyond Pleasure and Pain." *American Psychologist* 52, no. 12 (1997): 1280–1300.

2. Lyman W. Porter, Gregory A. Bigley, and Richard M. Steers, *Motivation and Work Behavior*, 7th ed. (Boston: McGraw-Hill/Irwin, 2003).

3. Marcus Buckingham and Curt Coffman, *First Break All the Rules: What the World's Greatest Managers Do Differently* (New York: Simon and Schuster, 1999).

4. D. Goleman, R. Boyatzis, and A. McKee, *Primal Leadership: Recognizing the Power of Emotional Intelligence* (Boston, MA: Harvard Business School Press, 2002).

5. Paul Hersey and Kenneth H. Blanchard, *Management of Organizational Behavior: Utilizing Human Resources*, 6th ed. (Englewood Cliffs, NJ: Prentice Hall, 1993); Kenneth H. Blanchard, Drea Zigarmi, and Patricia Zigarmi, *Situational Leadership II* (San Diego: Blanchard Training and Development, Inc, 1994).

6. Studs Terkel, *Working* (New York: Pantheon Books, 1974).

7. Barbara Ehrenreich, *Nickel and Dimed: On (Not) Getting by in America* (New York: Metropolitan Books, 2001).

8. Patricia Eileen Boverie and Michael S. Kroth. *Transforming Work: The Five Keys to Achieving Trust, Commitment, and Passion in the Workplace. New Perspectives in Organizational Learning, Performance, and Change.* (Cambridge, MA: Perseus, 2001).

9. *Wikipedia: The Free Encyclopedia*. s.v. "Rubicon." http://en.wikipedia.org/wiki/Rubicon (accessed September 21, 2006).

10. Lyn Corno, "The Best-Laid Plans: Modern Conceptions of Volition and Educational Research." *Educational Researcher* 22, no. 2 (1993): 14–22.

Chapter 3

1. Richard M. Wielkiewicz and Stephen P. Stelzner. "An Ecological Perspective on Leadership Theory, Research, and Practice." *Review of General Psychology* 9, no. 4 (2005).

2. James C. Collins and Jerry I. Porras, *Built to Last: Successful Habits of Visionary Companies,* 1st ed. (New York: HarperBusiness, 1994).

3. Malcolm Patterson, Peter Warr, and Michael West, "Organizational Climate and Company Productivity: The Role of Employee Affect and Employee Level," *The British Psychological Society* 77 (2004): 193–216.

4. Brian Ballou, Norman H. Godwin, and Rebecca Toppe Shortridge, "Firm Value and Employee Attitudes on Workplace Quality," *Accounting Horizons* 17, no. 4 (2003).

5. Bruce E. May, R.S.M. Lau, and Stephen Johnson, "A Longitudinal Study of Quality of Work Life and Business Performance," *South Dakota Business Review* 58, no. 2 (1999).

6. Matthew Boyle, "Happy People, Happy Returns," *Fortune* 153, no. 1 (2006).

7. Ingrid Smithey Fulmer, Barry Gerhant, and Kimberly S. Scott, "Are the 100 Best Better? An Empirical Investigation of the Relationship between Being a 'Great Place to Work' and Firm Performance," *Personnel Psychology* 56, no. 4 (2003).

8 Michelle Arthur, "Share Price Reactions to Work-Family Initiatives: An Institutional Perspective," *Academy of Management Journal* 46, no. 4 (2003).

9. Susan G. Bednar, "Elements of Satisfying Organizational Climates in Child Welfare Agencies." *Families in Society* 84, no. 1 (2003).

10. John P. Meyer and Natalie Jean Allen, *Commitment in the Workplace: Theory, Research, and Application. Advanced Topics in Organizational Behavior* (Thousand Oaks, CA: Sage, 1997).

11. Linda Rhoades and Robert Eisenberger, "Perceived Organizational Support: A Review of the Literature." *Journal of Applied Psychology* 87 (2002): 698–714.

12. *Navy SEALs*. s.v. "Introduction to Naval Special Warfare." http://www.sealchallenge.navy.mil/seal/introduction.aspx (accessed September 21, 2006).

13. Michelle Rivera. "Corporate Spotlight: Poudre Valley Health System." *Health Executive*. March, 2006. http://www.healthexecutive.com/spotlights/mar_2006/sl_Poudre.asp (Accessed September 28, 2006).

14. Michael Kroth and Patricia Boverie. "Poudre Valley Health System: A Transformational Work Environment." Presentation, Sixth International

Transformative Learning Conference, East Lansing, MI, October 6–9, 2005.

15. Geoff Colvin, "The 100 Best Companies to Work for 2006" [cover story], *Fortune* 153, no. 1 (2006).

16. Collins and Porras, *Built to Last: Successful Habits of Visionary Companies.*

17. Tom Peters, "Rule # 3 Leadership Is Confusing as Hell" [cover story], *Fast Company,* no. 44 (2001).

18. Russell Cropanzano and Deborah Rupp, "An Overview of Organizational Justice: Implications for Work Motivation," in *Motivation and Work Behavior,* ed. Lyman W. Porter, Gregory A. Bigley, and Richard M. Steers (Boston: McGraw-Hill Irwin, 2003).

19. Rhoades and Eisenberger, "Perceived Organizational Support: A Review of the Literature."

20. Jason A. Colquitt et al., "Justice at the Millenium: A Meta-Analytic Review of 25 Years of Organizational Justice Research," *Journal of Applied Psychology* 86, no. 3 (2001).

21. Amundson, Norman E., "Mattering: A Foundation for Employment Counseling and Training." *Journal of Employment Counseling* 30 (1993); Morris Rosenberg and Claire McCullough. "Mattering: Inferred Significance and Mental Health among Adolescents." *Research in Community and Mental Heath* 2 (1981).

22. Nancy K. Schlossberg et al., "The Mattering Scales for Adult Students in Postsecondary Education" *American Council on Education,* Washington DC: Center for Adult Learning and Educational Credientials, 1990. (ED341772).

23. Gregory Elliott, Suzanne Kao, and Ann-Marie Grant, "Mattering: Empirical Validation of a Social-Psychological Concept," *Self & Identity* 3, no. 4 (2004).

24. Lesley M. Wilkes and Marianne C. Wallis, "A Model of Professional Nurse Caring: Nursing Students' Experience," *Journal of Advanced Nursing* 27, no. 3 (1998).

25. Kristen Swanson, "What's Known about Caring in Nursing Science: A Literary Meta-Analysis," in *Handbook of Clinical Nursing Research,* ed. A. S. Hinshaw, S. Feetham, and J. L. F. Shaver (Thousand Oaks, CA: Sage, 1999).

26. Viktor Emil Frankl, *Man's Search for Meaning: An Introduction to Logotherapy* (Boston: Beacon Press, 1963).

27. Henry David Thoreau, *Walden* (New York: AMS Press, 1982).

28. John R. Wooden and Steve Jamison. *My Personal Best: Life Lessons from an All-American Journey.* (New York: McGraw-Hill, 2004)

29. Ernest Hilgard, "The Trilogy of Mind: Cognition, Affection, and Conation," *Journal of the History of the Behavioral Sciences* 16 (1980).

30. Marsha Sinetar, *Do What You Love, the Money Will Follow: Discovering Your Right Livelihood* (New York: Dell, 1989).

31. Kay R. Jamison, *Exuberance: The Passion for Life,* 1st ed. (New York: Knopf, 2004).

32. Upton Sinclair, *The Jungle* [Copyright Paperback Collection, Library of Congress] (New York: Signet Classic, 2001).

33. Studs Terkel, *Working.* New York: Pantheon Books, 1974,

34. Barbara Ehrenreich, *Nickel and Dimed: On (Not) Getting by in America.*

35. Jean Lipman-Blumen, "The Allure of Toxic Leaders: Why Followers Rarely Escape Their Clutches," *Ivey Business Journal* 69, no. 3 (2005): 1–8.

36. Jerry Krueger and Emily Killham, "Why Dilbert Is Right: Uncomfortable Work Environments Make for Disgruntled Employees—Just Like the Cartoon Says," *Gallup Management Journal Online* (2006). http://gmj.gallup.com/content/default.asp?ci=21802.

37. Gregory Berns, *Satisfaction,* 1st ed. (New York: Holt, 2005).

38. Marcus Buckingham and Curt Coffman, *First Break All the Rules: What the World's Greatest Managers Do Differently.*

39. Patricia Eileen Boverie and Michael S. Kroth. *Transforming Work: The Five Keys to Achieving Trust, Commitment, and Passion in the Workplace. New Perspectives in Organizational Learning, Performance, and Change.* Cambridge, MA: Perseus, 2001.

40. John R. Wooden and Steve Jamison, *My Personal Best: Life Lessons from an All-American Journey* (New York: McGraw-Hill, 2004).

41. Edward L. Deci and Richard Flaste, *Why We Do What We Do: The Dynamics of Personal Autonomy* (New York: Putnam's Sons, 1995).

42. Timothy Butler and James Waldroop, "Job Sculpting," *Harvard Business Review* 77, no. 5 (1999).

43. Amy Wrzesniewski and Jane E. Dutton, "Crafting a Job: Revisioning Employees as Active Crafters of Their Work," *Academy of Management.*

Chapter 4

1. Gregory A. Rich. "Salesperson Optimism: Can Sales Managers Enhance It and So What If They Do?" *Journal of Marketing Theory & Practice* 7, no. 1 (1999): 53; Martin E. P. Seligman, *Learned Optimism.* (New York: Pocket Books, 1998).

2. Rich. "Salesperson Optimism: Can Sales Managers Enhance It and So What If They Do?"; Seligman, *Learned Optimism.*

3. Christopher Peterson, Steven F. Maier, and Martin E. P. Seligman, *Learned Helplessness: A Theory for the Age of Personal Control* (New York: Oxford University Press, 1993); Seligman, *Learned Optimism.*

4. Albert Bandura, *Self-Efficacy: The Exercise of Control* (New York: Freeman, 1997).

5. Wooden and Jamison, *My Personal Best: Life Lessons from an All-American Journey.*

6. Jeffrey Pfeffer, "Put the Spotlight on Personnel," *Security Management* 43, no. 8 (1999).

7. Edwin A. Locke, "Linking Goals to Monetary Incentives," *Academy of Management Executive* 18, no. 4 (2004).

8. Edwin A. Locke, "Guest Editor's Introduction: Goal Setting Theory and Its Applications to the World of Business." *Academy of Management Executive* 18, no. 4 (2004).

9. Edwin A. Locke and Gary P. Latham, "Building a Practically Useful Theory of Goal Setting and Task Motivation." *American Psychologist* 57, no. 9 (2002).

10. Steven Kerr and Steffen Landauer, "Using Stretch Goals to Promote Organizational Effectiveness and Personal Growth: General Electric and Goldman Sachs," *Academy of Management Executive* 18, no. 4 (2004).

11. E. Tory Higgins, "Promotion and Prevention: Regulatory Focus as a Motivational Principle," in *Advances in Experimental Social Psychology,* ed. M. P. Zanna (New York: Academic Press, 1998).

12. Maarten Vansteenkiste, Willy Lens, and Edward L. Deci, "Intrinsic versus Extrinsic Goal Contents in Self-Determination Theory: Another Look at the Quality of Academic Motivation," *Educational Psychologist* 41, no. 1 (2006).

13. Gerard H. Seijts and Gary P. Latham, "Learning Versus Performance Goals: When Should Each Be Used?" *Academy of Management Executive* 19, no. 1 (2005).

14. D. Burton and T. Raedeke, *Sport Psychology for Coaches* (Champaign, IL: Human Kinetics, in press).

15. Steven Kerr, "On the Folly of Rewarding A, While Hoping for B," *Academy of Management Executive* 9, no. 1 (1995).

16. Heinz Heckhausen and Julius Kuhl, "From Wishes to Action: The Dead Ends and Short Cuts on the Long Way to Action.," in *Goal Directed Behavior: The Concept of Action in Psychology,* ed. M. Frese and J. Sabini (Hillsdale, NJ: Erlbaum, 1985); Peter M. Gollwitzer, Heinz Heckhausen, and Heike Ratajczak. "From Weighing to Willing: Approaching a Change Decision through Pre- or Postdecisional Mentation." *Organizational Behavior & Human Decision Processes* 45, no. 1 (1990): 41.

17. Karyll N. Shaw, "Changing the Goal-Setting Process at Microsoft," *Academy of Management Executive* 18, no. 4 (2004).

18. Edwin A. Locke, Gary P. Latham, and Miriam Erez. "The Determinants of Goal Commitment." *Academy of Management Review* 13, no. 1 (1988).

19. Karen Wilson Scott, "Congruous Autonomy: The 'Pull' of Personal Commitment to Extraordinary Involvement in a Pursuit," *MPAEA Journal of Adult Education* 33, no. 1 (2004).

20. Lyn Corno. "The Best-Laid Plans: Modern Conceptions of Volition and Educational Research." *Educational Researcher* 22, no. 2 (1993).

21. Ruth Kanfer and Phillip L. Ackerman, "Motivational Skills and Self-Regulation for Learning: A Trait," *Learning & Individual Differences* 8, no. 3 (1996).

22. Robert W. Renn, "Moderation by Goal Commitment of the Feedback–Performance Relationship: Theoretical Explanation and Preliminary Study," *Human Resource Management Review* 13, no. 4 (2003).

23. Audhesh K. Paswan, Lou E. Pelton, and Sheb L. True, "Perceived Managerial Sincerity, Feedback-Seeking Orientation and Motivation among Front-Line Employees of a Service Organization," *Journal of Services Marketing* 19, no. 1 (2005); Sumantra Ghoshal and Heike Bruch. "Going Beyond Motivation to the Power of Volition." *MIT Sloan Management Review* 44, no. 3 (2003).

Chapter 5

1. Jean Watson, *Assessing and Measuring Caring in Nursing and Health Science* (New York: Springer, 2002).

2. Swanson, "What's Known about Caring in Nursing Science: A Literary Meta-Analysis."

Chapter 6

1. Michael M. Lombardo, Robert W. Eichinger, and Center for Creative Leadership, *Eighty-Eight Assignments for Development in Place: Enhancing the Developmental Challenge of Existing Jobs* (Greensboro, NC: Center for Creative Leadership, 1989).

2. Sources for this case study were interviews with Melaleuca executives; the company's application to the Idaho Psychological Association Psychologically Healthy Workplace Award; and the article "Melaleuca Continues 20-Year Streak, Sales Top $702 million," *Idaho Business Review* (10 April 2006), p. 7A.

Index

About The Author

MICHAEL KROTH is Assistant Professor in the Department of Adult and Organizational Learning at the University of Idaho. As a long-time consultant he has provided corporate-level leadership development and succession planning programs, been the administrator of a corporate foundation, and served as a director of corporate community affairs. He is the Leadership Field Editor for the American Society for Training and Development's In-Practice on-line newsletter, is a past member of the ASTD International Program Advisory Committee, and a member of the National Speakers Association, presenting regularly at national and international conferences. He is co-author, with Patricia Boverie, of *Transforming Work: The Five Keys to Achieving Trust, Commitment, and Passion in the Workplace.*